ENGLISH GRAMMAR

the text of this book is printed
on 100% recycled paper

About the Author

Professor Curme was graduated from the University of Michigan, received an M.A. from DePauw University, and was awarded a degree as Doctor of Philosophy from Heidelberg University for a German grammar that he wrote in 1904. He also received a Doctorate of Laws from the University of Southern California and Doctorates of Letters from Northwestern and DePauw universities.

He was for nine years Professor of German Language and Literature at Cornell College; from 1896 to 1933 he was Professor of Germanic Philology at Northwestern University; and from 1933 until 1939 he lectured in German at the University of Southern California.

His writings include *Selected Poems from Premières et Nouvelles Meditations of Lamartine*, *Lessing's Nathan der Weise*, *A Grammar of the German Language*, *College English Grammar*, *English Syntax*, *Parts of Speech and Accidence*, and *Principles and Practice of English Grammar*.

He was a president of the Modern Language Association and a member of the Linguistic Society of America and the National Institute of Social Sciences.

ENGLISH GRAMMAR

by George O. Curme
Late Professor of Germanic Philology
Northwestern University

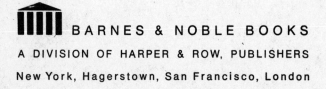 BARNES & NOBLE BOOKS

A DIVISION OF HARPER & ROW, PUBLISHERS

New York, Hagerstown, San Francisco, London

©

L. C. catalogue card number: 47–2452

ISBN: 0-06-460061-0

Formerly published under the title:
PRINCIPLES AND PRACTICE OF
ENGLISH GRAMMAR

This book is based in part upon
COLLEGE ENGLISH GRAMMAR
Published, 1925

Copyright, 1925, Harper & Row, Publishers, Inc.
Copyright renewed 1953, by Gertrude Curme Bragg
Assigned to Harper & Row, Publishers, Inc., 1953

Printed in the United States of America

80   12

PREFACE

This treatise on English grammar gives a rather full description of present usage and glimpses of the older usage found in our older masterpieces still widely read and studied. In this book English grammar is represented, not as a body of fixed rules, but as a part of the evolutionary process, as the stirring story of the struggles of the English-speaking people for a fuller expression of their unfolding intellectual life.

Although concise in statement, this outline will be found to be characterized by richness of detail, especially in difficult matters, so that the student can locate what he needs. It is more comprehensive than most college textbooks, treating various distinctive and important features of the English language that are commonly overlooked by school grammarians. Among the more significant of these might be mentioned *aspect* (§§ 39, 120–121), the *predicate appositive* (§ 53.C), and *infinite predication* (§ 125).

As all materials are methodically arranged, indexed, and supplied with cross references, *English Grammar* is suited either for reference use or for systematic study. As a textbook it is suited for fairly intensive courses in grammar.

The very fine Index is the work of Dr. Roger R. Walterhouse of Barnes & Noble Books. It will prove an unfailing source of help to all who use *English Grammar*.

GEORGE O. CURME

White Plains, New York

TABLE OF CONTENTS

INTRODUCTION: The English Language

TABLE OF CONTENTS

TABLE OF CONTENTS

TABLE OF CONTENTS

INTRODUCTION

THE ENGLISH LANGUAGE

THE ENGLISH LANGUAGE

1. Origin and Spread
2. Periods
    A. Old English
    B. Middle English
    C. Modern English

INTRODUCTION

THE ENGLISH LANGUAGE

1. Origin and Spread. English, though mixed in its vocabulary, containing a large number of words from different languages, is in its grammatical structure essentially a Germanic language. The Germanic tongues, German, English, Dutch, Danish-Norwegian, Icelandic, Swedish, belong to the Indo-European family of languages, comprising Indo-Iranic (Persian, Sanskrit with its different modern forms now spoken in British India), Baltic (Lithuanian, Lettish), Slavic (Russian, Polish, Czech, Serbian, Bulgarian), Celtic, Greek, and Latin, from the last of which have come modern Italian, French, Spanish, and Portuguese.

English is a branch of Low German, the speech of the lowlands of north Germany. About A.D. 450 different Low German tribes, Saxons, Angles, and Jutes — later collectively called English — began to invade England and to settle there. They gradually pushed back the Celts, who had possession when they came. Though Celtic is still represented in Great Britain by modern Welsh and Highland Scotch, the prevailing literary language has long been English, a literary speech that has gradually developed out of the earlier Low German dialects. The present literary language is in its essential features an outgrowth of the speech of the Midland.

English is now not only spoken in Great Britain, but has been carried by English colonists to Ireland and to many foreign lands and established there. Just as a transplanted tree is for a time stopped in its growth, transplanted English was for a time arrested in its development. This accounts for the retention of older sounds and forms of speech in the colonial forms of English, hence, of course, in our own American English, while in the mother country newer developments have taken their place. On the other hand, the new things and the

3

new needs of the new world have called forth new words and expressions, so that the vocabulary in the colonial lands is somewhat different from that of the mother speech. In spite of these differences the different English peoples are held together by the priceless heritage of their common literature.

2. Periods. The history of English is divided into the following three periods:

A. OLD ENGLISH. This period extends from 450 to 1150. It is characterized by full vowels in the endings and the use of more endings than were employed in the later periods: (plural of stan *stone*) nominative stan*as*, accusative stan*as*, dative stan*um*, genitive stan*a;* now *stones, stones, to the stones, of the stones.*

The vocabulary of English in this period was for the most part Low German. The Celtic influence was very slight and brought few words into the language, aside from many names of places, such as Avon (the Celtic name for river), Aberdeen (= mouth of river), etc. Between 800 and 1050 the Danes (i.e. Danes, Norwegians, Swedes) made frequent inroads into England, and from 1017 to 1042 Danish kings ruled there. They brought many words into our language and have influenced the grammatical structure somewhat; but the Danes were themselves a Germanic people, closely related to the English, so that these changes did not affect the general character of the language.

B. MIDDLE ENGLISH. This period extends from 1150 to 1500. It is characterized in part by the reduction of the older full vowels in the endings to one uniform unaccented *e:* Old English stan*as* (= stones), Middle English ston*es* (with a pronounced but unstressed *e*). In part, it is characterized by the loss of many endings. These changes were the results of forces that had long been at work in the language. For instance, in oldest English, case endings were necessary to indicate the grammatical relations; but later, after these relations were largely expressed by the word-order, they for the most part gradually disappeared as useless forms. From here on, the development of the language was often along different lines from those usually followed in older English. For instance, since the dative no longer had a distinctive form, it often became necessary to place the preposition *to* or *for* before it to mark it as a dative:

> A man of greet (great) honour,
> *To whom* that he was alwey (always) confessour.
> — Chaucer.

In 1066 an event — the Norman Conquest — occurred which led to great changes in our language. These Normans were originally Danes who during their occupation of Normandy (in northern France) had acquired the French dialect of this part of France. After their conquest of England they introduced French into all the seats of power and influence, so that French came into wide use. Alongside of French another foreign language was much used — Latin — in the learned professions, law, medicine, and divinity. For over two hundred years English was replaced in the higher literary language by French and Latin. But alongside of these two languages English continued to be used by the common people and was everywhere employed in popular literature. English feeling was not dead and in course of time grew strong, and gradually brought English back into literary use again. In the fourteenth century, the national feeling — greatly strengthened by the war with France — had become so strong and the use of English so widespread that Chaucer, the greatest of all the writers of this period, wrote in English, and from then on English gradually supplanted French and later also Latin.

The return to the use of English as the literary language brought many difficult problems. English had been long used merely for practical purposes and had thus lost the expressions for the higher things of literature, science, and religion, so that words had to be borrowed from French and Latin. Words were taken not only from Norman French, but after 1300 in much greater degree from Central (i.e. Parisian) French. Borrowings from the Latin and Central French continued in the following period described in C below. Thus, it has come about that we largely employ English words in our usual intercourse with one another but borrowed words in scientific or formal language. Even in the plainest conversation, however, we often cannot make ourselves understood without the aid of some borrowed words. Though borrowed words are usually everywhere necessary, it still remains true that English words — *father, mother, brother, sister, home, love, hate, life, death, God*, etc. — contain in large measure the power that moves the soul. Many carry the use of borrowed words too far and thus speak without power. Many who have little thought use big borrowed words to hide its thinness, often perhaps fooling themselves, thinking that they are expressing themselves effectively. Borrowed words are often useful in varying our expression and in making it accurate, but they can easily weaken our expression when used instead of our simple but powerful English words.

C. MODERN ENGLISH. This period extends from 1500 to the present time. It is in part characterized by the suppression of the weakly stressed *e* in the endings of words: *stones*, still as in Middle English written with *e*, which, however, is now silent.

Furthermore, this period has been increasingly characterized, on the one hand, by a simpler and compacter sentence structure and, on the other hand, by a finer differentiation of the forms of the language, which naturally resulted from the unfolding intellectual life of the English people and its growing need for fuller and more accurate expression. These developments will be described later in detail.

PART ONE

THE PARTS OF SPEECH

THE NOUN

3. Definition
4. Classification
   A. Common Nouns
   B. Proper Nouns
5. Common Noun Used as a Proper Noun
6. Proper Noun Used as a Common Noun
7. Compound Nouns and Derivative Nouns
   A. Compound Nouns
   B. Derivative Nouns

THE PRONOUN

8. Definition
9. Classification
   A. Personal Pronouns
   B. Reflexive Pronouns
   C. Reciprocal Pronouns
   D. Relative Pronouns
      1. Relative Pronoun with Antecedent
      2. Indefinite and General Relative Pronouns
   E. Indefinite Pronouns
   F. Interrogative Pronouns
   G. Limiting Adjectives Used as Pronouns
      1. Intensifying Adjectives
      2. "This," "This One," Etc.
      3. Indefinites
   H. Exclamatory Adjective Used as a Pronoun

THE ADJECTIVE

10. Definition
11. Classification
12. Compound Adjectives and Derivative Adjectives
    A. Compound Adjectives
    B. Derivative Adjectives
13. Classes of Limiting Adjectives
    A. Possessive Adjectives
    B. Intensifying Adjectives

C. Demonstrative Adjectives
D. Numeral Adjectives
   1. Cardinal Numeral Adjectives
   2. Ordinal Numeral Adjectives
   3. Multiplicatives
E. Relative Adjectives
   1. "Which"
   2. Indefinites, "Which," "What," Etc.
F. Indefinite Adjectives
G. Interrogative Adjectives
H. Proper Adjectives
 I. Exclamatory Adjectives

THE VERB

14. Definition
15. Classification
  A. Transitive Verbs
  B. Intransitive Verbs
  C. Linking Verbs
16. Compound Verbs
  A. Inseparable Compound
  B. Separable Compound
  C. Prepositional Compound

THE ADVERB

17. Definition
18. Classification
  A. Classification by Function
    1. Simple Adverb
    2. Sentence Adverb
    3. Conjunctive Adverb
    4. Interrogative Adverbs in Principal Propositions
  B. Classification by Meaning
    1. Adverbs of Place, Direction, Arrangement
    2. Adverbs of Time
    3. Adverbs of Manner
    4. Adverbs of Degree, Amount, Number
    5. Adverbs of Cause
    6. Adverbs of Inference and Result

PART ONE

THE PARTS OF SPEECH

THERE are eight parts of speech: noun, pronoun, adjective, verb, adverb, preposition, conjunction, interjection.

THE NOUN

3. Definition. A noun, or substantive, is the name of a living being or lifeless thing: *Mary, John, horse, cow, dog; hat, house, tree; London, Chicago; virtue.*

4. Classification. There are different classes of nouns:

A. COMMON NOUNS. A common noun is a name that can be applied to any one of a class of living beings or lifeless things: *teacher, student, mayor, president, king, man, lion, tiger, cow; house, tree, city, country,* etc.

A common noun may not only be the name of a thing with a definite form, but it may also be the name of a formless mass, a material, as *tea, wheat, sand, water, gold, paper* (but with different meaning in "this morning's *paper*").

A common noun may also be the name of a collection of living beings or lifeless things, here called a collective noun, as *nation, army, crowd,* a *herd* of cattle, a *row* of trees, a *chain* of mountains, etc.

A common noun may also be the name of a quality, action, state, or a general idea, here called an abstract noun: *hardness, kindness,* formed from the adjectives *hard, kind* by the addition of the suffix *-ness; warmth (warm + -th); youth (young + -th =* young state), but a concrete common noun in *a youth* and a collective noun in "*the youth* of the land"; formed from nouns in *friendship (friend + -ship), manhood, bondage, serfdom, slavery, hatred, fraternity* (but a concrete collective noun in "the members of *this fraternity*"); formed from verbs in *stroke* (from *strike*), *throw, growth, growing, singing, scolding, increase, decrease;* many

names of general ideas: *music, art, chemistry* (but concrete in
"*the chemistry* lying upon the table"), *grammar* (but concrete in
"*the grammar* lying upon the table").

B. PROPER NOUNS. A proper noun is the name of a particular living being or lifeless thing: Mary, John, Longfellow,
Shakespeare, Carlo (name of a dog), Chicago, London, England, Pennsylvania, January, Friday, Christmas, Macbeth
(name of a general), *Macbeth* (name of a drama), Hamlet
(name of a prince), *Hamlet* (name of a drama), etc.   A proper
noun begins with a capital.

5. Common Noun Used as a Proper Noun. A common
noun is often employed as a proper noun:

> Nelson's flagship was the *Victory.*

> Now *Nature* hangs her mantle green
> On every blooming tree.   — Burns.

6. Proper Noun Used as a Common Noun. A proper
noun may often be employed as a common noun: Virgil was
the Homer (i.e. great epic poet) of the Romans. He was a
Napoleon of finance. She was a regular Xantippe (an ill-
tempered woman, originally the name of Socrates' wife).
Lend me your Webster (dictionary). He bought a Packard
(automobile).

7. Compound Nouns and Derivative Nouns.

A. COMPOUND NOUNS. In the case of both common and
proper nouns a group of two or more nouns often forms a
unit, a compound: toothpick, tablecloth, sidewalk; George
Washington, James Russell Lowell, the White House, the
Northshore Hotel, *Vanity Fair* (the title of a novel by
Thackeray), etc. Notice that we do not always write real
compounds as one word.

B. DERIVATIVE NOUNS. Similar to compound nouns are
derivative nouns, i.e. nouns formed by adding to a common
or proper noun, an adjective, or to a verb a suffix, which in
many cases was originally an independent word. These suffixes

are: *-ness, -ship, -dom, -th, -er, -ing, -ess* (§ 95.A.2), etc.; the diminutive endings *-kin, -ling, -ette, -let, -ie, -y,* which are also much used to express endearment: dark*ness,* friend*ship,* wis*dom,* Christen*dom,* warm*th,* find*er,* writ*ing,* heir*ess;* lamb*kin,* gos*ling,* kitchen*ette,* rivu*let,* Kat*ie,* bird*ie,* kitt*y,* Kitt*y,* etc.

THE PRONOUN

8. Definition. A pronoun is a word used instead of a noun.

9. Classification. There are seven classes:

A. PERSONAL PRONOUNS. They are: *I, me, thou, thee, he, him, she, her, it; we, us, ye, you, they, them.*

The speaker employs *I* or *me* instead of his own name, or, when he includes others, he uses *we* or *us: I* know it. He knows *me. We* know it. He knows *us.*

You is used in direct address instead of the name of the person spoken to: *You* know it.

He, she, it, they, them are used instead of nouns that have been previously mentioned: I shall talk with *Henry* about the matter this evening and shall discuss *it* (referring to the antecedent *matter*) with *him* (referring to the antecedent *Henry*). *Henry* found that *he* (referring to the antecedent *Henry*) was mistaken. *Henry* and *James* found that *they* (referring to the antecedents *Henry* and *James*) were mistaken. John said *that he didn't do it,* and I believe *it* (referring to the antecedent *that he didn't do it*). These pronouns always have an antecedent, i.e. a noun, pronoun, clause, or sentence to which they refer.

My, mine, thy, thine, his, hers, its, our, ours, your, yours, their, theirs were once used as personal pronouns, as the genitive forms to *I, thou, he, she, it, we, you, they,* and are sometimes still so used (§§ 57.C.4 and 103.C). They are now usually possessive adjectives (§ 103.C).

B. REFLEXIVE PRONOUNS. They are: *myself, ourself* (= *myself;* see § 105), *thyself, yourself, himself, herself, oneself* or *one's self, itself; ourselves, yourselves, themselves.* They refer to the subject of the proposition in which they stand, indicating that the action performed by the doer passes back to him: He is worrying *himself* to death. For older forms which are still sometimes used here see § 97.

C. Reciprocal Pronouns. They are: *each other, one another*. They express mutual action or relation on the part of the persons indicated by the subject: These two never weary of *each other*. For older forms which are still sometimes used here see Syntax, § 98.

D. Relative Pronouns. There are two groups:

1. *Relative Pronoun with Antecedent*. The relative pronouns of this group, like the personal pronouns in A above, have an antecedent, but they differ from them in two points. The personal pronouns may stand in either a principal or a subordinate clause, but these relative pronouns always stand in a subordinate clause, where they have two offices to fill: They not only perform the function of a pronoun, referring back to the antecedent, but they also have the function of a conjunction, i.e. they have relative force, linking the subordinate clause to the principal clause. These relative pronouns are: *who* (*whom, whose*), *which, what, that*, and other less common ones enumerated in § 80.B: *He* makes no friend *who* never made a foe. I met a *man that* I knew. I have read the *book which* you lent me. *He is rich, which* I unfortunately am not. The antecedent in the last example is the whole principal proposition *He is rich*. *What* is similarly employed, but usually points to a following clause: We are going away this summer for a vacation, and, *what* is still better, *Father is going along*.

2. *Indefinite and General Relative Pronouns*. The meaning here is always indefinite or general, hence there can be no reference to a definite antecedent; but these pronouns have the same relative force as the relatives in 1, linking the subordinate clause in which they stand to the rest of the sentence. These pronouns are: *who, what; whoever, whosoever, whoso, what*(*so*)-*ever; which, whichever:* I do not know *who did it*. I did not see *whom he struck*. I did not see *to whom he gave it*. I do not know *what he meant*. He told the story to *whoever would listen*. *Whatever is worth doing at all* is worth doing well. As I have not yet read all the new books, I cannot tell you *which* (or more accurately *which one* or *which ones*) *I like best*. "Here are some new books. You may have *whichever one* (or *ones*) *you choose*."

The expression here is often elliptical: I tell you *what* [*the truth* or *the right course is*]. I know *what* [*to do,* i.e. I have a new idea].

E. INDEFINITE PRONOUNS. When we desire to convey an indefinite or general impression, we avoid the use of a noun and often employ instead of it an indefinite pronoun. We now often use thus the indefinite pronouns *somebody, anybody, everybody, nobody, something, somewhat, anything, aught, nothing, naught.* These words were originally indefinite nouns, but they have developed into indefinite pronouns, as can be seen by our hesitation to put an article or other modifying adjective before them. When they take a modifier, they become nouns and have a different meaning: "*Somebody* (pronoun) is ringing," but "He thinks himself *a somebody*" (noun). "She is hunting *something*" (pronoun), but "There was *an* indefinable *something* (noun) about his manner that always attracted my attention." As the pronouns of this group never have a plural, a form with a plural ending must be a noun: the thousand and one *nothings* of the day and hour. They are *nobodies. Somewhat* is not only a pronoun, but also an adverb, and more commonly so: This argument has lost *somewhat* (pronoun) of its force. He is *somewhat* (adverb) better this morning.

The older group of indefinite pronouns in G.3 below competes with this group without a difference of meaning. The clear concrete meaning of *body* (*person*) and *thing* has brought this group into favor. Similarly, the adverbial compounds *any place, some place, no place, every place*, etc. by reason of the concrete force of *place* are often used in popular speech instead of the literary compounds *anywhere, somewhere, nowhere, everywhere:* I can't find it *any place.* I am going *some place* today.

The indefinite pronouns of this group, though themselves compounds, enter into a close relation to the adverb *else*, which often follows them, forming with it new compound pronouns: *somebody else's* child, *nobody else's* business. Compare § 32.

F. INTERROGATIVE PRONOUNS. When the situation is so indefinite that we are aroused to inquire after the exact state of things, we do not use nouns at all but employ certain indefinite pronouns, which we now call interrogative pronouns, since by giving them strong stress and a peculiar intonation we indicate that they are intended to ask for an explanation of the indefinite situation and that we are expecting an answer. These pronouns are: *who* (*whose, whom*), *what, which* (*one*): *Who* did it? *What* did he want? "Here are the books. *Which one* is yours? or *Which* are yours?" These interrogatives are also used in rhetorical questions, i.e. questions which do not expect an answer but express the indefiniteness or uncertainty present in the mind of the speaker: Well, *what* in the world will happen now? They are often, however, employed with the force of a declarative sentence: *What is the use?* = *There is no use.*

These same forms are also used in indirect questions, i.e. indirect ways of asking a question, or indirect reports of them: "Tell me *who did it*," indirect form instead of "Who did it?" "Tell me *what he wanted*," an indirect form instead of "What did he want?" "Bring these hats to John and ask him *which one is his*," an indirect way of asking a question through another person. "I asked him *to whom he gave it*," an indirect report of the question "*To whom* did you give it?"

Notice that the interrogative pronouns *who, what, which* are identical in form with the indefinites *who, what, which* in D.2 above. The interrogatives have developed out of the indefinites and are still indefinites, differing only in that they by means of a stronger stress and peculiar intonation indicate that the speaker is asking for an explanation of the indefinite situation and is expecting an answer.

G. LIMITING ADJECTIVES USED AS PRONOUNS. There is a tendency for the substantive (§ 103) form of limiting (§ 11) adjectives to develop into pronouns. The reciprocal pronouns in C above were once the substantive forms of limiting adjectives used as pronouns, but they have further developed into real pronouns. The substantive forms of a number of limiting adjectives are used not only in adjective function but often also as pronouns. There are three groups:

1. *Intensifying Adjectives.* The intensifying adjectives, *myself, ourself* (= *myself;* see § 105), *thyself, yourself, himself, herself, ourselves, yourselves, themselves*, are often used for emphasis instead of the personal pronouns in § 9.A above: You are not *yourself*

16

(= *you yourself*) today. Did you ever know a woman pardon another for being handsomer than *herself* (= *she herself*)? (Syntax, § 105.)

2. *This, This One, Etc.* Instead of naming living beings or lifeless things we often indicate them by a gesture or a description, or by giving their position in a series, or by including each individual in the series, employing the following limiting adjectives, treating them as pronouns: *this, this one, these; that, that one, those; the one, the ones; such, such a one, such ones; the same, the same one* (or *ones*); *the former, the latter; the first* (*one*), *the second* (*one*), etc.; *the last* (*one*); *both; either; neither; the other; each one; all.* All of these pronouns except those that point out the person or thing by gesture have an antecedent: *This* is the picture of my wife and *that* the picture of her mother. "Which of these two *balls* do you want?" — "*The one* in your right hand." "*John* and *William* are both hard-working students. *The former* excels in mathematics, *the latter* excels in history." The problem has exercised the minds of the two *brothers*, and *each one* has solved it according to his temperament. She invited her *Sunday-school class* to her house, and *all* came.

Before a relative clause we usually employ in the plural the determinative (§ 13.C) pronoun *those* or now less commonly the personal pronoun *they* with determinative force: *Those* (or sometimes *they*) who do such things cannot be trusted. In the singular we use here the personal pronouns as determinatives: "*He* (or *she*) who does such things cannot be trusted," or in colloquial speech: "A man (or a woman) who does such things cannot be trusted." Compare p. 167. Similarly before a prepositional phrase: *She* (or more commonly *the girl*) with the auburn hair.

3. *Indefinites.* When we desire to convey an indefinite or general impression, we avoid the use of a noun and often employ instead of it an indefinite limiting adjective, treating it as an indefinite pronoun. These forms are: *all; any* (singular or plural); *anyone* (or earlier in the period simple *any*); *this one and that* (or *this and that one*, or *this one and that one*); *this, that and the other; this, that and the other one; everyone; some* (= *a fair amount* and *some people*, earlier in the period also with the meaning of

17

someone); *someone* (or early in the modern period simple *some*);
several; many; many a one; one; none (a singular or a plural, now
more commonly the latter); *no one; another, others; one — another; much; more; a little; little; less; few; a few; enough;* the
cardinal numerals, *two, three, fifty,* etc., when the reference is to
persons: *All* is not gold that glitters. I haven't *any* of his patience. Have you seen *any* of the latest hats? I should like to
have *some* of his patience. *Some* were captured, *others* were
killed. I chatted with *this and that one*. We talked about *this,
that and the other*. In our class there were *four* absent. There
were *five hundred* there.

H. EXCLAMATORY ADJECTIVE USED AS PRONOUN. The
exclamatory adjective *what a* is used as a pronoun: *What a one*
he is to make excuses!

THE ADJECTIVE

10. Definition. An adjective is a word that is used with a
noun or pronoun to describe or point out the living being or
lifeless thing, designated by the noun or pronoun: a *little* boy,
that boy, *this* boy, a *little* house.

11. Classification. There are two classes, descriptive and
limiting. A descriptive adjective expresses either the *kind* or
condition or *state* of the living being or lifeless thing spoken of:
a *good* boy, a *bright* dog, a *tall* tree; a *sick* boy, a *lame* dog. The
participles of verbs in adjective function are all descriptive
adjectives, since they indicate either an active or passive state:
running water, a *dying* soldier, a *broken* chair.

A limiting adjective, without expressing any idea of kind or
condition, limits the application of the idea expressed by the
noun to one or more individuals of the class, or to one or more
parts of a whole: *this* boy, *this* book, *these* books; *this* part of the
country.

In all the examples given above, the adjective stands before
the noun. The adjective in this position is called an adherent
adjective (§ 56.A). It may also follow the noun: There never
was a man *more just* (§ 56.A).

In all of the examples given above, the adjectives are used

attributively, i.e. are attributive adjectives, i.e. they stand before the noun or after it in direct connection with it; but the adjective can also stand after a linking (§ 15.C) verb as a predicate, i.e. a word which says something of the subject: The *tree* is *tall*. Here the adjective can be used also with a pronoun: John isn't here today; *he* is *sick*. The predicative use of the adjective is discussed in Syntax, § 54.B. The linking verb is lacking when the adjective says something of an object: I found him *sick*. The adjective is here called an objective predicate (Syntax, § 67.C.1).

12. Compound Adjectives and Derivative Adjectives.

A. COMPOUND ADJECTIVES. On account of the loss of its endings the modern English adjective has acquired a great facility to form compounds: an *up-to-date* dictionary, a *cut-and-dried* affair, a *plain-clothes* policeman, my *next-door* neighbor, a *large-scale* map, the *quarter-past-seven* train, *this*, *that and the other* newspaper. Notice that English compounds are not always written together as one word.

B. DERIVATIVE ADJECTIVES. Similar to compound adjectives are derivative adjectives, i.e. adjectives formed by adding to a noun, an adjective, or a verbal stem a suffix, which in most cases was originally an independent word. These suffixes are: *-en, -fold, -ful, -ish, -less, -ly, -some, -y, -able*, etc.: wood*en*, mani*fold*, hope*ful*, child*ish*, friend*less*, man*ly*, lone*some*, ston*y*, bear*able*, etc. To convert a group of words into an adjective we often connect the components by a hyphen and add the adjective suffix *-ed: warm-hearted, dark-haired*, etc.

13. Classes of Limiting Adjectives.
Descriptive adjectives are so simple in nature that they do not form classes. Limiting adjectives, on the other hand, form distinct groups:

A. POSSESSIVE ADJECTIVES. They are: *my, thy, his, her, its, our, your, their*. For variation in form in different functions see Syntax, § 103.C.

Possessive adjectives are often employed, not to express possession, but to convey the idea of appreciation or depreciation: He knows *his* Shakespeare. That boy has just broken *his*

19

third glass. *Your* true rustic turns his back on his interlocutor (G. Eliot).

B. Intensifying Adjectives. They are: *myself, ourself* (= *myself;* see § 105), *thyself, yourself, himself, herself, itself, ourselves, yourselves, themselves, oneself,* or *one's self.* They intensify the force of a preceding noun or pronoun, making it emphatic: Father *himself* admits it. One must decide such things *oneself* (or *one's self*). Compare Syntax, § 105.

In case the governing word is a noun, we often use *very* instead of these adjectives, but it always precedes the noun: He drew me out of the *very* jaws of perdition. To increase the intensity here we put *very* in the superlative: You have bought the *veriest* rubbish. We always use *very* when we desire not only to intensify the force of the word but also to emphasize the idea of identity or coincidence: You are the *very* man I am looking for.

C. Demonstrative Adjectives. They are: *this, these, that, those, the same, such, the, the one, yonder, yon* (archaic or poetic), and *both;* often also: *each, every, all,* which frequently point to definite individuals and hence are not always indefinite, as they are usually classed. As a number of these words vary their form according to the function they perform, they are treated in Syntax, § 103. Only a few simple examples are given here: *this* book and *that* one; *these* books and *those.*

When these demonstratives point forward to a following explanatory phrase or clause, they are called determinatives: *the* book on the table; *the* book I hold in my hand; this book and *the one* on the table; these books and *the ones* on the table; this book and *the one* you hold in your hand; *every* book on the table. We often use as determinatives also the indefinites *a, any, every, all* in F below and the relative adjectives in E.2 below. Compare Syntax, § 80.A.1.

a) The definite article and determinative *the* is sometimes still for archaic effect written *ye,* the *y* representing older *þ* and hence pronounced *th:* "ye old town."

b) Such or *such a* often indicates a high degree of a quality, sometimes standing alone before a noun, sometimes followed by an adjective which expresses the quality more accurately: I have never seen *such a storm*, or more accurately *such a terrible storm*, or with the adverb *so* instead of the adjective *such: so terrible a storm*. The adjective construction is the usual one before a plural noun: I have never seen *such children*, or more accurately *such good children* or *such bad children*.

D. NUMERAL ADJECTIVES. They indicate number. There are three classes:

1. *Cardinal Numeral Adjectives*. They are employed in counting: *three* dollars, *four* dollars, *fifty-five* dollars, *one hundred and fifty* dollars, etc. They are called *cardinal* (from Latin cardo *hinge*) because they are the most important words of number, on which the others hinge.

2. *Ordinal Numeral Adjectives*. They denote position or order in a series: the *first, second, third, last* day of the month.

3. *Multiplicatives*. They indicate multiplication: *twofold, tenfold*, etc.

E. RELATIVE ADJECTIVES. There are two groups:

1. *Which*, always pointing backward to a definite antecedent: We traveled together as far as Paris, *at which place we parted*.

2. The indefinites *which, what* (more indefinite than *which*), *whichever, whatever*. They are all determinatives (see C above) in that they point to the following explanatory clause, but at the same time they are relatives in that they link the clause in which they stand to the principal proposition. They introduce a substantive clause, i.e. a noun clause in the relation of a subject or object of the principal verb or an appositive to a noun: It is not known *which*, or *what, course he will pursue* (subject clause). I do not know *which*, or *what, course he will pursue* (object clause). The question *which*, or *what, course he will pursue* (appositive clause) has not yet been settled. I will approve *whichever*, or *whatever, course you decide upon* (object clause).

F. INDEFINITE ADJECTIVES. They are: *a, an; all; any; this, that and the other; every; some; many, many a, a great many; another;*

much; more; little, a little; less; few, a few; enough; several; sundry; divers. Examples: He has *much, little,* patience. Idle people jot down their idle thoughts and then post them to *this, that and the other* newspaper. He has helped *many a* man.

a) In American colloquial slang *some* is widely used also as a descriptive adjective expressing a high degree of excellence — a development out of the adverb *some* described in § 34.C (last par.): She is *some* girl. Often employed ironically: That is *some* car.

G. INTERROGATIVE ADJECTIVES. They are: *what* (indefinite), *which* (more definite, referring to two or more beings or things which are had distinctly in mind). Examples: *What* books have you bought? *Which* book did you finally select? In indirect questions (§ 9.F): I asked him *which* books I should read.

H. PROPER ADJECTIVES. Proper adjectives, i.e. adjectives derived from a proper noun, often do not denote a kind or a condition, but are limiting adjectives, identifying a being or thing: a *Harvard* student, the *United States* flag, the *German* universities, the *English* navy, etc. Notice that proper adjectives begin with a capital.

I. EXCLAMATORY ADJECTIVES. In exclamations *what* and *what a* are used: *What* nonsense! *What a* shame! *What a* beautiful day!

THE VERB

14. Definition. The verb is that part of speech by means of which we make an assertion or ask a question: The wind *blows. Is* the wind *blowing?*

15. Classification. There are three classes — transitive, intransitive, and linking.

A. TRANSITIVE VERBS. A transitive verb denotes an action which passes over from the doer of the action to the object of it: The boy *struck* his dog. The girl *loves* her pretty doll.

Where the action passes back to the doer we call the transitive verb a reflexive: She *is dressing* herself. He *overate* himself.

I *talked* myself hoarse. The object here is always a reflexive pronoun (§ 9.B).

B. INTRANSITIVE VERBS. An intransitive verb denotes a state or simple action without any reference to an object: John *is sleeping*. I *dream* every night. He often *acts* rashly. "The sun *is melting* (transitive) the snow," but "The snow *is melting*" (intransitive).

Transitive verbs are often used intransitively without an object when the thought is directed to the action alone: Mary *is dressing* (herself). He *hid* (himself) behind a tree. He *overeats* (himself). He likes *to give*. Compare § 109.

C. LINKING VERBS. Although we very commonly make assertions and ask questions by means of verbs, they are not absolutely necessary, and in fact we often do without them: *A sad experience! Our sister dead! John a cheat! Everything in good order.* This is an old type of sentence, once more common than now. It is employed when the thing predicated of the subject is an adjective, noun, or prepositional phrase. It was originally thought sufficient to place the predicate adjective, noun, or prepositional phrase alongside of the subject, before it or after it. Early in the development of the Indo-European (§ 1, 1st par.) languages it became common to join the predicate to the subject by means of the copula *be:* The boy *is* tall. He *is* a carpenter. Everything *is* in good order. Such a verb performs merely the function of announcing the predicate. It does not itself predicate, it merely *links* the predicate to the subject. In course of time there have developed a large number of such linking verbs, as *seem*, *look*, *get*, etc., and the list is growing. The linking verbs, or copulas, are treated in detail in Syntax, § 53.B.

16. Compound Verbs. A verb often enters into a close relation with an adverb, preposition, prepositional phrase, or an object, forming with it a unit, a compound. There are three classes:

A. INSEPARABLE COMPOUND. Adverb and verb often form a firm, inseparable compound in which the stress rests upon the verb, often with figurative meaning: *upróot*, *uplíft*, *undernóurish*, *overchárge*, etc. A preposition often forms such a compound with a verb: The river *is overflówing* its banks. Compare § 19 (last par.). Where the preposition or adverb is no longer in use outside of these compounds, as in the case of *be-* (= *over*, *upon*), it is called a prefix: to *bemóan* (= moan over). Also the frequentative suffixes *-le* and *-er* are common: crack*le*, flick*er*, etc. A compound with a prefix or a suffix is called a derivative.

Such compounds and derivatives are very common in foreign verbs: *pervade*, *coöperate*, *proceed*, *precede*, etc.

B. SEPARABLE COMPOUND. The verb often enters into a close relation with a more strongly stressed element, usually an adverb, prepositional phrase, or an object, forming with it a unit in thought, a real compound, although the parts are often separated and are not written together: His father *sèt* him *úp* in business. I *tòok* him *to tásk* for it. He *tòok párt* in the play.

C. PREPOSITIONAL COMPOUND. This newer group of compounds is described in § 20 (3rd par.).

THE ADVERB

17. Definition. An adverb is a word that modifies a verb, an adjective, or another adverb: The girl is improving *remarkably*. The girl is *remarkably* beautiful. The girl is improving *remarkably* fast. We walked *almost* four miles (adverbial accusative; § 68.B). It is *less than* two miles (adv. acc.) away. It is *more than* ten miles away. Compare § 68.

Adherent (§ 56.A) and appositive (§ 56.A) adjectives which modify verbal nouns are in a formal sense adjectives, but they have the force of adverbs: his *late* arrival, his last visit *here*.

18. Classification. Adverbs may be classified from different points of view:

A. CLASSIFICATION BY FUNCTION. There are three groups:

1. *A Simple Adverb* modifies a single word or group: He came *yesterday*. He is *very* industrious. He runs *very* fast. We walked *almost* four miles.

2. *A Sentence Adverb* modifies a whole sentence or clause: **He** is *undoubtedly* an able man. For fuller treatment see Syntax, §§ 53.C.4; 70; 70.B.

3. *A Conjunctive Adverb* not only modifies some word in the proposition in which it stands, but also links the proposition in which it stands to the rest of the sentence: We played **an** hour; *then* we went home. For fuller information see Syntax. § 75.A.

In such sentences both propositions are independent. Where, however, one of the propositions is logically subordinate, the old conjunctive adverb has been drawn into the subordinate clause and now serves there as the subordinating conjunction: "I met him *as* (contraction of *all so*, i.e. *quite so*) *I was coming home*," originally "I met him *so: I was coming home.*" Compare pp. 176–177. In older English, corresponding to the definite conjunctive adverb *so*, were the indefinites *where*, *whence* (now usually *where — from*), *whither* (now usually *where*), *when*, *why*, *how*, etc., which, like *so*, were early drawn into the subordinate clause and now serve there as subordinating conjunctions of place, time, etc., or as relative adverbs with the force of conjunctions binding the subordinate clause to the principal proposition, either as indefinite relative adverbs or in indirect questions (§ 9.F) as interrogative adverbs: I shall go *when* (subordinating conjunction of time) *he calls me.* I do not know *when* (indefinite relative adverb) *he did it.* I'll ask him *when* (interrogative adverb) *he did it* (indirect question). Compare §§ 85.A; 77.A; 79.A; 82.A.

4. *Interrogative Adverbs in Principal Propositions.* In indefinite situations where we desire to ask for information, we employ indefinites, not only as interrogative pronouns (§ 9.F) and interrogative adjectives (§ 13.G), but also as interrogative adverbs, namely *when*, *where*, *whence* (or in plain prose usually *where — from;* see § 19, next to last par.), *whither* (or in plain prose usually *where*), *why*, *how:* When did he go? *Where* does he live? "*Whence* did he come?", or more commonly "*Where* **did** he come *from?*" *Whither* (or more commonly *where*) did he go? *Why* did he do it? *How* did he do it?

25

B. Classification by Meaning.

1. *Adverbs of Place, Direction, Arrangement.* They are: *here, there, in, out, up, down, around; first*(*ly*), *secondly*, etc.; *where* (interrogative), *whither* (interrog.; in poetry and choice prose) or now more commonly *where; whence* (interrog.; in poetry and choice prose) or now more commonly *where — from;* etc.: He lives *here.* "Is your father *in?*" "No, sir, he has just gone *out.*" He went *in. Where* does he live? In popular speech many say "*Where* is he *at?*" to express rest and "*Where* did he go *to?*" to express motion and direction, but in literary language we say here: "*Where* is he?" and "*Where* did he go?", preferring the more simple construction, although it is not so expressive. But even in literary language we must say: "*Where* did he come *from?*", for otherwise the thought would not be clear. Where we use *where* and a preposition (*at, to,* or *from*), *where* ceases to be an adverb and becomes a noun (§ 19, next to last par.).

In colloquial speech *any place, some place, no place, every place,* are often used instead of the literary forms *anywhere, somewhere, nowhere, everywhere* (§ 9.E, 2nd par.).

2. *Adverbs of Time.* They are: *now, then, immediately, when* (interrogative), etc.: It is not raining *now. When* are you going?

3. *Adverbs of Manner.* They are: *well, slowly, fast, neatly, how* (interrogative), *so*, etc.: He walked *slowly. How* did you do it?

4. *Adverbs of Degree, Amount, Number.* They are: *very, nearly, almost, much, little, once, twice, so,* etc.: She is *very* kind. We are *nearly* there. He *almost* died. He worries *much.* He works *little.* He struck me *twice.*

5. *Adverbs of Cause.* They are: *why* (interrogative), *for what reason* (interrogative), etc.: *Why* did you do it?

6. *Adverbs of Inference and Result.* They are: *therefore, hence, so, thus,* etc.: No man will take counsel, but every man will take money: *therefore* money is better than counsel (Swift). There was no one there, *so* I went away. Compare § 75.A.5.

THE PREPOSITION

19. Definition and Function. A preposition is a word that connects a noun or pronoun with a verb, adjective, or another noun or pronoun by indicating a relationship between the things for which they stand: He stood *by* the *window*. He stood *behind me*. In the first example the preposition *by* connects the intransitive (§ 15.B) verb *stood* with the noun *window*. In the second example, the preposition *behind* connects the intransitive verb *stood* with the pronoun *me*. In both examples the prepositional phrase, i.e. the preposition and its object (i.e. the word governed by the preposition, the word following it), forms an adverbial element modifying the intransitive verb. The adverbial prepositional phrase is also common in connection with a transitive (§ 15.A) verb and its object: He is writing a letter *by the window*.

The adverbial prepositional phrase indicates some circumstance of place, as in these examples, and various other circumstances, as those of time, manner, degree, cause, purpose, result, means, agency, etc.: I wrote a letter *before breakfast* (time). I wrote the letter *with care* (manner). I am taller than you *by three inches* (degree). He was beheaded *for treason* (cause). John works *for grades* (purpose). He worked himself *into a frenzy* (result). The gardener trimmed the trees *with a knife* (means or instrument). The trees were trimmed *by the gardener* (agency).

In "He is shooting *at a mark*" the prepositional phrase made up of the preposition *at* and its object *mark* stands in a little closer relation to the intransitive verb than an adverbial element, forming the necessary complement of the verb, which we call a prepositional object. Compare p. 120 and § 66.

After the copula (§ 15.C) *be* the prepositional phrase is an adjective element with the force of a predicate adjective: The country is *at peace* (= *peaceful*).

In "She is fond *of music*" the preposition *of* connects the noun *music* with the adjective *fond*. The prepositional phrase *of music* is the necessary complement of the adjective *fond*, hence is its object. Compare § 66.

In "The girl *with dark hair* is my sister" the preposition *with*

27

connects the noun *hair* with the noun *girl*. The prepositional phrase *with dark hair* is an attributive adjective element since it modifies the noun *girl*. It is here equal in force to the descriptive (§ 11) adjective *dark-haired:* The *dark-haired* girl is my sister. The prepositional phrase here often has the force of a limiting (§ 11) adjective, pointing out one or more individuals: the tree *behind the house*. After verbal nouns (i.e. nouns made from verbs) the prepositional phrase, though in a formal sense an adjective element, often has the force of an object or an adverb: a mother's love *for her children* (with the force of an object); a walk *in the evening* (with the force of an adverb of time).

The object of the preposition is always a noun or a pronoun, which is uniformly in the accusative (§ 25.B): He went with my *brother* and *me*. The preposition usually stands before its object, but it may stand at the end of the sentence or clause: *Whom* (object of the preposition *with*) do you play *with* (preposition)? Compare § 131. The object of the preposition is often an adverb or a clause which is used as a noun or pronoun. As a noun: for *ever*, until *now*, after *today*, between *now* and *then*. *Where* did he come from? The day before *he came* (= *his coming*) was very beautiful. I have a little insight into *what he is doing*. He wrote me about *what he was doing*. As a pronoun: I saw him a month ago, since *when* (§ 80.C) I haven't seen anything of him.

In the preceding examples the preposition either stands before a noun or pronoun forming with it a phrase, or stands at the end of the sentence or clause. These are the most common uses of the preposition; but with a number of words the preposition is the first component of a compound verb, and its object stands after the verb: The enemy *over*ran the whole country. A great principle *under*lies this plan. Water *per*meates the ground. Compare § 16.A.

20. Inflectional Prepositions. Prepositions have played a conspicuous rôle in the development of our language. Their numbers are ever increasing. In Syntax, § 127, a list of those now in use is given. There are now so many of them that we have a wide range of choice in shading our thought. Some do not differ from others in meaning, as *with regard to*, or *with respect to;* they simply serve to vary our expression.

Some prepositions, however, are in certain grammatical relations perfectly rigid, and cannot be replaced by others with the same or similar meaning. They have often lost a good deal of their original concrete meaning and are no longer felt as prepositions, for they have developed into inflectional particles which indicate definite grammatical relations, often taking the place of older inflectional endings. Thus we now can say "I gave the book *to my friend*" instead of "I gave *my friend* the book." The words *my friend* are in the dative and once had a distinctive ending to indicate the dative relation. Now, as adjectives and nouns have lost their old distinctive dative ending, we often employ the preposition *to* to indicate the dative relation. Similarly, we often use the preposition *of* as an inflectional sign to indicate the genitive relation: "the father *of the boy*" instead of "*the boy's father*." Compare Syntax, § 66.A.

The inflectional preposition is not only placed before words, but often also after them in case of verbs: You can *depend upon* him. The preposition, as *upon* in this example, which once belonged to the word following it, is now often felt as belonging to a preceding intransitive verb, serving as an inflectional particle with the office of converting the intransitive into a transitive. That the preposition and the verb have fused into one word, a real compound, can be seen in passive form, where the preposition remains with the verb: He can be *depended upon*.

THE CONJUNCTION

21. Definition. A conjunction is a word that joins together sentences or parts of a sentence: Sweep the floor *and* dust the furniture. He waited *until* I came.

22. Classification. There are two general classes — coördinating and subordinating. Coördinating conjunctions are treated in detail in Syntax, § 75.A–B, subordinating conjunctions in §§ 77.A; 78.A; 79; 80.B; 82.A; 83.A; 84.A; 85.A; 86; 87; 88.A; 89.A; 90.A; 91.A.

THE INTERJECTION

23. Definition. An interjection is an outcry to express pain, surprise, anger, pleasure, or some other emotion, as *Ouch! Oh! Alas! Why!* In general, interjections belong to the oldest forms of speech and represent the most primitive type of sentence. Thus they are not words but sentences. Sentences are older than words (Syntax, § 71).

PART TWO

ACCIDENCE

INFLECTION OF NOUNS

24. Number
   A. Formation of the Plural of English Nouns
      1. By Adding an *s*-Sound to the Singular
      2. By Adding *-en* to the Singular
      3. By a Change of Vowel
      4. By Retaining Singular Form
   B. Foreign Plurals
      1. Words in *-a* with a Plural in *-ae*
      2. Words in *-us* with a Plural in *-i*
      3. Words in *-um* with a Plural in *-a*
      4. Words in *-ex*, Etc., with a Plural in *-es*
      5. Words in *-on* with a Plural in *-a*
      6. Words in *-ma* with a Plural in *-mata*
      7. *Species*, *Series*, Etc.
      8. Italian Words with the Plural in *-i*
      9. French Words
     10. Hebrew Words
   C. Two Forms of the Plural with Differentiated Meaning
   D. Plural of Compound Nouns
      1. Old Compounds
      2. Syntactical Compounds
      3. Titles
25. Case
   A. Nominative
   B. Accusative
   C. Dative
   D. Genitive
26. Gender

INFLECTION OF PRONOUNS

27. Case
28. Personal Pronouns
29. Reflexive Pronouns
30. Reciprocal Pronouns
31. Relative Pronouns
   A. *Who* and *Who*-Forms
   B. Indefinite *Which* and *Whichever*

32

INFLECTION OF ADJECTIVES

INFLECTION OF VERBS

Forms of Inflection

Tense Formation

INFLECTION OF ADVERBS

UNINFLECTED PARTS OF SPEECH

PART TWO

ACCIDENCE

A CCIDENCE is the study of the inflection of words, i.e.
the change of form in words to indicate the part they play
in the sentence. In English, the inflection is not so important a
factor in the expression of our thought as it once was. The
part a word plays in the sentence is now often indicated, not
by its form, but by its position in the sentence. The subject
of the sentence usually stands before the verb, the object after
it: The mother (subject) loves her child (object). Verbs once
had many more endings than they now have: Old English *ic
lufige*, *we lufiath*, now *I love*, *we love*. Today the singular and the
plural of the verb have the same form in the first person while
in Old English the endings of the verb indicated singular or
plural. We now feel that the subjects *I* and *we* are sufficient to
make the thought clear. Our language has become simpler
and yet, as we shall see later, is now often more accurate and
expressive than Old English was in spite of its greater richness
of form.

On the other hand, we now often use more words to express
ourselves than our ancestors. In Old English the superlative
of the adjective always was a single word with a superlative
ending, *-est* or *-ost*. We now often put *most* before the simple
adjective to form the superlative: "Mary is the *most béautiful*
and Jane the *most belóved*," but "The sisters are all beautiful,
but Mary is the *móst beautiful*." Notice the accents. To emphasize the quality, we stress the adjective, but we stress *most* to
emphasize the idea of degree. This shading of the thought was
impossible in Old English, since there was only one form here.
Alongside of the new superlative, however, we still often employ the old simple form: Of the sisters Mary is the *prettiest*.
Thus in English we often find the old and the new side by side.
The simple form with an ending we call a synthetic form, the

new form with an additional word an analytic form. The old synthetic forms are, in general, best preserved in poetic language, where there is usually a strong tendency to prefer the old, as hallowed by the use of our older masters.

In this treatise on accidence, the inflection of words, i.e. their forms or lack of forms, is treated in the usual order of the parts of speech, nouns, pronouns, adjectives, verbs, adverbs, prepositions, conjunctions, interjections. In the Syntax, the manner of using these forms will be described. Accidence and syntax are closely related in actual speech, in fact inseparable, but for practical purposes they are separated in this book as much as possible. It is thought helpful to the student to arrange for him in systematic shape all the forms of the language, the bare forms, free from syntactical discussion as much as possible, so that he may always have for ready reference a complete outline of all the formal means of expression in the language.

INFLECTION OF NOUNS

Nouns are inflected to indicate *number*, *case*, and *gender*.

24. Number. Number is that form of a word which indicates whether we are speaking of *one* or *more than one*.

English nouns have two numbers — the singular and the plural: The *bird* (singular) is singing. The *birds* (plural) are singing.

A. FORMATION OF THE PLURAL OF ENGLISH NOUNS. The plural is formed:

1. *By Adding an* S-*Sound to the Singular*. We now feel this as the "regular" plural ending, hence we always employ it with new words. In older English, -*es* was the usual ending, but we now in most nouns shorten it to -*s:* boy*s*, hat*s*, etc. Letters, figures, signs used in writing, and parts of speech other than nouns when used as nouns take -'*s* in the plural instead of -*s:* Dot your *i*'*s* and cross your *t*'*s*. There are two *9*'*s* in 99. The *I*'*s* and *my*'*s* and *me*'*s* in his speech pass beyond the bounds of modesty and good taste. The *pro*'*s* and *con*'*s*.

The older fuller form -*es* is still written in the following groups of nouns:

a. After sibilants (*s, ss, c, sh, tch, ch, g, dg, x, z*): gas*es*, mass*es*, vic*es*, dish*es*, ditch*es*, church*es*, ag*es*, edg*es*, box*es*, topaz*es*. Here -*es* always indicates a distinct syllable. In words in which a silent -*e* follows a sibilant, as in *rose, horse*, we add only -*s* in the plural, but we pronounce -*es*.

b. In the case of nouns ending in the singular in -*y* preceded by a consonantal sound. Here, however, before the addition of -*es* in the plural *y* is changed to *i*: lad*y*, pl. lad*ies;* soliloqu*y*, pl. soliloqu*ies;* fl*y*, pl. fl*ies*. But the plural of *fly* (carriage) and the plural of proper names in -*y* are regular: *flys, Marys, Murphys*.

Notice that the plural -*es* here does not mean a distinct syllable as in a. The *e* of the plural ending is silent.

c. In the case of nouns of English origin ending in the singular in -*f* or -*fe* preceded by *l* or any long vowel except *oo*. Here, however, before the addition of -*es* in the plural the *f* is changed to *v*: cal*f*, pl. cal*ves;* wol*f*, pl. wol*ves;* thie*f*, pl. thie*ves;* wi*fe*, pl. wi*ves*. Notice that the plural -*es* here does not mean a distinct syllable as in a. The *e* of the plural ending is silent.

Words ending in -*f* preceded by *oo*, as *roof, hoof*, have the regular plural in -*s*: *roofs, hoofs*. Likewise borrowed words in -*f* or -*fe*: *chief, chiefs;* strife, strifes. *Beef*, though a French word, has become thoroughly naturalized and may have either the English plural *beeves* or in American English, *beefs*.

Wharf, dwarf, scarf form the plural with -*fs* or -*ves*. *Staff* has two plurals with different meaning: *staffs, staves*. Compare C below.

d. A number of common nouns in -*o* preceded by a consonant take -*es* in the plural, especially: *echo, mosquito, Negro, no, potato, tomato, veto*. A currently increasing number take either -*es* or -*s*: *banjo, bravo, buffalo, calico, cargo, fresco, grotto, halo, lasso, mango, memento, motto, portico, proviso, stiletto, zero*. All nouns in -*o* preceded by a vowel and a large number preceded by a consonant take -*s*, as: *bamboo, cuckoo, cameo, curio, embryo, folio, Hindoo*, etc.; *canto, casino, chromo, contralto, dynamo, octavo, piano, quarto, rondo, solo, soprano, torso, tyro*, etc.

Notice that the plural -*es* here does not mean a distinct syllable as in a above. The *e* of the plural ending is silent.

2. *By Adding* -en *to the Singular: ox*, pl. *oxen*. This plural, common in older English, is now in its simple form restricted to *ox*. *Children, brethren, kine* (archaic plural of *cow*) are double plurals, resulting from adding the plural ending -*en* to an old plural once in use, *cildru, brothru, cy* (old plural of *cu* cow).

3. *By a Change of Vowel: foot, feet; goose, geese; louse, lice; man, men; woman, women; mouse, mice; tooth, teeth.*
The plural of *Northman* is *Northmen*, but *Norman* has the regular plural *Normans.* The foreign words *Mussulman, Ottoman*, have nothing to do with English *man* and hence have regular plurals: *Mussulmans, Ottomans.*

4. *By Retaining Singular Form.* In a large number of words the plural has the same form as the singular: *one deer, several deer; one sheep, two sheep.* Other examples are given in § 94.A and D (last par.). *Swine* is usually a plural: throw pearls before *swine.* It is now used in the singular only as a term of abuse: You *swine* you! The use of a plural with the same form as the singular, once more common than now, is still common in the second component of compounds: a ten-*pound* baby, a ten-*foot* pole, a three-*year*-old. Many nouns made from adjectives have the same form for singular and plural (§ 108).

B. FOREIGN PLURALS. Nouns that have not been thoroughly naturalized retain their original plurals. Some of them have a tendency more or less strong to assume the regular English plural in -*s* — a tendency that should be encouraged. There are different groups:

1. *Words in* -a *with a Plural in* -ae : *alumna, alumnae; formula, formulas* or *formulae; larva, larvae; nebula, nebulae* or *nebulas; vertebra, vertebrae* or *vertebras.*

2. *Words in* -us *with a Plural in* -i: *alumnus, alumni; bacillus, bacilli; cumulus, cumuli; focus, focuses* or *foci; fungus, fungi* or *funguses; gladiolus, gladioli* or *gladioluses; hippopotamus, hippopotamuses* or *hippopotami; magus, magi; nucleus, nuclei; radius, radii; stimulus, stimuli; terminus, termini* or *terminuses.* But

apparatus has the plural *apparatus* or *apparatuses; hiatus* the plural *hiatuses* or *hiatus; genus* the plural *genera; octopus* the plural *octopuses*, not *octopi* as given by some grammarians.

3. *Words in* -um *with a Plural in* -a: *addendum, addenda; agendum, agenda; bacterium, bacteria; candelabrum, candelabra* or *candelabrums; curriculum, curriculums* or *curricula; datum, data; dictum, dicta* or *dictums; erratum, errata; memorandum, memoranda* or *memorandums; stratum, strata* or *stratums*.

4. *Words in* -ex, -ix, -yx, -is, -sis *with a Plural in* -es, which, however, is not added to the singular, but to an altered or shortened form of it, or, on the other hand, is often after English fashion added to the regular singular form: *apex, apexes* or *apices; index, indexes* or *indices; vertex, vertexes* or *vertices; vortex, vortices* or *vortexes; administratrix, administratrices; appendix, appendixes* or *appendices; executrix, executrices* or *executrixes; radix, radices* or sometimes *radixes; calyx, calyxes* or *calyces; axis, axes; amanuensis, amanuenses; analysis, analyses; basis, bases; crisis, crises; ellipsis, ellipses; hypothesis, hypotheses; oasis, oases; parenthesis, parentheses; synopsis, synopses; thesis, theses*.

5. *Words in* -on *with a Plural in* -a: *automaton, automatons* or *automata; criterion, criteria; phenomenon, phenomena*.

6. *Words in* -ma *with a Plural in* -mata: *dogma, dogmas* or now rarely *dogmata; stigma, stigmas* or *stigmata*.

7. *Species, Series, Abatis, Chamois, Corps*, have the same form for singular and plural, but in *chamois* and *corps* the final *s* is silent in the singular and in the plural is pronounced in the case of *corps*, unpronounced or pronounced in the case of *chamois*. *Forceps* is either a singular or a plural: this or these forceps, a pair of forceps.

Cyclops has a variant form *Cyclop*. *Cyclops* has the plural *Cyclopes* or *Cyclopses; Cyclop* has the plural *Cyclops*.

8. *Italian Words with the Plural in* -i: *bandit, bandits* or *banditti; conversazione, conversaziones* or *conversazioni; virtuoso, virtuosos* or *virtuosi*.

9. *French Words: madame, mesdames; monsieur, messieurs; beau, beaus* or *beaux; bureau, bureaus* or *bureaux*.

10. *Hebrew Words:* *cherub*, *cherubim* or sometimes with a double plural, *cherubims; seraph*, *seraphs* or *seraphim* or sometimes with a double plural, *seraphim*. Compare C below.

C. Two Forms of the Plural with Differentiated Meaning: *brother*, pl. *brothers* (by blood), *brethren* (of a religious or secular order or community); *cherub*, pl. *cherubs* (darlings), *cherubim* (angels); *cloth*, pl. *cloths* (different pieces or kinds of cloth), *clothes* (the collection of one's garments); *die*, pl. *dies* (stamps), *dice* (cubes used in games); *genius*, pl. *geniuses* (people of genius), *genii* (fabulous spirits); *penny*, pl. *pennies* (individual coins), *pence* (collectively, as in "Can you give me six pennies for this sixpence?"); *index*, pl. *indexes* (tables of contents), *indices* (algebraical signs); *seraph*, pl. *seraphs* (sweet singers), *seraphim* (angels); *staff*, pl. *staves* (musical term), *staffs* (military or newspaper staffs, flagstaffs, etc.).

In older English, *pease* is a singular as well as a plural. The old singular form is still sometimes used in *pease-pudding* (now usually *pea-pudding, pea-soup*, etc.). From the plural *pease* was formed the new singular *pea*, a so-called back-formation. To this new singular there were for a long time two plurals, *peas* (individual peas) and *pease* (for a mass of peas), now usually *peas*.

For further discussion see Syntax, § 94.A.1.

D. Plural of Compound Nouns. There are three groups:

1. *Old Compounds.* Our oldest compounds and most of our newer ones are forms representing a unit of thought, hence are treated as simple nouns, the final element, if a noun, assuming the plural form that it would have as a simple word: *toothpick, toothpicks; horseman, horsemen; washer-woman, washer-women; bird's-nest, bird's-nests.* If the final element is not a noun, the plural usually ends in *-s: stowaways, bucketfuls, godsends, merry-go-rounds.*

Inflection usually takes place only in the final element, but in a few compounds containing two nouns as components both nouns have plural form: *maidservants, girl cashiers*, etc., but *menservants, men friends, women students*, etc. It would be more in accordance with our modern feeling, as described in § 56.C

(2nd par.), to construe the first element of such compounds as an adjective.

2. *Syntactical Compounds.* Although in the old compounds in 1 the components stand in a syntactical relation, the relation is often not indicated by their form; hence we can easily add the plural sign at the end of the group. But in many compounds where the syntactical relation is indicated by the form, especially where the first component is a noun which is modified by a genitive, prepositional phrase, adverb, or adjective, we plainly feel the force of the noun and give it plural form if there is a reference to more than one: *men-of-war, brothers-in-law, commanders-in-chief, lookers-on, passers-by, coats-of-mail, courts-martial, poets laureate, billets-doux.* In a number of such compounds, however, the concrete force of the noun is felt so little and the oneness of the compound is felt so strongly that the regular plural ending *-s* is added at the end: *will-o'-the-wisps, jack-in-the-pulpits* (American plant), etc.; and often *court-martials* instead of *courts-martial.*

3. *Titles.* For the plural of titles see Syntax, § 94.E.

25. Case. A case is that form or position of a noun or a pronoun which marks it as the subject or the object of a verb, adjective, or preposition, or as playing the part of an adjective or adverb. Once the Germanic (§ 1) languages indicated these grammatical relations by *inflectional endings,* i.e. the endings which the nouns, pronouns, and adjectives assumed to show the part they were playing in the sentence. Of the many endings once used, English has, in the case of nouns, preserved only one, namely the *-s* of the genitive. We now express these relations by the *position* of the noun with regard to the verb or preposition, or by means of *inflectional prepositions* (§ 20), which have taken the place of the old inflectional endings.

There are four cases, nominative, accusative, dative, genitive:

A. NOMINATIVE. We employ this case to indicate the subject, predicate, or a noun in direct address. The subject relation is indicated by placing the noun before the verb: The *wind* blows. The *winds* blow. The subject nominative usually as here stands before a finite verb, i.e. a verb that agrees with its subject in number and person. In subordinate clauses, however, the subject nominative sometimes stands before a predicate participle, adjective, noun, adverb, or prepositional phrase: Off we started, *he remaining behind* (= *while he remained behind*). This nominative is called the absolute nominative. The construction is described in detail in § 73.

The predicate noun is recognized by its position after a linking (§ 15.C) verb: He is my *brother*.

The nominative of address is known by its peculiar intonation and its independent position in the sentence, having a close relation to the thought, but without any relation to the grammatical structure: O *Mary*, go and call the cattle home!

B. ACCUSATIVE. We employ this case to mark a noun or pronoun as the object of a transitive (§ 15.A) verb, a preposition, or an adjective. The object relation is indicated by placing the noun or the pronoun after the verb, preposition, or adjective: The dog bit my *brother* and *me*. He is sitting by *me* on the *sofa*. This book is worth (adjective) *reading*.

A full discussion of the use of the accusative as the object of verbs is given in Syntax, § 63.B. The various uses of the accusative as the object of prepositions are given in § 19. *Worth* is the only adjective that takes an accusative object. Adjectives usually have as object a prepositional phrase, a so-called prepositional object consisting of a preposition and its object: She is fond *of music*. He is eager *for gain*. Compare § 19. Also an intransitive (§ 15.B) verb may have a prepositional object: He is shooting *at a mark* (§ 66).

An accusative is often used adverbially, as a modifier of a verb, modifying it without indicating the direction of an activity toward an object: He stayed *an hour*. For further discussion see Syntax, § 68.B.

A noun or pronoun which is predicated of an accusative subject is in the accusative: The President made him *a general*. He thought Richard to be *me*. I supposed it to be *him*. These constructions are explained in §§ 67.C; 82.B.

C. DATIVE. We employ this case to indicate that an action or feeling is directed toward a person or thing to his or its advantage or disadvantage. This relation is indicated in two ways:

We place the noun or pronoun between the verb and an accusative: The mother is making *her boy* a new coat. The mother is sewing for her boy; she is making *him* a new coat. The dative is distinguished here by its position, not by its form.

Or we place the inflectional preposition (§ 20) *to* or *for* before the simple noun (or pronoun), preposition and noun (or preposition and pronoun) together forming a dative with the same force as the old dative with an inflectional ending: "The mother is making a new coat *for her boy John*. She will give his old one *to his little brother*." "The mother is sewing *for her boy;* she is making a new coat *for him*. She will give it *to him* when he comes home from school." The prepositions *to* and *for* are not the only ones used here. By the choice of different prepositions we can shade our thought better than was possible in Old English by the use of one ending. For further discussion see Syntax, §§ 63.A; 64.A,B,C.

D. Genitive. The attributive genitive, i.e. the genitive that modifies a noun or pronoun, plays the part of an adjective. It expresses many related ideas, *origin, possession, subject, object, material, composition, characteristic, measure, apposition, a whole from which a part is taken: Shakespeare's* (origin) dramas; *John's* (possession) hat; *mother's* (subject) love for us; *Caesar's* (object) murderers; an idol *of gold* (material); a flock *of birds* (composition); a *child's* (characteristic) language; an *hour's* (measure) delay; the gift *of song* (apposition); a piece *of bread* (whole from which a part is taken).

There are four distinct genitive forms, often differentiated in use. These are described in § 57.A.1,2,3,4.

For the further discussion of the attributive genitive see Syntax, § 57.

The genitive is sometimes used adverbially, i.e. as a modifier of a verb: I was taken *unawares* by his question. *Of late years* we see very little of each other. For fuller information see Syntax, § 68.B.

26. Gender. Gender was once an important feature in the inflection of English nouns, but now plays a rather modest rôle. The subject is treated in detail in Syntax, § 95.

INFLECTION OF PRONOUNS

27. Case. The cases of pronouns have the same force as those of nouns, as described in § 25.A,B,C,D.

The seven classes are presented here in the same order as in § 9.

28. Personal Pronouns. These pronouns have three persons: the first person representing the speaker; the second the person spoken to; the third the person or thing spoken of. The forms for the third person have in the singular three genders (§ 95.A.1,2,3), masculine, feminine, neuter.

Their inflection is as follows:

	FIRST PERSON	SECOND PERSON		THIRD PERSON		
		Old Form	*Common Form*	*Masc.*	*Fem.*	*Neut.*

SINGULAR

Nom.	I	thou	you	he	she	it
Acc.	me	thee	you	him	her	it
Dat.	me / to me / for me	thee / to thee / for thee	you / to you / for you	him / to him / for him	her / to her / for her	it / to it / for it
Gen.	mine / my / of me / of mine	thine / thy / of thee / of thine	yours / your / of you / of yours	his / of him / of his	hers / her / of her / of hers	its / of it

PLURAL

Plural of All Three

Nom.	we	ye	you	they
Acc.	us	you	you	them
Dat.	us / to us / for us	you / to you / for you	you / to you / for you	them / to them / for them
Gen.	ours / our / of us / of ours	yours / your / of you / of yours	yours / your / of you / of yours	theirs / their / of them / of theirs

44

The use of the dative forms is described in §§ 63.A; 64.A,B,C.

Of the above forms the simple genitives are now more commonly used as adjectives than as pronouns (Syntax, §§ 103.C; 57.C.4). The double genitive *of ours*, *of yours*, etc. is widely used. See § 57.A.3.

For the use of the second person forms see Syntax, § 51.H.

29. Reflexive Pronouns. These pronouns (§ 9.B), *myself, yourself*, etc., have no change of form in the accusative, and in the dative take *to* or *for* before them except before an accusative, where they still have their old simple form: She is dressing *herself*. He is true *to himself*. "He bought a new hat *for himself*," or "He bought *himself* a new hat." The form itself indicates the number and person and in part also the gender. For older forms which are sometimes still used here see Syntax, § 97.

30. Reciprocal Pronouns. These pronouns (§ 9.C), *each other, one another*, have the old *s*-genitive alongside of the newer *of*-genitive, but in the dative have only the newer form with *to* or *for:* They never weary of *each other's* company, or the company *of each other*. They are kind *to each other*. They love *each other* (acc.) dearly. For the use of these forms see Syntax, § 98.

31. Relative Pronouns. These pronouns (§ 9.D.1,2), *who, which, that, what*, etc., have all, except *who* and the *who*-forms, as *whoever*, etc., lost their old inflectional forms, even the genitive ending -*s*, which is still common in nouns. Hence the case relations here are indicated by modern means: The subject stands before the verb, and the dative and the genitive have inflectional prepositions (§ 20) before them as case signs, *to* or *for* before the dative and *of* before the genitive: He is the boy *that* (nom.) gave it to me. He is the boy *that* (dat.) I gave it *to*, or with the suppression of the relative pronoun: He is the boy I gave it *to*. He is the boy *that* (dat.) I bought the new coat *for*. In the case of the relative pronoun *that*, the case sign *to* or *for* stands at the end of the clause, as explained in Syntax, § 80.A.1.

The *of*-genitive here often follows the governing noun, always so when the governing noun stands in a prepositional phrase: This is the tree in the shade *of which* we often rest. *That*, however, has no genitive form.

Relative pronouns which are the object of a verb have a position in the sentence different from that of all other objects. As they have conjunctive force, i.e. as they link the clause in which they stand to the rest of the sentence, they must stand at or near the beginning of the clause, hence cannot follow the verb. They indicate the grammatical relations here by a peculiar word-order. If the verb follows the relative immediately or soon, the relative is a nominative: He is the boy *that* (nom.) did it. That is *what* (nom. sing.) caused it. *What* (nom. plural) have often been censured as Shakespeare's conceits *are* completely justifiable (Coleridge). If a noun or other pronoun follows the relative, the relative is in the object relation: He is the boy *that* (acc.) I saw do it. That is *what* (acc.) he wants. He is the boy *that* (acc.) the dog bit.

If the relative pronoun is the object of a preposition, it stands at the beginning of the clause after the preposition, or it stands in the first place in the clause and the preposition in the last place: "This is the pen *with which* I write," or "This is the pen *which* I write *with*," or "This is the pen I write *with*" (Syntax, §§ 80. A.1; 131).

A. "Who" and "Who"-Forms. These pronouns are inflected as follows, the same form in each case serving as a singular and a plural:

Nom.	who	whoever	whosoever
Acc.	whom	whomever	whomsoever
Dat.	{ to whom { for whom	{ to whomever { for whomever	{ to whomsoever { for whomsoever
Gen.	{ whose { of whom	{ whosever { whoever's (colloquial)	whosesoever

As we have abandoned the use of the old case forms in relative pronouns — except the *who*-forms given above — and now employ the modern means of expression described above, there is a strong tendency in colloquial speech to abandon also these special *who*-forms and use the modern forms also here: I don't know *who* (instead of *whom*) he plays *with*. I will go with *whoever I like*, instead of *whomever I like* [*to go with*].

46

But of course: I will go with *whoever* is going my way. The relative pronoun always has the case form required by the construction of the clause in which it stands. Thus in the last example it is nominative since it is subject. In the preceding example it is the object of the preposition *with* understood. We should withstand the strong drift here toward the modern forms and use the more expressive older ones.

One old *who*-form is an exceedingly useful form, namely the genitive *whose*. The modern genitive *of whom* is at times useful, in the partitive genitive relation is even necessary, as in "He has two sons, *of whom* the elder is his junior partner." In general, however, the old short form *whose* is the favorite genitive even in colloquial speech, which is elsewhere not friendly to the older use of distinctive endings and prefers the modern means of expression: He has two sons *whose* friendship I much prize. I will not hurt a hair of her head, *whose ever* (older form, now more commonly *whosever* or *whoever's*) daughter she may be.

The *who*-forms are often followed by the appositive adverb *else:* I don't know *who else* (i.e. distinct from him) could have done it. Relative pronouns often enter into a close relation to *else*, forming with it a compound. I don't know *whose else* (older usage), or now usually *who else's*, child it could be. If it isn't his child, I don't know *whose else* (still in use when there is, as here, no noun following), or *who else's*, it could be. His love will never fail, *whoever else's* (or *whosoever else's*) may.

For the use of these forms, see the cross references in Syntax, § 99.

B. INDEFINITE "WHICH" AND "WHICHEVER." Differing from all other relative pronouns these words are limiting (§ 11) adjectives used as pronouns; hence they may have the *one*-form, like other limiting adjectives in substantive (§ 103) function: Here are two hats, but I don't know *which one* is mine. "Here are some new books. I don't know *which ones* to select." It has a genitive singular in -*s:* All three boys have a good record at school, but I do not know *which one's* is the best (§ 103).

32. Indefinite Pronouns. Of these pronouns (§ 9.E) only the forms in -*body*, i.e. *somebody, anybody, everybody, nobody,* have preserved the old genitive in -*s*, which they retain alongside of the newer *of*-form: I don't want *anybody's* help, or the help *of anybody*. The other forms have preserved the old *s*-genitive only when used as the subject of the gerund: I haven't heard of *anything's* (or *anything*, an acc.; see § 124.B) being wrong. Elsewhere we employ the modern means of expressing the grammatical relations: subject before verb and object after it; *to*-dative or *for*-dative; *of*-genitive. These words have no plural.

These pronouns are often followed by the appositive adverb *else:* It wasn't he; it was *somebody else* (i.e. distinct from him). These compound pronouns often enter into a close relation with *else* here, forming with it a compound indefinite pronoun: It can't be *anybody else's* hat, instead of older *anybody's else* hat. That is my business and *nobody else's*, or sometimes as in older English *nobody's else*.

33. Interrogative Pronouns.

There are three interrogative pronouns, *who, what, which*. The last of these is a limiting (§ 11) adjective used as a pronoun; hence, like other limiting adjectives in substantive (§ 103) function, it may have a *one*-form: Here are two hats. *Which one* is yours? "You have read the latest novels. *Which*, or *which ones*, are the best?" It has a genitive singular in -*s:* "All three brothers, they say, have a good record at school." — "*Which one's* is the best?"

What is not inflected. The grammatical relations are shown by the word-order: subject before the verb; the object before a verb which is followed by the subject: *What* (subject) is worrying you? *What* (subject) are their names? *What* (object) does he want? *What* and *who* are predicates when they stand before a linking (§ 15.C) verb which is followed by the subject: *What* is he? *Who* is he? Often also in exclamations: *What* was my astonishment when I saw her there!

When *what* is the object of a preposition it stands at the beginning of the sentence after the preposition, or much more commonly it stands in the first place, and the preposition in the last place: *About what* are they talking?, or *What* are they talking *about?*, or She is asking him *what* they are talking *about* (indirect question).

Who inflects as follows, the same form in each case serving as a singular and a plural:

Nom.	who
Acc.	whom
Dat.	to whom *or* for whom
Gen.	whose

As we have in general abandoned the use of the old inflectional endings in favor of modern means of expression, there is also here in colloquial speech a strong tendency to employ modern forms — except in the genitive relation, where the old form is well preserved: "*Who* (instead of *whom*) did you meet?" "*Who* did you give it *to?*", instead of "*Whom* did you give it *to?*", or "*To whom* did you give it?" "*Who* did you get it *from?*", instead of "*Whom* did you get it *from?*", or "*From whom* did you get it?" We should withstand the very strong drift here toward the modern forms and use the more expressive older ones. In the genitive relation we still prefer the older form: *Whose* car is it?

The *who*-forms are often followed by the appositive adverb *else: Who else* (i.e. distinct from those mentioned) were there? The interrogative often enters into a close relation to *else*, forming with it a compound: *Whose else* (older usage), or now usualy *who else's*, son could he be? It is my book; *whose else* (still widely used when there is, as here, no noun following), or now also *who else's*, could it be?

34. Limiting Adjectives Used as Pronouns. The three groups given in § 9.G.1,2,3 are inflected as follows:

A. Intensifying Adjectives. The intensifying adjectives (§ 9.G.1) *myself, ourselves, yourself, yourselves, themselves,* etc., have all lost their old case endings and even when used as pronouns must indicate the case relations by modern means: *yourself,* a subject when standing before the verb, but an object when following a preposition or any verb except a linking (§ 15.C) verb, where it is a predicate; *to,* or *for, yourself,* dative. For examples see Syntax, § 105 (2nd par.).

The form of these pronouns always indicates the number and the person.

49

B. "THIS ONE," ETC. Of the words in this group (§ 9.G.2) *this one, that one, the one, such a one, the same one, the former, the latter, the first one, the second one*, etc., *the last one, either, either one, neither, neither one*, and *each one* still have in the singular the old *s*-genitive alongside of the newer *of*-genitive: John and Sam and *the latter's* sister, or the sister *of the latter*. All the other forms in this group indicate the case relations by modern means, also the forms given above when used in the plural: I know most of the students present, but I don't know the names *of these*, or the names *of the last ones* in the row.

Some words indicate the singular and the plural by their forms: *this, these; that, those; the one, the ones; such a one, such ones; the same (one), the same (ones); the first (one), the first (ones); the last (one), the last (ones)*. The meaning of *both* and *all* indicates the plural. Both *the former* and *the latter* remain unchanged in the plural, the connection alone indicating the number: The struggle between Alfred and the Danes resulted in the overthrow *of the latter*. *Either* and *neither* are usually employed only in the singular, but *neither* is not infrequently used as a plural (§ 55.A.1.e).

C. INDEFINITES. Of the words in this group (§ 9.G.3) *anyone, this (one)* and *that one, this, that* and *the other one, everyone, someone, many a one, one, no one, another* still have in the singular the old *s*-genitive alongside of the newer *of*-genitive: *someone's* boy, or the boy *of someone*. *Others* is the only word that has the old genitive in the plural: She thinks only of *others'* good, or the good *of others*. All the other forms of this group regularly indicate the case relations by modern means, also usually the forms given above when used in the plural.

Two indicate the plural by their form: *others* and *this, that* and *the other ones*. Four indicate the plural by their meaning: *several, many, few, a few*. *None* is either singular or plural, more commonly the latter: None *know*, or *knows*, it so well as I. In the singular it is usual to employ *nó one: Nó one* knows it so well as I. *Not óne*, or colloquially *not a óne*, is more emphatic than *none* or *no one:* There is none, no, *not óne* in whom I trust (M. H. Hewlett). No one came to the meeting, no, *not a óne*.

Also *all, any, some, more* are either singular or plural. *Less* is a singular but *less than* and *more than* are often adverbs: There were *less than* (adverb) sixty (= sixty people) there, or *fewer* (= fewer people) *than* sixty there. *More than* (adverb) one has found it so.

All, any, none, some (= *a fair amount*), *much, more, little, a little, less, enough* are used as neuter pronouns: I don't want *any* of your nonsense. It is *none* of my business. I should like to have *some* of your patience. The accusative of these neuter pronouns is much used adverbially (§ 68.B.), especially with a comparative: He cares *little* about it. It is *much* too large. Is he resting *any* better today? He is *none* the worse for his fall. He is *some* (colloquial acc. for the literary adverb *somewhat*) better this morning.

In American colloquial slang adverbial *some* is much used to express a high degree: "He is going *some*," originally a modest statement, *some* (= *a little*) indicating modestly a high degree. By this development it has come about that the word *some* indicates both a low and a high degree. Compare § 13.F.*a*.

INFLECTION OF ADJECTIVES

35. Older Usage and Modern Usage. In Old English, adjectives indicated by their inflection case, gender, number, and the degrees of comparison, the comparative and the superlative. In the course of the Middle English (§ 2.B) period the inflectional endings for case, gender, and number entirely disappeared.

These inflectional endings had scarcely disappeared when it became apparent that something valuable had been lost. The inflectional endings for case, gender, number, had served the useful purpose of linking the adjective to its governing noun. The lack of an ending was not felt when the adjective stood immediately before the noun, as in "a *black* sheep," but in substantive function, i.e. when the adjective stood alone separated some distance from its governing noun, the lack of the ending was sorely missed: "My brother bought a white sheep, and I bought a *black*." The need of something after *black* to link it to its governing noun *sheep* was felt as early as the fourteenth century, and people began to put the numeral *one* after it: My brother bought a white sheep, and I bought a *black one*. The linking force of *one* was felt much more strongly than its original meaning *one*, so that the plural *ones* was employed to link the adjective to a plural noun: My brother bought two white sheep, and I bought two *black ones*.

Thus *ones* in this example has entirely ceased to have a relation to the numeral *one*, for it means *two*. It has the same force as the old inflectional ending that once stood in the same place, except that it is not associated in any way with gender or case. In spite of the fact that it has always been written as an independent word, it has become an inflectional ending of the adjective with the function of linking it to its governing noun.

The use of *one* here began to spread, since its usefulness was at once recognized, and it is still spreading. A more detailed description of present usage here is given in Syntax, § 103, 103.A.1.a.

The older use of inflectional forms to express the comparative and superlative degrees survives, but the form of expression has changed considerably. A detailed description of present usage is given in Syntax, § 104.

INFLECTION OF VERBS

The English verb has forms called voices, moods, tenses, aspects, numbers, and persons, which represent the action suggested by the verb as limited in various ways, such as in person, number, time, manner of conception, etc. A verb that can be limited in all these ways is called a finite verb: I *go*, he *goes*, they *go*, he *went*, he *may* go, he *might* go, etc. The infinite forms of the verb — the participle (§ 122), the infinitive (§ 123.A), and the gerund (§ 124) — are limited in fewer ways.

Forms of Inflection

36. Voice. There are two voices, the active and the passive.

A. ACTIVE VOICE. The active voice indicates that the subject does something, or is, or is becoming, something: Mary *makes* good bread. Two men *are painting* our house. Mr. Smith *is* a banker. John *is becoming* tired.

INFLECTION OF VERBS: VOICE   [§ 36.C.4

B. Passive Voice. The passive voice represents the subject
as acted upon: John *was punished* for disobeying his mother.
Our house *is being painted*. Only transitives (§ 15.A) can form
a passive.

C. Formation of the Passive. The active verb is often a
simple form, but the passive is always a compound, made in the
following ways:

1. *Common Literary Form.* The common literary form is made
by prefixing some form of the copula *be* (*is, are, was, were*, etc.)
to the past participle: Our house *is painted* every year. Here
the reference is to an act. But the same form is often used to
express a state: Our house *is painted*. The door *was shut* (state)
at six o'clock, but I don't know when it *was shut* (act). For
full inflection see § 45.A.

2. *Colloquial Form.* The present literary passive is the weak-
est part of our language, since it cannot express our thought
accurately. In our colloquial speech, where we are not as much
under restraint as in the literary language, we often yield here
to the impulse to express ourselves more precisely and use the
copula *get* instead of *be:* Our house *gets painted* every year.
John tried to cheat, but he *got caught* at it. We feel the *get*-
passive as an *actional* passive, expressing an act, and the *be*-
passive as a *statal* passive, expressing a state: "As I passed by,
my coat *got caught* (act) on a nail," but "I had to stop since
my coat *was caught* (state) on a nail." This fine distinction
deserves to be carried into the literary language.

3. *"Become"-Form.* Instead of *get* we often employ *become* as
a passive auxiliary with a different shade of meaning as *become*
serves not only as a passive auxiliary here but also retains its
original effective aspect (§ 121.B) force, representing the act
as the result of a development: He *became seized* with a profound
melancholy (McCarthy, *History of Our Own Times*). This newspaper *has* already *become* widely *read* in this community.

4. *Progressive Forms.* We employ the progressive form of the
copula *be, get,* or *become* in connection with the past participle
to indicate that the subject is receiving the action continuously:

Our house *is being* (or colloquially *getting*) *painted*. This news-paper *is becoming* widely *read* in this community. These three forms are used only in the present and the past tense. Else-where they are replaced by the old form described in *a* below. For full inflection see § 45.B.

a) Older Progressive. There is an older progressive passive which is still in limited use. It is made by prefixing a form of the copula *be* to the present participle: There *is* a new bridge *building*. It is still exclusively used in the present perfect, past perfect, future, and future perfect. Compare § 45.B.

The progressive passive is treated more fully in Syntax, § 110.

37. Mood. Moods are the changes in the form of the verb to show the various ways in which the action or state is thought of by the speaker.

There are three moods:

A. INDICATIVE MOOD. This form represents something as a fact, or as in close relations with reality, or in interrogative form inquires after a fact. A fact: The sun *rises* every morning. In a close relation to reality: I shall not go if it *rains*. The indica-tive *rains* here does not state that it *is* raining, but indicates that the idea of rain is not a mere conception, but something close to a reality, for the speaker feels it as an actual problem in his day's program with which he has to reckon and is reck-oning.

B. SUBJUNCTIVE MOOD. This form represents something as not actually belonging to the domain of fact or reality, but as merely existent in the mind of the speaker as a desire, wish, volition, plan, conception, thought; sometimes with more or less hope of realization, or, in the case of a statement, with more or less belief; sometimes with little or no hope or faith: I desire that he *do* it as soon as possible. O that he *were* alive and *could see* all this blessing that has come from his life! If I *were* in his place, I *would do* it. I fear that he *may come* too late.

The subjunctive is treated in considerable detail in Syntax, §§ 111–115.

C. IMPERATIVE MOOD. This form is the mood of command, request, admonition, supplication, entreaty, warning, prohibition. It now has many forms. One of them, the simple imperative, is one of the oldest forms of our language: *Go! Run!*

The imperative is treated in considerable detail in Syntax, §§ 116–117.

38. Tense. Tenses are the different forms which a verb assumes to indicate the time of the action or state. There are six tenses, present, past, present perfect, past perfect, future, future perfect: *I return* (present), *returned* (past), *have returned* (present perfect), *had returned* (past perfect), *shall return* (future), *shall have returned* (future perfect). For formation see §§ 41–45.

The meaning and use of these tenses are described in detail in Syntax, §§ 119; 112.

39. Aspect. Aspect indicates the aspect, the type, the character of the action. This subject is discussed more fully in Syntax, §§ 120–121. The three English aspects are described briefly below.

A. TERMINATE ASPECT. This aspect, a prominent feature of English, takes the common form of the verb and represents an act as a whole, as a fact, as habitual, customary, characteristic, or as a general truth: I *slept* eight hours last night. Dogs *bark*. Water *runs* down hill (a fact, a general truth). The time of the act may be short, but·it must be a whole act: He *shot* a duck.

B. PROGRESSIVE ASPECT. This aspect, also a prominent feature of English, takes the progressive form (§ 44.B) and represents an act or action as going on: He *is sleeping*. He *is working* in the garden. The fire *is crackling* on the hearth.

C. POINT-ACTION ASPECT. This aspect calls attention, not to an act as a whole, but to only one point, either the beginning or the final point.

There are thus two classes:

1. *Ingressive Aspect.* This point-action type directs the attention to the initial stage of the action or state: It is *beginning* (or

starting) to rain. He *went to sleep* as soon as he lay down. The boat *slowed up* (began to go slower) as it came in.

This aspect is further treated in Syntax, § 121.A.

2. *Effective Aspect*. This point-action aspect directs the attention to the final point of the activity, to a result that has been effected, to a goal that has been reached: They *ate up* everything that was on the table. "I *hunted up* (indicating attainment) my old friend Collins." For fuller treatment see Syntax, § 121.B.

With the progressive form point-action verbs indicate a preparing to begin or end, complete: Baby *is waking up*, i.e. is preparing to be awake. He *is working out* a plan (is preparing to work out a plan).

40. Number and Person. There are two numbers, singular and plural: *thou singst, ye sing; he singeth, they sing; thou sangst, ye sang; he sings, they sing*. In poetry we can in the indicative distinguish between singular and plural in the second and third persons of the present tense and in the second person of the past tense, but in ordinary language only the third person indicative of a present tense form can indicate the number, as in the last example. The one verb *be* can go a little farther in indicating the number — a survival of the older usage, which in verbs carefully distinguished the singular and the plural in all tenses and moods. *Be* still keeps the numbers distinct in the first and third persons indicative in both the present and the past tense: I *am*, he *is*, we *are*, I *was*, he *was*, we *were*. In poetic and biblical style we can always distinguish between singular and plural in the second person: *thou givest, ve give; thou gavest, ye gave*.

Elsewhere we do not distinguish singular and plural. We now feel that the subject makes the idea of number clear: *I sing, we sing; you* (speaking to a definite person) *sing, you boys sing, I sang, you* (speaking to a definite person) *sang, he sang, we sang, you boys sang, they sang, if he sing, if they sing*. The subject here makes also the idea of person clear.

As can be seen by the examples given above, the few endings that verbs now have indicate not only the number, but also the person and the mood. The absence of an ending in the third person singular of any present tense form usually marks it as a subjunctive: he *comes* (indicative), if he *come* (subjunctive). Only two verbs have here an especial subjunctive form: if he *be*, if he *have* (regularly formed from *have*, while the indicative *has* is an irregular, contracted form).

Tense Formation

English originally had only two tenses — the present and the past — and in one sense still has only two tenses, for the four additional tenses — present perfect, past perfect, future, future perfect — have been formed by combining a present or a past tense with a participle or an infinitive, so that every tense in our language contains a present or a past tense.

41. Formation of the Present Tense.

A. REGULAR INFLECTION. The formation of this tense is simple and there are comparatively few irregularities. The common form for the second person singular is the second person plural form, which is now used also for the singular. Compare § 51.H. The use and omission of the endings are treated in § 40. As there are few irregularities almost any verb can serve as a model:

SINGULAR

Indicative	*Subjunctive*
1. I walk	I walk
2. you walk (old form, thou walk*est*)	you (thou) walk
3. he walk*s* (old form, walk*eth*)	he walk

PLURAL

1. we walk	we walk
2. you walk (old form, ye walk)	you (ye) walk
3. they walk	they walk

Imperative

walk

Present Participle walking	*Present Infinitive* (to) walk

Present Gerund walking

57

1. *Ending of Third Person Singular.* After a sibilant (*s, ss, c, sh, tch, ch, g, dg, x, z*) or a vowel not preceded by a vowel, *-es* is added instead of *-s:* (*e* pronounced) pass*es*, push*es*, lunch*es;* (*e* silent) go*es*, do*es*, but tip-toe*s*, taboo*s*.

In words in which a silent *e* follows a sibilant, as in *splice, singe, pledge,* we add only *-s*, but we pronounce *-es:* splic*es*, sing*es*, pledg*es*.

2. *Dropping of* E. An *e* at the end of a verb is dropped before a vowel in the ending: *love,* but *loving.* Notice, however, that we irregularly write *singeing* (from *singe,* to distinguish it from *singing,* from *sing*), *shoeing, hoeing, canoeing.*

3. *Doubling of Consonants.* A final consonant preceded by an accented short vowel is doubled before a vowel in the ending: *shop,* but *shopping.*

4. *Time Relations.* The present participle, infinitive, and gerund are not confined to reference to present time. The situation indicates the time: the *rising* sun (present time). My train starts at six, *arriving* (future time) in Chicago at ten. I came late, arriving (past time) after all the others. I expect *to arrive* (future) late.

B. Irregularities in Formation of Present Tense:

1. *BE.*

SINGULAR

Indicative	Subjunctive
1. I am	I be
2. you are (old form, thou art)	you (thou) be
3. he is	he be

PLURAL

1. we are	we be
2. you are (old form, ye are)	you (ye) be
3. they are	they be

Imperative

be

Present Participle being   *Present Infinitive* (to) be

Present Gerund being

a) In older English the form *be* was sometimes used also as an indicative: Here *be* my keys (Shakespeare, *Merry Wives,* III, iii, 172). This older usage survives in popular speech.

2. *HAVE.*

SINGULAR

Indicative	*Subjunctive*
1. I have	I have
2. you have (old form, thou hast)	you (thou) have
3. he has (old form, hath)	he have

PLURAL

1. we have	we have
2. you have (old form, ye have)	you (ye) have
3. they have	they have

Imperative

have

Present Participle having   *Present Infinitive* (to) have

Present Gerund having

3. *DO.*

SINGULAR

Indicative	*Subjunctive*
1. I do	I do
2. you do (old forms, doest [full verb], dost [auxiliary])	you (thou) do
3. he does (old forms, doeth, doth)	he do

PLURAL

1. we do	we do
2. you do (old form, ye do)	you (ye) do
3. they do	they do

Imperative

do

Present Participle doing   *Present Infinitive* (to) do

Present Gerund doing

4. *Present and Past Tenses of Past-Present Verbs.* There is a group of verbal forms which were originally past tenses, but have come to have the meaning of the present tense. They are: *can, dare, may, shall, will, must, ought,* and the archaic *wot* (= *know*). Most of these words, after becoming a present tense, developed a new past tense. *Must* is the subjunctive of one of these new past tense forms. It now serves as a present tense, having supplanted the present form.

These verbs, like other verbs, once belonged to regular inflectional systems, but have come down to us as shattered fragments.

Can, dare, may, shall, wot, are old past indicatives; *will, must, ought,* old past subjunctives.

Will once had a variant form, *wol,* which survives in *won't* (= *wol not*).

Ought is an old past subjunctive of *owe.* The present subjunctive of *must* survives in archaic *mote:* So *mote* (= *may*) it be! *Ought* is a past subjunctive of modesty, still widely used: You *ought* to do it, *lit.* I think you owe the doing of it. Shakespeare used the old past indicative *ought* (now *owed*).

Wot, an old past indicative used as a present, survives in the infinitive *to wit,* now with the meaning *namely.* The present participle survives in the adverb *unwittingly.* The new past *wist,* once common, is still found in the Bible (Mark, IX.6). As *wot* (= modern *know*) did not have subjunctive force as did the other verbs in this group, it disappeared from the group and from the language — replaced by *know.*

The verb *need* has been drawn into this group under the influence of its meaning, which is similar to that of *must.* In the meaning *to be without, want,* it is always a regular verb: He *needs, needed,* men and money. Elsewhere, there is fluctuation between the regular inflection of its tenses and the inflection of past-present verbs, as described in § 123.G.3.a.iv.

Dare, on the other hand, is manifesting a tendency to leave this group. It is always a regular verb throughout in the sense of *challenge:* He *dares, dared,* me to do it. Elsewhere, there is fluctuation between the regular inflection of its tenses and the inflection of past-present verbs, as described in § 123.G.3.a.iii. Also *will* is a regular verb when we feel its meaning as related to the noun *will:* God *wills, willed,* that man should be happy.

What has drawn verbs of such different origin together? They are all verbs that do not state facts, but merely present conceptions, representing something as possible, necessary, desirable, befitting. These are ideas closely related to those expressed by the subjunctive, so that they have come to be felt as modal auxiliaries, as subjunctives, and, as subjunctives, naturally take no -*s* in the third person singular. The oldest of these forms once had an indicative alongside of the subjunctive in both the present and the past tense, the indicative with more positive force than the subjunctive. The old past indicatives could refer to the past, while our present past tenses, *could, durst, might, should, would,* prevailingly point to the present or the future, differing from the present tenses only in the *manner* of the conception, as described in Syntax, § 112. When a past tense that does not depend upon a past indicative points to the present or the future, it must be a subjunctive. Thus these verbs are losing their power to point to the past and are gradually becoming inflectional forms used in connection with an infinitive to express subjunctive ideas, modal auxiliary and infinitive together having the force of a simple subjunctive, pointing to the present or the future: If it *should rain,* I *would stay* at home. It *might rain.* I *could do* it if I had time. *Could* and *would* are still, not infrequently, used as past indicatives, referring to the past; but this can be done only when the context clearly indicates that the reference is to past time, for these forms cannot of themselves point to the past: I *couldn't* find him yesterday. I tried to persuade him yesterday, but he *wouldn't* consent to it. *Must, ought, need,* have not yet developed a past tense in their function as modal auxiliaries. The present tense form here must also serve as a past tense. The old form *durst* is now usually replaced by *dare,* which, like *must,* serves both as a present and a past tense.

Although these verbs now for the most part have the force of subjunctives, they have in poetic style an ending in the second person singular, *thou mayst, thou mightest,* etc., which is contrary to usage with real subjunctives for the present tense. The original words in this group were indicatives and, of course, were entitled to a consonantal ending in the second person singular. Later, by the force of analogy an ending became established here in all of these words except *must*.

These verbs inflect in the present and the past tense as follows:

PRESENT TENSE

SINGULAR

1.	can	dare	may
2. {	can	dare	may
	(canst)	(dar(e)st)	(may(e)st)
3.	can	dares, dare	may

PLURAL for All Persons

can	dare	may

SINGULAR

1.	shall	will	must
2. {	shall	will	must
	(shalt)	(wilt)	(must)
3.	shall	will	must

PLURAL for All Persons

shall	will	must

SINGULAR

1.	ought	need	wot †
2. {	ought	need	wot †
	(ought(e)st)	(need(e)st)	(wottest) †
3.	ought	needs	wot † (wotteth †, wots †)
		need	

PLURAL for All Persons

ought	need	wot †

PAST TENSE

SINGULAR

1. could	dared dare (durst)	might
2. could (couldst)	dared dare (durst) (daredst)	might (might(e)st)
3. could	dared dare (durst)	might

PLURAL for All Persons

could	dared dare (durst)	might

SINGULAR

1. should	would	must
2. should (shouldst)	would (wouldst)	must (must)
3. should	would	must

PLURAL for All Persons

should	would	must

SINGULAR

1. ought	needed need
2. ought (ought(e)st)	needed need (needest)
3. ought	needed need

PLURAL for All Persons

ought	needed need

a) The inflection of *shall* and *will*, as given above, holds only for the use of these forms as modal auxiliaries. For their use in the future tense see Syntax, § 119.E.1.

42. Formation of the Past Tense. There are two types of inflection — the weak and the strong.

A. FORMATION OF WEAK PAST.

1. *Regular Inflection.* This type of inflection forms the past tense and past participle with the suffix *-ed,* in which *e* is silent except after *d* and *t:* (with silent *e*) work, *worked* (past tense and past participle); (with pronounced *e*) hand, *handed;* hunt, *hunted.* Contrary to this principle, however, the *e* in a number of distinctively *adjective* participles is pronounced: *learned, beloved, accursed,* etc. In "on *bended* knees" the old adjective form is still used, while we elsewhere use the newer contracted form, even in adjective function, as in "a *bent* twig." The old full form with pronounced *e* is also preserved in derivative adverbs, *assuredly, avowedly,* etc. In all such cases where the *e* is pronounced, the *d* of the suffix is sounded as *d;* but where the *e* is silent, the *d* is sounded as *d* only after voiced consonants, as in *warmed, oiled, feared, robbed, raised,* elsewhere being pronounced *t,* as in *crossed, watched, locked, jumped, scoffed.*

A final consonant, preceded by an accented short vowel, is doubled before *e* of the ending *-ed:* drop, drop*ped;* but envelop, envelo*ped.*

After a consonant, *y* becomes *ie* before *-ed:* rel*y,* rel*ied;* but pla*y,* pla*yed.*

Final silent *e* is dropped before *-ed:* love, lov*ed.*

This class comprises all the verbs in the language except about one hundred. This is the only living type. All new verbs are inflected weak. Many verbs, once strong, have become wholly or partially weak.

The past of *love* may serve as an example:

SINGULAR

Indicative	Subjunctive
1. I loved	I loved
2. you loved (thou lovedst)	you loved (thou lovedst)
3. he loved	he loved

64

PLURAL

1. we loved   we loved
2. you loved   you (ye) loved
   (old form, ye loved)
3. they loved   they loved

2. *Irregularities in the Weak Past.* The weak type of inflection is much simpler than it once was, but older conditions have left traces behind, so that there are still a number of irregularities.

In older English, the vowel of the tense and participial suffix was sometimes suppressed, which led to the shortening of a long root vowel: sweep, *swept;* leave, *left;* etc.

In a number of verbs ending in -d the -ded of the past tense and participle is contracted to -t: bend, *bent;* build, *built;* etc.

In a number of verbs ending in -d and -t the suffix is dropped, leaving the present and the past tense and past participle alike: *cut* (present), *cut* (past), *cut* (past participle). There are a large number of such verbs: *bid* (make an offer), *burst, cast, cost, cut, hit, hurt, let, put, rid, set, shed, shut, slit, split, spread, thrust.* Some of these verbs: *bid, burst, let, slit,* are strong verbs which have been drawn into this class under the influence of their final -d or -t. Alongside of the literary forms *burst, burst, burst* are the colloquial and popular forms *bust, busted, busted,* which have become especially common in the meaning *to break.* In a few cases we use either the full or the contracted form: *bet, bet* or *betted, bet* or *betted; knit, knitted* or *knit, knitted* or *knit; quit, quit* or *quitted, quit* or *quitted; shred, shredded* or *shred, shredded* or *shred; sweat, sweat* or *sweated, sweat* or *sweated; wed, wedded* or *wed, wedded* or *wed; wet, wet* or *wetted, wet* or *wetted.* The compound *broadcast* is sometimes regular: *broadcast, broadcasted, broadcasted.* In America we say *spit, spit, spit,* but in England the parts are *spit, spat, spat.* In the literary language the British forms are now often used also in America. In older English, the list of the short weak forms was longer, as attested by their survival in certain adjective participles: "a *dread* foe," but "The foe was *dreaded*"; "*roast* meat," but "The meat was *roasted.*" The extensive use of these short forms is in part explained by the fact that in the third person singular the -s of the present tense distinguishes the two tenses: he *hits* (present) hard; he *hit* (past)

hard. Elsewhere we gather the meaning from the situation.
As the past tense is the tense of description, there is here usually
something in the situation that makes the thought clear. As
this simple type of inflection is usually not unclear, it is spreading to the strong past, which in loose colloquial or popular
speech now often has the same vowel as the present tense: He
give (instead of *gave*) it to me yesterday.

In a number of words ending in *-l* or *-n* the ending is either
-ed or *-t*, the latter especially in England: *spell, spelled* or *spelt;
learn, learned* or *learnt;* etc.

Had and *made* are contracted from *haved* and *maked*.

In a large number of words the difference of vowel between
the present and the past gives them the appearance of strong
verbs, but the past tense ending *-t* or *-d* marks them as weak:
bring, brought; tell, told; etc.

An alphabetical list of all irregularities follows. In a number
of cases the irregularities are only orthographical, as in *dressed*
or *drest*. Where there is fluctuation in usage the more common
form is given first. Sometimes the variant (i.e. the second form)
is an old strong form, retiring from general service, now serving
preferably in figurative use, as in the case of *shorn*, or, in the case
of others now only employed in poetic style; sometimes, on the
other hand, it is a vigorous, new, more regular form which is
working its way to the front. Wherever the form is obsolete,
it is marked by a sword (†). Wherever the form is especially
preferred, or only used, in adjective function, there is an asterisk (*) after it. Some of the verbs were once strong and still
have strong forms. The irregular *proven* was once used even
by good writers and is still so in adjective function: "his *proven*
ability," but it is now in general avoided in choice English.

Present	Past	Past Participle
		accursĕd*
		accurst*
bend	bent	bent
bereave	bereaved	bereaved
	bereft	bereft
beseech	besought	besought
bet	bet	bet
	betted	betted

Present	Past	Past Participle
bid (too high, five dollars, for public favor)	bid	bid
bleed	bled	bled
blend	blended	blended
	blent	blent
bless	blessed	blessed
	blest	blest
breed	bred	bred
bring	brought	brought
build	built, builded†	built, builded†
burn	burned	burned
	burnt	burnt
burst	burst	burst
buy	bought	bought
cast	cast	cast
catch	caught	caught
cleave	clove	cloven
(split)	cleft	cleft
	clave†	cleaved
cleave	cleaved	cleaved
(adhere)	clave	
clothe	clothed	clothed
	clad	clad
cost	cost	cost
creep	crept	crept
crow	crowed	crowed
	crew	
curse	cursed	cursed
		cursĕd*
cut	cut	cut
deal	dealt	dealt
dip	dipped	dipped
	dipt	dipt
dream	dreamed	dreamed
	dreamt	dreamt
dress	dressed	dressed
	drest	drest
drop	dropped	dropped
	dropt	dropt

Present	Past	Past Participle
dwell	dwelt	dwelt
	dwelled	dwelled
feed	fed	fed
feel	felt	felt
flee, fly (*Brit.*)	fled	fled
gild	gilded	gilded
	gilt	gilt
gird	girded	girded
	girt	girt
grave	graved	graved
		graven*
have (§ 41.B.2)	had	had
hear	heard	heard
heave	heaved	heaved
	hove	hove
hew	hewed	hewn
		hewed
hit	hit	hit
hurt	hurt	hurt
keep	kept	kept
kneel	knelt	knelt
	kneeled	kneeled
knit	knitted	knitted
	knit	knit
lade†	laded †	laden
		laded †
lay	laid	laid
lead	led	led
lean	leaned	leaned
	leant	leant
leap	leaped	leaped
	leapt	leapt
learn	learned	learned
	learnt	learnt
leave	left	left
lend	lent	lent
let	let	let
light (*set fire to*)	lighted	lighted
	lit	lit
light (*descend*)	lighted	lighted
	lit	lit

68

Present	Past	Past Participle
lose	lost	lost
make	made	made
mean	meant	meant
meet	met	met
melt	melted	melted
		molten*
mow	mowed	mowed
		mown
owe	owed, ought†	owed
	ought (subj.; § 41.B.4)	own* (in obs. sense *possess*)
pay	paid	paid
pen (*confine*)	penned	penned
		pent*
plead	pleaded	pleaded
	plead	plead
prove	proved	proved, proven*
put	put	put
quit	quit	quit
	quitted	quitted
read	read	read
reave	reaved	reaved
	reft	reft
reeve	reeved	reeved
	rove	rove
		roven
rend	rent	rent
rid	rid	rid
rive	rived	riven
		rived
roast	roasted	roasted
		roast*
saw	sawed	sawed
		sawn
say	said	said
seek	sought	sought
seethe	seethed	seethed
	sod†	sodden*
sell	sold	sold
send	sent	sent
set	set	set

Present	Past	Past Participle
sew	sewed	sewed
		sewn
shape	shaped	shaped
		shapen†
shave	shaved	shaved
		shaven*
shear	sheared	sheared
	shore	shorn
shed	shed	shed
shoe	shod	shod
show	showed	shown
		showed
shred	shredded	shredded
	shred	shred
shrive	shrived	shrived
	shrove	shriven
shut	shut	shut
sleep	slept	slept
slit	slit	slit
smell	smelled	smelled
	smelt	smelt
sow	sowed	sown
		sowed
speed	sped	sped
speed (causative; also intrans., *go too fast*)	speeded	speeded
spell	spelled	spelled
	spelt	spelt
spend	spent	spent
spill	spilled	spilled
	spilt	spilt
spit	spat	spat
	spit	spit
split	split	split
spoil	spoiled	spoiled
	spoilt	spoilt
spread	spread	spread
stave	staved	staved
	stove	stove
stay	stayed	stayed
	staid	staid

Present	Past	Past Participle
strew	strewed	strewed
		strewn
sweat	sweat	sweat
	sweated	sweated
sweep	swept	swept
swell	swelled	swelled
		swollen
teach	taught	taught
tell	told	told
think	thought	thought
thrive	thrived	thrived
	throve	thriven
thrust	thrust	thrust
toss	tossed	tossed
	tost	tost
wash	washed	washed
		washen†
wax (*become*)	waxed	waxed
		waxen†
wed	wed	wed
	wedded	wedded
weep	wept	wept
wet	wet	wet
	wetted	wetted
won†		wont* (am *wont* to act with energy)
		wonted* (He acts with his *wonted* energy.)
wont (He *wonts* to act with energy.)	wonted	
	wont	
work	worked	worked
	wrought	wrought
writhe	writhed	writhed, writhen†
		wreathen†

B. Formation of Strong Past. Strong verbs form the past tense without a suffix, by changing the root vowel: eat, *a*te; know, kn*e*w

They form the past participle with the suffix *-en* or *-n*: eat*en*, know*n*. The vowel of the past participle may be either the same as that of the past tense, or the same as that of the present tense, or it may be different from that of both: tread, tr*o*d, tr*o*dden; sh*a*ke, shook, sh*a*ken; swim, swam, swum.

In many verbs the suffix of the past participle has disappeared: bind, bound, *bound*. The older form of the participle in *-en* is often preserved in adjectives: "The ship has *sunk*," but "a *sunken* ship."

The past tense of *see* may serve as an example:

SINGULAR

Indicative	*Subjunctive*
1. I saw	I saw
2. you saw (old form, thou sawest)	you saw (thou sawest)
3. he saw	he saw

PLURAL

1. we saw	we saw
2. you saw (old form, ye saw)	you (ye) saw
3. they saw	they saw

a) Past Tense of *Be*. There is only one verb in the language in which the vowel of the past subjunctive differs from that of the indicative and in which the vowel of the plural of the past indicative differs from that of the singular:

SINGULAR

Indicative	*Subjunctive*
1. I was	I were
2. you were (old form, thou wast)	you were (thou wert)
3. he was	he were

PLURAL

1. we were	we were
2. you were (old form, ye were)	you (ye) were
3. they were	they were

1. *Classes of Strong Verbs.* There were once seven well-defined classes of these verbs, grouped together on the basis of the vowels of their present and past tense and their past participle. For many centuries there have been many forces working upon the vowels and the words themselves, affecting them in many

ways, thus breaking up the classes. Moreover, there is a trend in the direction of the weak inflection, so that parts of certain strong verbs are now weak. Consequently, what we have left of the old classes is merely scattered clusters of words which still cling together. Thus after the model of *drive, drove, driven* we still inflect *ride, rise, arise, shrive* (A.2 above), *smite, stride, write, thrive* (A.2 above), *strive*. There are also other groups of verbs which cling together, but there are so many irregularities that it is thought best to put all the strong verbs into an alphabetical list (B.2 below) for convenient reference.

2. *List of Strong Verbs.* There are now less than one hundred strong verbs in our language. For many centuries there has been a steady loss in favor of the weak class. In only a few cases have weak or foreign verbs been drawn into the strong class. The weak verbs *chide, hide* and the foreign verb *strive*, which are similar in sound to the strong verb *ride*, have been influenced by it and have become strong. Similarly, *wear* has become strong under the influence of *tear*. Also *dig*, once with the past tense and past participle *digged*, has become strong. The weak class has made another important contribution to the strong. The old weak verb *wend, went, went* with the transitive meaning *direct* (one's way, course) and the intransitive meaning *go* has furnished the old strong verb *go* with a past tense, relinquishing to it its past tense *went* for use as an intransitive and reforming its parts to *wend, wended, wended* for use in its old transitive meaning.

In the following list are given only such strong verbs as are still prevailingly strong. Old strong verbs that are now prevailingly weak but have strong forms alongside of the weak are given in A.2 above with irregular weak verbs. Where there is fluctuation in usage, the more common form is given first. The variant (i.e. the second form) may be a less common strong form, or, on the other hand, a vigorous weak form, as in the case of *waked*, which is pushing to the front and will, without doubt, ultimately prevail. Sometimes, as in case of *weaved*, the weak form has not yet come into wide use. The verb *shine* is strong only as an intransitive. The causative (§ 109.a) *shine* is always weak. In the case of one old verb, only the form for the first and the third person of the past tense survives, namely *quoth* (= *said*), now only used archaically or in quoting contemptuously, always with the inverted word-order: *quoth he* (or *she*, etc.). Forms now used only as adjectives have an asterisk after them. The adjective form *broke*, past participle of *break*, is much used in the sense *out of money*, but has not been given in the table below since it belongs exclusively to colloquial and popular speech.

Present	Past	Past Participle
abide	abode	abode
arise	arose	arisen
awake	awoke	awoke
	awaked	awaked
be (§ 41.B.1)	was (§ 42.B.a)	been
bear (*bring forth*)	bore	born
bear (*carry*)	bore	borne
beat	beat	beaten, beat
beget	begot	begotten
begin	began	begun
behold	beheld	beheld
		beholden*
bespeak	bespoke	bespoken
		bespoke (Brit.)
bid (one welcome or	bǎde	bidden
defiance, bid one go,		bid
bid fair to succeed)		bǎde
bind	bound	bound
		bounden*
bite	bit	bitten
		bit
blow	blew	blown
break	broke	broken
chide	chided	chided, chidden
	chid	chid
choose	chose	chosen
cling	clung	clung
come	came	come
dig	dug	dug
do (§ 41.B.3)	did	done
draw	drew	drawn

Present	Past	Past Participle
drink	drank	drunk
		drunken*
drive	drove	driven
eat	ate	eaten
fall	fell	fallen
fight	fought	fought
find	found	found
fling	flung	flung
fly	flew	flown
forbear	forbore	forborne
forbid	forbade	forbidden
		forbid
forget	forgot	forgotten
—	—	forlorn*
forsake	forsook	forsaken
freeze	froze	frozen
get	got	got
		gotten
		gotten*
		(ill-gotten)*
give	gave	given
go	went	gone
grind	ground	ground
grow	grew	grown
hang (*suspend*)	hung	hung
hang (*execute*)	hanged	hanged
	hung	hung
hide	hid	hidden
		hid
hold	held	held
know	knew	known
lie	lay	lain
—	—	lorn*
ride	rode	ridden
ring	rang	rung
rise	rose	risen
run	ran	run
see	saw	seen
shake	shook	shaken
shine (**intrans.**)	shone	shone
shoot	shot	shot

Present	Past	Past Participle
shrink	shrank	shrunk
	shrunk	shrunken*
sing	sang	sung
sink	sank	sunk
	sunk	sunken*
sit	sat	sat
slay	slew	slain
slide	slid	slid
		slidden*
sling	slung	slung
slink	slunk	slunk
smite	smote	smitten
speak	spoke	spoken
spin	spun	spun
	span	
spring	sprang	sprung
stand	stood	stood
steal	stole	stolen
stick	stuck	stuck
sting	stung	stung
stink	stank	stunk
	stunk	
stride	strode	stridden
strike	struck	struck
strike (figurative)	struck	stricken
string	strung	strung
strive	strove	striven
swear	swore	sworn
swim	swam	swum
swing	swung	swung
take	took	taken
tear	tore	torn
throw	threw	thrown
tread	trod	trodden
		trod
wake	woke	waked
	waked	woke
		woken
wear	wore	worn
weave	wove	woven
	weaved	weaved

Present	Past	Past Participle
win	won	won
wind (*turn, twine*)	wound	wound
wind (*sound*)	wound, winded	wound, winded
wring	wrung	wrung
write	wrote	written

43. Formation of the Compound Tenses. A compound tense is formed by the use of a present or a past tense of an auxiliary in connection with a participle or an infinitive. The treatment of the different compound tenses follows.

A. PRESENT PERFECT. This tense is made up of the present tense of the auxiliary *have* and the past participle of the verb to be inflected.

SINGULAR

Indicative	Subjunctive
1. I have taken	I have taken
2. you have taken	you have taken
(thou hast taken)	(thou have taken)
3. he has taken	he have taken
(he hath taken)	

PLURAL

1. we have taken	we have taken
2. you (ye) have taken	you (ye) have taken
3. they have taken	they have taken

Participle having taken   *Infinitive* (to) have taken
       Gerund having taken

a) Time Relations. As there are no participial, infinitival, or gerundial forms corresponding to the past perfect tense, the present perfect forms must serve both as a present perfect and a past perfect: *Having been* (= *as I have been*) sick so much, I have learned to take good care of my health. *Having finished* (= *after I had finished*) my work, I went to bed. Compare Syntax, §§ 122; 123.D; 124.A.

77

B. Past Perfect. This tense is made up of the past tense of the auxiliary *have* and the past participle of the verb to be inflected.

SINGULAR

Indicative	*Subjunctive*
1. I had taken	I had taken
2. you had taken	you had taken
(thou hadst taken)	(thou hadst taken)
3. he had taken	he had taken

PLURAL

1. we had taken	we had taken
2. you (ye) had taken	you (ye) had taken
3. they had taken	they had taken

C. Future. There are two entirely different types of expression in English to indicate future time.

1. *Present Tense Used as a Future.* In oldest English the present tense was the usual form employed to express future time, and it is still commonly employed for this purpose where an adverb of time or the situation makes the thought clear: The ship *sails* tomorrow. Wait until I *come.* For fuller statement see Syntax, § 119.A.5. As this old means of expression is not accurate enough for higher purposes, it has long been common to employ an especial form to express future time, the future tense described in 2 below.

This is true, however, only for the indicative. No especial future form for the subjunctive has developed, nor has there been any need for such, for the old type of expression had great possibilities of development.

In oldest English, the simple present subjunctive was much used to express future time, and it can often still be used in choice language: We shall have passed Dover tomorrow if the wind *keep* favorable. The simple subjunctive has for the most part been gradually replaced by modal auxiliaries, which contain more shades of meaning than the old simple forms. The old type of expression, however, has been retained. In this old type there are two tenses of the subjunctive employed for reference to the future — the present and the past — which

78

differ only in the *manner* of the conception, the present tense expressing a greater degree of probability: It *may* rain. It *might* rain. As the uncertainty in the outcome of future events is great, the past tense form of the subjunctive is a pronounced favorite. In conditional sentences we employ *should* in the condition and in the conclusion *should* in the first person and *would* in the second and third persons to indicate a probable result: If it *should* rain tomorrow, *I should*, or *he would*, be very much disappointed. *Would* here in the first person of the conclusion represents the future act as intended: If it *should* rain tomorrow, *I would* stay at home. A modest opinion as to a future result is expressed by *should* in the third person: If everything goes right, the work *should* be done by tomorrow evening.

The use of the subjunctive forms is treated in detail in Syntax, §§ 111–115.

2. *Future Indicative.* This form is made up of the present tense of the auxiliary *shall* or *will* and the simple infinitive of the verb to be inflected. In independent declarative sentences *shall* is employed in the first person and *will* in the second and the third:

SINGULAR

1. I shall take
2. you will take
   (thou wilt take)
3. he will take

PLURAL

1. we shall take
2. you (ye) will take
3. they will take

There are peculiar difficulties connected with the use of the indicative of this tense, since the employment of *shall* and *will* in the different persons varies according to the form of the sentence and the meaning to be conveyed. This subject is treated in detail in Syntax, § 119.E.1.

D. FUTURE PERFECT. This tense is differently formed in the indicative and the subjunctive:

1. *Future Perfect Indicative*. This form is the same as the future indicative, described in C.2 above, with the exception that the present perfect infinitive is used instead of the present infinitive:

SINGULAR

1. I shall have taken
2. you will have taken
   (thou wilt have taken)
3. he will have taken

PLURAL

1. we shall have taken
2. you (ye) will have taken
3. they will have taken

For the use of this form see Syntax, § 119.F.

2. *Future Perfect Subjunctive*. To express the probable completion of an act in the future we employ the past subjunctive *should* in the first person and the past subjunctive *would* in the second and third persons in connection with a perfect infinitive: *I should have finished* (or *he would have finished*) the work by tomorrow evening if everything had gone right. The use of *would* in the first person represents the completion of the future act as intended: I *would* have gone tomorrow evening if things had gone right. A modest opinion as to a future result is expressed by *should* in the third person: If things go right, they *should have completed* the work by tomorrow evening, or they *should complete* the work by tomorrow evening.

44. Full Inflection of Active Verb.

A. COMMON FORM

Present

Indicative	Subjunctive
I take	take
you take	take
(thou takest)	(take)
he takes	take
(he taketh)	
we take	take
you (ye) take	take
they take	take

Imperative take

Participle	*Infinitive*
taking	to take
(§ 41.A.4)	(§ 41.A.4)

Gerund taking (§§ 41.A.4; 124.A)

Past

Indicative	*Subjunctive*
I took	took
you took	took
(thou tookest)	(tookest)
he took	took
we took	took
you (ye) took	took
they took	took

Present Perfect

Indicative		*Subjunctive*	
I have	taken	have	taken
you have		have	
(thou hast)		(have)	
he has		have	
(he hath)			
we have		have	
you (ye) have		have	
they have		have	

Imperative have done

Participle	*Infinitive*
having taken	(to) have taken
(§ 43.A.*a*)	(123.D)

Gerund having taken (§ 124.A)

Past Perfect

Indicative		*Subjunctive*	
I had	taken	had	taken
you had		had	
(thou hadst)		(hadst)	
he had		had	
we had		had	
you (ye) had		had	
they had		had	

Future	Future Perfect
Indicative	*Indicative*
I shall take	shall have taken
you will take	will have taken
(thou wilt take)	(wilt have taken)
he will take	will have taken
we shall take	shall have taken
you (ye) will take	will have taken
they will take	will have taken
For subjunctive see § 43.C.1.	For subjunctive see 43.D.2.

B. Progressive Form (§ 120)

Present

Indicative		*Subjunctive*	
I am		be	
you are		be	
(thou art)		(be)	
he is	taking	be	taking
we are		be	
you (ye) are		be	
they are		be	

Imperative	*Infinitive*
be taking	(to) be taking

Past

Indicative		*Subjunctive*	
I was		were	
you were		were	
(thou wast)		(wert)	
he was	taking	were	taking
we were		were	
you (ye) were		were	
they were		were	

82

Present Perfect

Indicative		*Subjunctive*	
I have been		have been	
you have been		have been	
(thou hast been)		(have been)	
he has been	taking	have been	taking
(he hath been)			
we have been		have been	
you (ye) have been		have been	
they have been		have been	

Participle	*Infinitive*
having been taking	(to) have been taking

Past Perfect

Indicative		*Subjunctive*	
I had been		had been	
you had been		had been	
(thou hadst been)		(hadst been)	
he had been	taking	had been	taking
we had been		had been	
you (ye) had been		had been	
they had been		had been	

Future	Future Perfect
Indicative	*Indicative*

Indicative		*Indicative*	
I shall be		shall have been	
you will be		will have been	
(thou wilt be)		(wilt have been)	
he will be	taking	will have been	taking
we shall be		shall have been	
you (ye) will be		will have been	
they will be		will have been	

The future and future perfect subjunctive forms are treated in § 43.C.1, D.2.

C. *Do*-Form (§ 53.A.3.*c*)

Present

Indicative	*Subjunctive*
I do take	do take
you do take	do take
(thou dost take)	(do take)
he does take	do take
(he doth take)	
we do take	do take
you (ye) do take	do take
they do take	do take

Past

Indicative	*Subjunctive*
I did take	did take
you did take	did take
(thou didst take)	(didst take)
he did take	did take
we did take	did take
you (ye) did take	did take
they did take	did take

45. Full Inflection of Passive Verb.

A. Common Form

Present

Indicative		*Subjunctive*	
I am		be	
you are		be	
(thou art)		(be)	
he is	taken	be	taken
we are		be	
you (ye) are		be	
they are		be	

Imperative	*Infinitive*
be taken	(to) be taken

Gerund being taken

Participle being taken

84

Past

Indicative		Subjunctive	
I was		were	
you were		were	
(thou wast)		(wert)	
he was	} taken	were	} taken
we were		were	
you (ye) were		were	
they were		were	

Present Perfect

Indicative		Subjunctive	
I have been		have been	
you have been		have been	
(thou hast been)		(have been)	
he has been	} taken	have been	} taken
we have been		have been	
you (ye) have been		have been	
they have been		have been	

Participle	Infinitive
having been taken	(to) have been taken

Gerund   having been taken

Past Perfect

Indicative		Subjunctive	
I had been		had been	
you had been		had been	
(thou hadst been)		(hadst been)	
he had been	} taken	had been	} taken
we had been		had been	
you (ye) had been		had been	
they had been		had been	

Future		Future Perfect	
Indicative		*Indicative*	
I shall be		shall have been	
you will be		will have been	
(thou wilt be)		(wilt have been)	
he will be	} taken	will have been	} taken
we shall be		shall have been	
you (ye) will be		will have been	
they will be		will have been	

a) Time Relations. The different tenses of the verbal forms indicate accurately the time of the action, but in case of adjective forms the time relations are indicated only by the situation: this *broken* (a present state) chair; a bridge *destroyed* (past perfect) two hours before by the enemy; a feat often *performed* (present perfect) by me. *Having been deceived* (= *since I have been deceived*) so often, I am now on my guard. *Having been more strongly opposed* (= *since they had been more strongly opposed*) than they expected, they retreated. Compare § 122.B.

B. Progressive Form

Present

Indicative		Subjunctive
I am being		
you are being		
(thou art being)		
he is being	} taken	(*lacking*)
we are being		
you (ye) are being		
they are being		

Imperative, Infinitive, Participle, Gerund, are lacking.

Past

Indicative		Subjunctive	
I was being		were being	
you were being		were being	
(thou wast being)		(wert being)	
he was being	} taken	were being	} taken
we were being		were being	
you (ye) were being		were being	
they were being		were being	

Present Perfect

Indicative	Subjunctive
(§ 110)	
it has been building	it have been building
they have been building	they have been building

Participle	Infinitive
having been building	(to) have been building

86

Past Perfect

Indicative	*Subjunctive*
(§ 110)	
it had been building	it had been building
they had been building	they had been building

Future	Future Perfect
Indicative	*Indicative*
(§ 110)	(§ 110)
it will be building (§ 110)	it will have been building
they will be building	they will have been building

INFLECTION OF ADVERBS

46. Forms. In older English certain cases of nouns indicated an adverbial relation to a verb or an adjective. Examples have been given in § 25.B,D. Adverbs now often have the suffix -*ly* to indicate their use as adverbs: She sings *beautifully*. Often an adverb has no distinctive mark, its position after or before a verb, adjective, or other adverb alone indicating its adverbial function: He runs *fast*. He is *pretty* slow. He works *pretty* slowly.

A fuller treatment is given in Syntax, §§ 68.A–D; 70.A,B.1–2.

The adverb is regularly inflected to indicate the comparative and superlative degrees. This subject is treated in Syntax, § 69.

UNINFLECTED PARTS OF SPEECH

47. Prepositions, Conjunctions, and Interjections. Three parts of speech, prepositions, conjunctions, and interjections, have no distinctive forms to indicate their function.

The position of the preposition before a word indicates that it brings this word into relation with another word (§ 19). It often has a characteristic position at the end of the sentence or clause: What do you write *with?* This is the pen I write *with* (Syntax, § 131). For list of prepositions, see Syntax, § 127.

A conjunction links an independent proposition, or a subordinate clause, or parts of a sentence to the rest of the sentence.

Its position immediately before a group of words indicates its function: He came early, *but* soon went away. Wait *until* I come. Conjunctions are treated in Syntax, §§ 75.A,B; 77.A; 78.A; 79.A; 80.B; 82.A; 83.A; 84.A; 85.A; 86; 87; 88.A; 89.A; 90.A; 91.A.

Pure conjunctions are regularly uninflected, but there are certain inflected pronouns which perform the function not only of pronouns but also of conjunctions (§§ 9.D; 75.B).

Interjections, *O!*, *Ouch!*, etc., are recognized by the peculiar tone which accompanies the spoken words (Syntax, § 71).

PART THREE

SYNTAX OF THE SENTENCE

I

THE SIMPLE SENTENCE, ITS KINDS AND PARTS

II

CLASSES OF SENTENCES

I. THE SIMPLE SENTENCE, ITS KINDS AND PARTS

KINDS OF SENTENCES

48. Classification
  A. The Exclamatory Sentence
  B. The Declarative Sentence
  C. The Interrogative Sentence

ESSENTIAL ELEMENTS OF A SENTENCE

49. Subject and Predicate
50. Forms of the Subject
  A. A Noun
  B. A Pronoun
  C. An Infinitive or Gerund
  D. An Adjective
  E. Another Part of Speech
  F. A Group of Words
  G. A Whole Clause
51. Use of Pronominal Subjects
  A. Situation *It* as Subject
  B. Impersonal *It* and *There*
  C. Anticipatory *It* and *There*
  D. Pronouns Used as General or Indefinite Subject
  E. Editorial *We*
  F. Plural of Majesty
  G. *We = You*
  H. *Thou, Thee, Ye, You*
52. Omission of Subject
  A. In Imperative Sentences
  B. In Set Expressions
  C. When Subject Is Suggested by the Situation
53. Forms of the Predicate
  A. A Finite Verb of Complete Predication
    1. Suppression of the Verb
    2. Use of *Do* to Avoid the Repetition of the Verb
    3. Use of the Periphrastic Form with *Do*
    4. Position of the Verb

B. A Verb of Incomplete Predication + Complement
C. A Predicate Appositive
54. Predicate Complement
    A. Predicate Noun
        1. Nominative after Verbs of Incomplete Predication
        2. Nominative and Appositive Introduced by *As*
        3. Expressions Employing a Prepositional Phrase
        4. Complement after Linking Verbs Indicating Development
        5. Predicate Genitive
    B. Predicate Adjective and Participle
    C. Predicate Pronoun and Adverb *So*
    D. Predicate Infinitive
        1. Normal Prepositional Form
        2. Modal Form
        3. Predicate Infinitive to Express Purpose
    E. Predicate Gerund
    F. Predicate Adverb and Prepositional Phrase
55. Agreement between Subject and Predicate
    A. Number
        1. Singular Subject
        2. Plural Subject
        3. Singular Abstract Subject Modified by Two Adjectives
        4. After *More Than*
        5. Affirmative and Negative Subject
        6. Plural Idea
        7. Subject a Clause
    B. Person
        1. Subjects of Different Persons in Apposition
        2. Subjects of Different Persons Connected by *Or*
        3. Affirmative and Negative Subjects
        4. Person and Number of Verb in Relative Clause
    C. Gender
    D. Case

SUBORDINATE ELEMENTS OF A SENTENCE

Attributive Adjective Modifiers

56. Attributive Adjectives and Participles
    A. Forms
    B. Position and Stress
    C. Nouns, Adverbs, Etc., Used as Adjectives
    D. Repetition of Limiting Adjective

57. Attributive Genitive
    A. Forms
        1. The *S*-Genitive
        2. The *Of*-Genitive
        3. The Double Genitive
        4. The Uninflected Genitive
    B. Stress
    C. Categories
        1. Genitive of Origin
        2. Possessive Genitive
        3. Subjective Genitive
        4. Objective Genitive
        5. Genitive of Material or Composition
        6. Descriptive Genitive
        7. Appositive Genitive
        8. Partitive Genitive
58. An Appositive as Modifier of a Noun
    A. Loose Apposition
        1. Appositive Nouns
        2. Pronouns as Appositives
        3. Appositive to a Sentence or Clause
    B. Close Apposition
59. A Prepositional Phrase as Modifier of a Noun
60. An Infinitive as Modifier of a Noun
    A. Infinitive with Original Force
    B. Infinitive with Force of Relative Clause
    C. Infinitive with Force of Appositive
61. An Adverb as Modifier of a Noun
62. A Clause as Modifier of a Noun

Objective Modifiers

63. Accusative Object
    A. Form and Position
    B. Meaning and Use of Accusative with Verbs
        1. Noun and Pronoun as Object
        2. Metonymic Object
        3. *It* and *So* as Object
    C. Passive Form of Statement
    D. Object of an Adjective
64. Dative Object
    A. Dative as Sole Object
    B. Dative as Indirect Object

II. CLASSES OF SENTENCES

THE COMPOUND SENTENCE

75. Structure and Connectives
    A. Coördinating Conjunctions
       1. Copulative Connectives
       2. Disjunctive Connectives
       3. Adversative Connectives
       4. Causal Connectives
       5. Illative Connectives
       6. Explanatory Connectives
    B. Pronouns and Adverbs as Conjunctions
    C. Parataxis

THE COMPLEX SENTENCE: SUBORDINATE CLAUSES

76. Classification by Form and Function
    A. Full and Abridged Clause
    B. Classification by Function

Subject and Predicate Clauses

77. Subject Clause
    A. Conjunctions
    B. Abridgment of Subject Clause
78. Predicate Clause

Adjective Clause

79. Attributive Substantive Clause and Its Abridgment
    A. Clause with Force of Appositive to a Noun
    B. Clause with Force of Attributive Prepositional Phrase
    C. Clause with Force of a Genitive
80. Attributive Adjective Clause
    A. Classification
       1. Asyndetic Relative Clause
       2. Relative Clause with Expressed Relative
    B. List of Relative Pronouns
    C. Descriptive and Restrictive Relative Clauses
    D. Personality and Form
    E. Case of Relative and Its Agreement with Its Antecedent
    F. Position and Repetition of the Relative
    G. Abridgment of Relative Clause

PART THREE

SYNTAX OF THE SENTENCE

I. THE SIMPLE SENTENCE, ITS KINDS AND PARTS

A SENTENCE is an expression of a thought or feeling by means of a word or words used in such form and manner as to convey the meaning intended.

KINDS OF SENTENCES

48. Classification. There are three kinds:

A. THE EXCLAMATORY SENTENCE, uttering an outcry, or giving expression to a command, wish, desire, in its written form often closing with an exclamation point: *Oh! Ouch! What a noise the engine makes! Look! Don't you touch that! Come in. Write soon.* This is probably the oldest form of the sentence. For the many forms that the imperative sentence may have, see § 116.

B. THE DECLARATIVE SENTENCE, stating a fact, or asserting something as a fact: *A day has twenty-four hours. Kind words are the music of the world.*

C. THE INTERROGATIVE SENTENCE, asking a question, in its written form closing with an interrogation point. In a question requiring *yes* or *no* for an answer the personal part of the verb usually stands in the first place: *Are you going?* If, however, the question is asked in a tone of surprise, the form is that of a declarative sentence; but it is spoken with rising tone: *You are going?* We may also employ the declarative form when we do not understand a statement and ask for the repetition of it: *He went where? = Where did you say he went?* Compare § 53.A.4.a.

Elsewhere the question is introduced by an interrogative pronoun (§ 9.F), an interrogative adjective (§ 13.G), or an interrogative adverb (§ 18.A.4). Compare § 53.A.4.a.

ESSENTIAL ELEMENTS OF A SENTENCE

49. Subject and Predicate. It is usually considered that there are two essential elements in every sentence — the subject and the predicate: *Fred won.* The subject is that which is spoken of, in this sentence *Fred*. The predicate is that which is said of the subject, in this sentence *won*. In a normal sentence both subject and predicate are present, but sometimes the one or the other may be absent, and yet the sentence may be a complete expression of thought: *Yes. No. Oh! Ouch! Fred!* (calling out for him to come in). Compare §§ 23; 71.

In such sentences nothing is omitted. They represent a primitive type of sentence which prevailed before the development of the sentence with two essential elements. We still often find this old type of sentence useful.

50. Forms of the Subject. The complete subject often consists of a group of words: *The stately ship* dropped her anchor. The noun round which the other words are grouped is called the *subject word*, in this sentence *ship*. The subject word is always in the nominative case.

The subject may be:

A. A Noun: The *sun* is rising.

B. A Pronoun: *He* is writing.

The pronominal subject is often used in questions in connection with a noun subject, so that there is a double expression of the subject: Your *friends*, what will *théy* say? (F. C. Philips.) Under the pressure of thought the subject here springs forth first as the most important thing, before the usual grammatical structure occurs to the mind and is later repeated in the usual position of the subject in the form of a personal pronoun.

Similarly in declarative sentences, the subject thus often springs forth suddenly, before it is felt as subject and is then repeated as a personal pronoun, especially in older English: The *Lord* your God, which goeth before you, *he* shall fight for you (Deuteronomy, I.30). This older literary usage survives in loose colloquial speech: *Papa, he* said I might.

C. An Infinitive or Gerund: *To read* good books improves the mind. *Reading* good books improves the mind.

We now usually employ the prepositional form of the infinitive, but the simple form was once used here and survives in old saws: [it is] Better *bend* than *break*. The old form has been preserved since it is felt as an imperative.

D. An Adjective: No *good* will come of it. *Rich* and *poor* rejoiced. Compare § 108.

E. Another Part of Speech: the *ups* and *downs* of life. *Under* is a preposition.

F. A Group of Words: *Early to bed, early to rise* makes man healthy, wealthy, and wise.

G. A Whole Clause: *Whoever knows him well* respects him.

51. Use of Pronominal Subjects. Attention is here called to a few important points:

A. Situation "It" as Subject. *It* is much used as subject to point to something definite which is more or less clearly defined by the situation: *It* is John (words spoken upon hearing footsteps in the hall). *It* (i.e. the distance) is ten miles to the nearest town. This *it* often refers to the thought contained in a preceding statement: John came home late; *it* provoked his father.

B. Impersonal "It" and "There." We now say "*It* rained yesterday," but originally there was no *it* here, no subject at all, for reference was made to an activity without any desire to bring it into relation to a subject. The force of such sentences has not changed, for the *it* here has no meaning. It has been inserted to conform the sentence in a mere formal way to the usual type of sentence with subject and predicate. In spite of the *it* the verb has no real subject, indeed we still as in earlier times desire in such sentences merely to call attention to an activity or state in and of itself: *It* is snowing. *It* is cold. *It* is winter. *It* is a beautiful morning. *It* is Christmas. The old type of sentence without *it* survives in archaic *methinks*, literally *There is a thinking going on to me*, where *me* is a dative of reference (§ 64.C.2).

Instead of a predicate verb here we often employ a predicate noun, as being more concrete, introducing the sentence with *there* instead of *it:* "*It frosted* heavily last night," or "*There* was a heavy *frost* last night."

C. ANTICIPATORY "IT" AND "THERE." When we desire to emphasize a subject, we often withhold it for a time, causing the feeling of suspense and thus calling especial attention to it. Here anticipatory *it*, or in the case of a noun subject also *there*, serves as a provisional subject, pointing forward to the real subject: *There* once lived in this house *an interesting old mán. It* is necessary *to exért yourself*, or *that you exért yourself. It* is no use, or of no use, or *there* is no use, *to sáy anything*, or *sáying anything*.

Anticipatory *it* is also often employed when the subject leaves the first position so that a predicate noun, pronoun, adjective, or adverb may be brought near the beginning of the sentence for emphasis, provided, however, that the logical subject is a singular noun denoting a lifeless thing, or is a clause: *It* is indeed béautiful, this *view* of the mountains! *It* is hárd wórk *keeping the grass green this time of year. It* is immatérial *what names are assigned to them. It* is séldom *that I ever see him any more.* Compare § 77.A.*a*.

D. PRONOUNS USED AS GENERAL OR INDEFINITE SUBJECT. These are: *one, we, you*, and *they*, the last one usually excluding the speaker, hence often used by him to assert something modestly, representing it as coming from others: "*One* doesn't like to be snubbed," or "*You*, or *we*, don't like to be snubbed." In Japan *they* generally marry without love. *They* say best men are moulded out of faults (Shakespeare).

E. EDITORIAL "WE." This form is sometimes used by a speaker or writer to avoid the egotism of *I: We* would first speak of the Puritans, the most remarkable body of men perhaps which the world has ever produced (Macaulay). It will be easier to explain this later on, when *we* have said something about what is called the history of language (Wyld, *The Growth of English*). Instead of *we* some writers employ here a noun with the third person of the verb: The *author* would remark, etc.

In editorials *we* often has associative force, the writer speaking for the whole staff; hence it is here a real plural.

F. PLURAL OF MAJESTY. *We* is often used instead of *I* by kings, especially as a formal term in official decrees. It originally had associative force including the ruler's associates and advisers.

G. "WE" = "YOU." *We* is often used with the force of *you:* Are *we* down-hearted today? Often sarcastically: How touchy *we* are!

H. "THOU," "THEE," "YE," "YOU." The old usage of indicating the number in the pronouns of address, as given in § 28, survives only in poetry and biblical language.

In Middle English under French influence, the plural form was often used as a mark of respect in speaking to a single person of rank or distinction. Later, it became a mere mark of politeness. At first, *ye* was used for subject and *you* for object, but later *you* replaced *ye* in the subject relation. With the growth of democratic feeling the polite address *you* spread and finally in the eighteenth century became general in the common intercourse of life, so that now the plural *you* is the usual form for addressing either a single person or more than one In the language of Quakers the subject form *thou* has been largely replaced by the object form *thee* just as in the literary language the subject form *ye* has been replaced by the object form *you*. In older English it was common for all three persons of the verb to end in -*s*. This usage has passed away in the literary language, but the -*s* has become fixed in the second person in the language of Quakers: Thee *knows* best.

52. Omission of Subject. The subject is omitted:

A. AS A RULE IN IMPERATIVE SENTENCES: Hand me that book! Compare § 116.A.1,2,3.

B. IN THE FIRST PERSON IN A FEW SET EXPRESSIONS: [I] Thank you.

C. WHEN SUBJECT IS SUGGESTED BY THE SITUATION. As in oldest English there is still often no subject expressed, since it is suggested by the situation. Accustomed as we are to feel that every sentence must have a subject, we might understand here a situation *it* (§ 51.A) or some other pronoun as subject, but in reality in natural speech we simply trust to the situation to make our thought clear: He will do it as soon *as possible*. The conditions are *as follows*. He bought more than *was necessary*. *As regards* wheat, prices are rising. He came earlier *than usual*.

53. Forms of the Predicate. The predicate can be:

A. A FINITE (p. 52) VERB OF COMPLETE PREDICATION, i.e. a finite verb that has full verbal meaning, predicating something, hence quite distinct from the copulas described in B below, which have little more than linking force: Simplicity *attracts*. Riches *vanish*. He frequently *tells* us interesting stories. As in the last example the verb often has modifiers. The verb with all its modifiers constitutes the complete predicate.

The verb is not always a simple word as in the preceding examples but is often made up of an auxiliary and another verb-form, both together usually called the verb-phrase: I *have* just *finished* my work. I *shall* soon *finish* my work. I *can-not finish* my work today. Though the auxiliary has finite form as far as possible, i.e. like a simple verb indicates person and number, and the verb proper is in a formal sense dependent, the verb proper contains the basal thought.

In our colloquial speech there is a marked tendency to clothe the chief idea of the predicate in the form of a noun instead of a verb of complete predication: "After dinner we *had a quiet smoke*" instead of "We *smoked quietly*." "I *got a good shaking up*" instead of "I *was shaken up thoroughly*." We *got a good snub*. "The matter is *under consideration*" instead of "The matter *is being considered*." There is here as elsewhere a tendency to concreter forms of expression. A noun seems nearer to popular and colloquial feeling than the abstracter verb. The verbs that are used here in colloquial speech are all of the nature of the copulas described in B below. They merely serve to connect the predicate noun, the real predicate, with the subject.

1. *Suppression of the Verb*. The verb or some part of the verb-phrase often becomes an unimportant element in a sentence and on account of the overtowering importance of some other part of the complete predicate is so little felt that it may be

suppressed: [sit] Down in front! "Have you done it?" — "Of course, I have" [done it]. I guess I [had] better go in.

Sometimes still, as in older English, a dependent infinitive of a verb of motion is suppressed after an auxiliary: Let me [get] off at Jackson Street. Murder will [come] out.

2. *Use of "Do" to Avoid the Repetition of the Verb.* This is a convenient device: He has never acted as he *should have done*. He behaves better than you *do*.

3. *Use of the Periphrastic Form with "Do."* In older English *do* with a dependent infinitive is often used in the present and the past tense instead of the simple form of the verb: Thus conscience *does make* (now *makes*) cowards of us all (Shakespeare). There is here no difference of meaning or function between the simple form and the one with *do*. This old undifferentiated usage ceased about 1750, although it lingers on in legal and biblical language.

The *do*-form is still widely used in the present and the past tense of verbs of complete predication, but it has become differentiated from the simple form by having acquired three distinct functions of its own:

a. A stressed *do*-form is used in questions, declarative statements, and commands wherever there is a desire to emphasize the idea of actuality, the truthfulness of a claim, realization or a desire of realization: *Dóes* he believe it? *Díd* he see it? "Why didn't you téll him?" — "I *díd* tell him." I am so happy to learn that you *dó* intend to come. *Dó* finish your work (desire of realization).

b. An unstressed *do* is used in commands, questions, and in declarative sentences with inverted word-order, wherever there is a desire to see activity proceed, or to inquire after it, or in declarative sentences to call especial attention to it and thus emphasize it: Do fínish your work! Does he belíeve it? Did you téll him? Where did he cóme from? When did he finally gó? Bitterly did we repént our decision.

The *do*-form was so often used in questions for the sake of securing a pure verbal form to stress and emphasize, that it has become associated with question form and is now used in any question, even where the verbal idea is not emphatic: Whére did you buy it? Whóm did you meet?

c. A *do*-form is used in the negative form of questions, declarative statements, and commands when simple *not* is the negative: Doesn't he live here? He doesn't live here. Dón't go yet! Don't tóuch me! The use of *do* here is explained in large measure by our desire to get the sentence adverb *not* before the real verb, the infinitive, as described in § 70.B.

A careful study of the stress in a, b, c will show how valuable our *do*-forms are in shading our thought. When we desire to emphasize actuality or desire of realization, we stress *do;* to call especial attention to the verbal activity, we stress the verbal form. This was not possible in the old simple form that was once used here.

4. *Position of the Verb.* In declarative sentences, the verb of complete predication normally follows the subject.

Deviations from this norm and other features of English word-order relating to the position of the verb are given below:

a. An emphatic adverb or object may stand in the important first place, the personal part of the verb in the second place, and the subject in the third place — the old inverted word-order: Séven tímes did this intrepid general repeat his attacks. Néver had I even dreamed of such a thing. This word-order has become fixed in all questions in which there is an interrogative adverb or object, whether the interrogative adverb or object be emphatic or not: Whén did he come? When did he cóme? Whóm did you meet? Whom did you méet?

The old inverted word-order is now, however, as a living force pretty well shattered. It is now only regularly employed after a negative or a question, as in the above examples. Elsewhere, except of course the case described in b below, the tendency to put the subject before the verb asserts itself also here: "The gallant fellow fought for appearance, and *dówn* he went," not now as formerly "*dówn* went he." *This* I know. There survives here, however, a part of the original construction, namely the placing of an important adverb or object in the first place in the proposition.

b. Often a stressed or unstressed element takes the first place so that the subject may be withheld for a time to create the feeling of suspense and thus call attention to it and render it emphatic: Then came the *dréaded énd*. Now comes my *bést trick*. "You have acted selfishly," replied the *óld mán*. Outwardly this looks like the inverted order described in a, but the difference becomes apparent when a weak unstressed pronoun is subject: "You have acted selfishly," *he replied*. I conversed with him a while; then *I went* into the house.

c. In questions expecting *yes* or *no* for an answer and in imperative sentences, the personal part of the verb stands in the first place: *Did* you see him? *Hand* me the newspaper, please. In older English, the part of the verb containing the verbal meaning stood in the first place: *Discern'st* thou aught in that? (Shakespeare, *Othello*, III, iii, 101). The idea of action is important in both questions and commands; hence in older English the verb was put into the important first place in both kinds of sentences. This older usage survives in commands. In questions, we now express emphasis in a different way: we put an auxiliary in the first place and withhold for a time the part of the verb containing the verbal meaning, to call especial attention to it and thus emphasize it: Do you actually knów it? But also the declarative form is used in questions (§ 48.C).

Also in narrative, action is prominent, so that there is a natural tendency here to bring the verb forward as near the important first place as possible. It now often stands at the head of the sentence after the expletive *there* and later on after *then:* "There *sailed* a bold mariner over the sea . . . Then *came* unfavorable winds." In older English the verb stood in the first place, and this usage survives in choice, lively narrative: *Came* Christmas by which, at the outset, everybody knew it (i.e. the war) would be over and it was not over. *Came* June 1915 . . . (Hutchinson, *If Winter Comes*, p. 256).

B. A VERB OF INCOMPLETE PREDICATION + COMPLEMENT. The predicate may be also a finite form of a verb of incomplete predication in connection with a predicate complement, i.e. a predicate noun, adjective, participle, etc., the verb assuming in a mere formal way the *function* of predication, the complement serving as the real predicate: He *is a coward*. Shakespeare *was a dramatist*. I *am mad*. To err *is human*. Night *became day*. She *seems happy*. I *felt depressed*.

A verb of incomplete predication is called a copula or a linking verb, a verb which of itself has little meaning, merely linking the real predicate to the subject. If such verbs had much concrete meaning, they couldn't serve as links, because they would attract attention to themselves away from the real predicate. Yet they all have a little concrete meaning, each verb containing something not found in the others, thus differentiating our expression. The following are the most common of these linking verbs: *appear, become, come, fall, feel, get, go, grow, happen, keep, leave off, lie, look, loom, prove, rank, remain, rest, run, seem, sit, smell, sound, stand, stay, taste, turn, turn out*, etc.

These verbs have become copulas only as the result of a long development, gradually losing their original concrete meaning. Some of them still serve in their old capacity as verbs of complete predication as well as in their new capacity as linking verbs: "He *fell* (full verb) as a brave soldier at the front," but "He *fell* (linking verb = *became*) heir to a large estate." "The cow *has run* or *gone* (full verbs) into the barn," but "The cow or the spring *has run* or *gone* (linking verbs = *has become*) dry."

a) Appositional Type of Sentence. Originally there was no linking verb between the subject and the predicate adjective, noun or adverb. In primitive expression it was considered sufficient to place the predicate adjective, noun, or adverb alongside of the subject, either before or after it, the predicate word lying next the subject like an appositive explaining it, predicating something of it. In colloquial speech this old type of sentence is still common: Poor fellow! A man overboard! Everybody gone? Our sister dead? Compare § 15.C.

This old type, however, has great disadvantages for higher literary purposes: it cannot indicate time or modal relations. The introduction of a large number of linking verbs which had forms for the expression of tense and mood was a marked improvement of speech. But we still always use this old type when we predicate a noun, adjective, or adverb of an object:

He called me *a liar*. He thought me *crazy*. I found him *upstairs*.
See § 67.C.1.a.

b) Position of Linking Verbs. In declarative sentences,
linking verbs normally follow the subject, but for the sake of
emphasis an emphatic predicate noun or adjective or an emphatic object takes the first place, followed usually by the subject and the linking verb: *Cantankerous chap* Roger always was.
Lucky it is that we know her name. "If you telegraph at once,
he can be stopped," said the Inspector. And *stopped* he was.
This *threat* he was quite unable to carry out.

If, however, the subject is emphatic, it is often, as in A.4.b
above, withheld for a time to call attention to it. It then
stands after the verb: "You have acted selfishly," was her *cold
retort*.

C. A PREDICATE APPOSITIVE. The predicate may be also a
verb of complete predication in connection with a predicate
complement, i.e. a predicate noun, adjective, participle, prepositional phrase, etc., here called a predicate appositive: He
was born *a* (or *as a*) *child* of poor parents, he died *the* (or *as the*)
richest man in the state. He came home *sick*. He returned much
depressed. She asked him *in tears* to come again. Tonight he
appears *as Hamlet*. She acted *as hostess*. He got a job *as chauffeur*.
He has a good position *as teacher of Latin*. He came late *as usual*.
He heard a whimpering *as from a frightened child*. The predicate
appositive, as indicated by its name, is placed alongside of the
predicate, before it or after it, or within it between the subject
and the verb, or before the predicate adjective or noun. It has
in general the character of terseness and spontaneity as it often
adds a brief offhand remark, words thrown in as it were to
complete or explain or comment on the statement or often also
to modify it. It is often preceded by *as* (contraction of *all so*,
i.e. *quite so*), which here as elsewhere points to a following
explanatory remark. Instead of this *as*-phrase, an *as*-clause is
often used.

1. *Abridged Adverbial Clause with Form of Participle, Gerund, or
Infinitive*. The predicate appositive often not only adds a remark about the subject, but also has the force of an adverbial

clause, thus sustaining relations to both the subject and the principal verb: *Being sick* (= *as I was sick*), I stayed at home. *Having finished my work* (= *after I had finished my work*) I went to bed. He is having a hard time *getting used to this rough life* (= *while he is getting used to this rough life*). He hurt himself *playing leapfrog* (predicate appositive instead of a clause of manner). I beat him *jumping* (predicate appositive instead of a clause of manner). Don't bother *answering this* (predicate appositive instead of a clause of manner) or *as to answering this* (gerundial clause after a preposition, another terse predicate appositive short cut). The children never played *without quarreling* (predicate appositive gerundial clause after a preposition instead of a clause of pure result). He went early *to get a good seat* (predicate appositive infinitival clause instead of a clause of purpose). Sometimes the predicate appositive clause is introduced by a distinctive subordinating conjunction: He was drowned *while bathing in the river*. The predicate appositive is a pronounced favorite in terser language and is still growing lustily, crowding out in this field ever more and more the regular subordinate clause. As it is often a short cut, it is often called abridged clause. The predicate appositive is treated in greater detail under the various adverbial subordinate clauses under the heading "Abridgment." (See §§ 84.B; 85.B; 86.A–E; 87.A, B; 88.C; 89.B; 90.B; 91.B; 92.A.)

2. *A Predicate Appositive after a Predicate Noun or Pronoun or Adjective.* The predicate appositive is used not only after a verb of complete predication but also after a predicate noun or pronoun or adjective: He is a good neighbor, *always ready to lend a helping hand and do a good turn*. She was like a bird, *full of joy and music*. *Far from being kind*, he was most cruel. I was late *getting home last night*. Are you through *asking questions?* (participial predicate appositive instead of a clause of restriction introduced by *as: as regards asking questions*). I am proud of him *acting so unselfishly* (predicate appositive causal clause). What is he *to give himself such airs?* (infinitival predicate appositive, instead of a clause of pure result). What a one he is *to make excuses!* (infinitival predicate appositive instead of a clause of restriction, *as regards the making of excuses*). Between her eyes

there was a driven look *as of one who walks always a little ahead of
herself in her haste* (explanatory remark).   It is ten miles from
here *as the crow flies* (explanatory remark).

3. As-*Phrase or* As-*Clause with Adverbial Force.*   The *as*-phrase
or *as*-clause may often according to the context be construed as
indicating cause, manner, extent, degree, or purpose: He
settled in Boston *as a place of culture* (cause).   He was shunned *as
a man of doubtful reputation* (cause).   The horse was useless *as
wanting an eye* (cause).   They criticized the boy *as showing no
interest in his work* (cause).   I like my present work *as preparing
the way to my future career* (cause).   They parted *friends* or *as
friends* (manner).   They rose *as one man* (manner).   They employed him *as chauffeur* (manner).   It was (as) long *as my arm*
(extent).   He was (as) strong *as a horse* (degree).   His face was
(as) white *as a sheet* (degree).   I scattered salt hay over my
strawberry plants *as a protection against winter* (purpose).

4. As-*Phrase or* As-*Clause with the Force of a Sentence Modifier.*
The explanatory *as*-phrase or *as*-clause is often a sentence adverb (§ 70) explaining or commenting on the statement.   Here
it stands before or after the main clause or within it between
the subject and the verb: *As things stand*, we cannot hope to
finish before winter.   *As you well know*, I do not approve of such
conduct.   "*As I remember it*, he was very sick at that time," or
"He was very sick at that time *as I remember it*."   "*As a rule* the
families around here are large," or "The families around here
are large *as a rule*."   It has been raining for a fortnight and *as a
result* the rivers are all over their banks.   Paine's purpose, *as he
himself asserted*, was to stay the growth of atheism.   His burial,
as the evening papers announce (or *as announced by the evening papers*),
will take place tomorrow.   "*As you perceive from his accent*, he is a
foreigner," or "He is a foreigner *as you perceive from his accent*."
"We are in grave danger *as I see it*," or "*As I see it*, we are in
grave danger."

5. As-*Clause after Verb or Predicate Adjective to Express Actuality.*
The *as*-clause is often inserted after a verbal form or a predicate
adjective to stress the act or the quality as an actual fact: The
canceled check decides the question, showing *as it does* that he

received the money. I did not feel that I could go further than to indicate to you *as I clearly did* that I was willing to discuss the matter with you. Stupid *as he is*, he never loses sight of his profit.

6. *Certain Limiting Adjectives Used as Predicate Appositives.* In the preceding examples the predicate appositive adjectives are all descriptive (§ 11) adjectives, but also limiting (§ 11) adjectives are used as predicate appositives: These books are *all* or *both*, or *many of them*, new.

All and *both* were originally predicate appositives, which accounts for their peculiar position when used attributively: *all these books, both these books*, but *these two books; all my family,* but *my entire family*. After the analogy of *six of these books, two of these books* we now often say *all of these books, both of these books.*

54. Predicate Complement. The predicate complement may be:

A. PREDICATE NOUN:

1. In the nominative after verbs of incomplete predication:

a. After the linking verbs enumerated in § 53.B: Socrates was *the son* of a sculptor. She fell *a prey* to the angry waves.

The infinitive *to be* is often added to the finite form of a number of these verbs which have considerable concrete force to mark them more clearly as linking verbs: He *seemed* (or *seemed to be*) a happy man. Young Pen *looked to be* a lad of much more consequence than he was really (Thackeray).

If the complement is predicated of an accusative subject it must be in the same case as its subject, i.e. in the accusative: I believed him to be *John*. There is distinctive form here only in case of pronouns: A boy whom I believed to be *him* just passed. *Whom* do you suppose them to be. Compare §§ 67.C; 82.B. On the other hand, if the complement is predicated of the genitive subject of a gerund, it is in the nominative: I was sure of its being *he*. Compare § 124.

b. After the passive forms of the transitives (§ 67.C.1.a) which take a predicate accusative in the active, as in "They made him *a general*": He was made *a general*.

2. The predicate nominative is often introduced by *as* — now a very common form of the predicate complement and the regular form after the passive of the new prepositional compounds (§ 20, last par.): He is considered *our*, or *as our*, most trustworthy man. He is looked upon *as our richest citizen*.

Similarly, the predicate appositive (§ 53.C) is often introduced by *as:* They met *as friends*, but parted *as enemies*. The *as* that here introduces a predicate appositive noun is somewhat different in meaning from the predicate appositive adjective *like* that takes after it the dative object (§ 63.D) of a noun: "*As* a true friend, he stood by me to the end"; but "*Like a* friend, he came to me and exchanged a few words with me, but I knew he was inwardly not friendly disposed toward me." The *as* here expresses complete identity, oneness with, while *like* indicates mere similarity.

3. Instead of introducing the predicate complement by *as*, as in 2 above, we still after a few verbs in certain set expressions employ a prepositional phrase introduced by the preposition *for*, a usage which was once much more common: He passes *for an accurate scholar*. He was taken *for his brother*.

4. After linking verbs containing the idea of growth, development, or a change of position or condition the predicate complement indicates the final stage of the development, or the new position or state: He became the *president* of the company.

The simple predicate is only common after *become*. Usually a preposition, or, after certain words having a good deal of concrete meaning, the infinitive form *to be*, stands before the predicate complement to indicate more clearly the idea of a final stage, or a new position or state: He grew *into a pale and slender boy*. The machine got *to running* (gerund), or sometimes simple *running* (predicate participle), in contrast to "The machine was *running*." A rumor does not always *prove*, or *prove to be*, a fact. Compare § 124.C.3.c.

5. *Predicate Genitive*. A predicate genitive is found after certain linking verbs to indicate characteristic, measurement, origin, possession, material, etc. — usually the *of*-genitive, but quite commonly the *s*-genitive to indicate possession: The

matter is *of considerable importance*. The chimneys are *of the same height*. He was not *of the poor class*. Nature has denied him (i.e. Lord Curzon) the wit that is *Lord Rosebery's*. I don't want what is *John's* or *anybody else's*. The house is *of stone*.

In present-day English, the predicate genitive of characteristic is often felt as a predicative descriptive adjective, so that the genitive sign *of* naturally and properly drops out: The two boys are [*of*] *the same size, age, temperament*. Similarly in the appositive relation after a governing noun, where the appositive has the force of a predicate: He is a boy [who is *of*] *the same age* as my boy.

An objective predicate genitive of characteristic, i.e. a genitive of characteristic which is predicated of an object, is used after *show, represent, regard*, etc.: He showed himself *of noble spirit*. The predicate genitive here is always without a copula linking it to its subject, the preceding accusative. This is the old appositional type of sentence described in § 53.B.a. The objective predicate genitive is often felt as a predicate adjective and the *of* drops out: He has a daughter [*of*] *the same age*. *What color* shall I paint your door? Compare § 67.C.1.a.

B. PREDICATE ADJECTIVE AND PARTICIPLE. The predicate complement may be an adjective or participle: He is *poor*. She fell *ill*. He looks *unhealthy, ill, sick, bad* (not *badly*), *well* (adjective). He looks *well* (adjective) in that black suit. "He looks cold" (adj.), but "He looked at me *coldly*" (adv.). He ranks *high* as a general. It came *easy* to me. It feels *cold, warm*. I feel *cold, warm, contented, independent, indisposed, well* (adj.), *ill, sick, bad* (not *badly*). I feel *bad* (not *badly*) about it. "It smells *bad*" (adj.), but "It smells (i.e. stinks) *badly* or *disgustingly* (adverbs). It tastes *bad*. Your sentence sounds *well* (adj.), *bad*. It sounds *good* to hear your voice again. He seems (to be) *contented*. We stand *committed* to this action.

a) Predicate Noun with the Force of an Adjective. In the predicate a noun often loses its concrete force, no longer representing an individual person, but now a general abstract idea, often without an article: He was *fool* (= *foolish*) enough to marry her. "They turned *traitor*," where the idea is so abstract that the noun does not take plural form, although the reference is to more than one; but the plural idea more commonly demands plural form: They were *masters* of the situation.

The predicate noun here does not usually agree with its subject in gender, but the masculine form, as the more abstract of the two genders, is employed with reference to both sexes: She was *master* of the situation. Of course, the feminine form is regularly employed when the predicate noun refers to something specifically feminine: She is more *mother* than *wife*.

C. Predicate Pronoun and Adverb "So." The predicate complement may be a pronoun: It was *he*. It was *they*. It was *we*. We all desire to be free, but in this world, constituted as it is, we shall never be *that*.

Where the reference is to the idea contained in some preceding statement or word, we often use as a predicate pronoun the demonstrative *that*, as in the last example, but the personal pronoun *it* and the adverb *so* are often used with similar force: "I don't like my teacher." — "Why [is that] *so?*" She is shy, but it's a peculiarity of hers that she never looks *it* and yet is intensely *so*. He is poor and *so* am I. *So* is also predicated of an object: She made life interesting, just because she found it *so*.

a) Case of Predicate Pronoun. In choice language we should resist the strong colloquial drift to put an inflected predicate pronoun into the accusative; the nominative is the proper form: It is *he*.

D. Predicate Infinitive. There are three classes of infinitives here:

1. *Normal Prepositional Form.* There are two groups:

a. The prepositional form is used after linking verbs: To be good is *to be happy*. He seems *to have* ability.

Descriptive force is sometimes imparted here by employing as predicate a present participle instead of an infinitive: Her whole being seemed *hanging* on his words.

b. In our modern English a predicate infinitive is often employed after the passive form of many verbs: He was found *to be sleeping* (fact), or He was found *sleeping* (with descriptive force). It was ordered *sent*, or *to be sent*, to my house. He was believed *to be rich*. Compare § 67.C.1.b.(i).

2. *Modal Form*. After the linking verbs *be, remain, fall*, and *seem* the infinitive often assumes a peculiar modal force in the predicate, expressing the possibility, fitness, or necessity of an action, the last idea in its broadest sense, including all that takes place under the constraint of circumstances, or in the natural order of things, or in accordance with the decree of destiny or the will of another, or in accordance with some plan or agreement: An account of the event *is to* (= *can*) *be found* in the evening papers. Such women *are to* (= *ought to*) *be* admired. I *am to* (= *must*) *become* a burden to you all. These things *are* never *to be spoken of*. He *is* soon (adverb of time) *to leave us*. This modal infinitive can be used only after a present or a past tense.

We also employ the modal infinitive to predicate something of an object, but we must here use the appositional type of sentence (§ 53.B.*a*), which is without a linking word to connect the predicate with its accusative subject: I find plenty *to do* (= *that ought to be done*). I have much *to do*. This modal infinitive can be used after any tense.

3. *Predicate Infinitive to Express Purpose*. After the linking verb *be* the *to*-infinitive is sometimes used as a predicate appositive (§ 53.C) to express purpose: I have been down town *to buy* a new hat. In all such cases the copula still has a good deal of concrete force. In older English, the original concrete force often disappeared entirely, so that the infinitive became a real predicate complement with the force of the predicative present participle in the progressive form: "I have been all this day *to avoid* (now *avoiding*) him " (Shakespeare, *As You Like It*, II, v, 33).

This older usage survives after the ingressive linking verbs *set in, set about, start, start in, start out:* It set in *to rain* (or *raining*). After the flood they set about *to repair* (or *repairing*) the damage. The baby started (started in, started out) *to cry*, or *crying*.

E. PREDICATE GERUND. The gerund is often used as a predicate complement, usually with the same force as the prepositional infinitive: To build on any other foundation (than religion) is *building* upon sand (Southey), or to build upon sand.

F. PREDICATE ADVERB AND PREPOSITIONAL PHRASE. An adverb or a prepositional phrase is often used as a predicate complement: My day's work is *over*. Don't strike a man when he is *down*. He is *in good condition*. In many compounds the preposition *on* is reduced to *a*, as in *afoot, away, ashore*, etc., all originally prepositional phrases, hence still freely used as predicate complement: He is *ashore*.

55. Agreement between Subject and Predicate. The predicate agrees with the subject in number and, where it is possible, in person, gender, and case.

A. NUMBER.

1. *Singular Subject*. If the subject is singular, the verb is also singular: The tiniest hair *casts* a shadow.

a. The verb is always singular which follows situation *it* (§ 51.A) or an anticipatory subject *it* which points to a following clause, even though the reference is to more than one: "Where does all that noise come from?" — "It's the children playing upstairs." It *was* my two brothers *who were hurt* (subject clause).

b. If a subject in the singular is associated by means of *with, together with, as well as, no less than, like, but, except*, with other words which logically, though not formally, constitute a part of the subject, the subject is now usually in the singular, often in contrast to older usage: The bat together with the balls *was* stolen. The girl, as well as the boys, *has* learned to ride. Man, no less than the lower forms of life, *is* a product of the evolutionary process. Nobody but John and William *was* there.

c. In contrast to older usage, the number of the copula is now regulated by a mere mechanical principle. It now has the number of the noun that precedes it, whether it be subject or predicate: Her principal anxiety (predicate, but now treated as the subject) *was* her children (real subject, but now treated as predicate). It is often difficult to distinguish subject and

115

predicate in such cases, so that a mechanical rule is easier to follow.

d. Collective nouns and words denoting part or number take a singular or a plural verb according as the idea of oneness or plurality is uppermost in the mind: "The Senior Class *requests* (as a unit) the pleasure of your company," but "The Senior Class *are* unable to agree upon a president." "The greatest part of his life *was* spent in philosophical retirement," but "The greatest part of the Moguls and Tartars *were* as illiterate as their sovereigns." "The number of cases *grows* less each year," but "A large number of them *are* on our side."

e. The singular is now the regular form after *each one*, *everybody*, *everyone*, *either*, since they are felt as presenting the subjects separately: Everyone *has* his hobby.

None was originally a singular and is sometimes still so used, but it is now more commonly felt and used as a plural: None *are* so deaf as those who will not hear. In the singular it is now usually replaced by *no one*. Compare § 34.C.

Neither as the negative form of *either* should be a singular referring to two persons or things taken separately and this conception is perhaps the prevailing one; but in the negative form there is often a pronounced plural idea, which often in our best writers finds expression in plural form: Neither of them *is* worthy of this position. Neither of the sisters *were* very much deceived (Thackeray). Do you mean to say neither of you *know* your own numbers? (H. G. Wells). Compare 2.e below.

The singular is also used after the above list of words when used as limiting adjectives: Every boy and girl *is* taught to read and write. Every limb and every feature *appears* with its appropriate grace.

f. For the number of the verb after *kind of*, *sort of* see § 94.D.

2. *Plural Subject*. If the subject is plural, or if there are several subjects, the verb is plural: The boys in our class *are* more numerous than the girls. A strong wind and a full sail *bring* joy to the sailor.

a. When the verb precedes a number of subjects, it is often in older English in the singular agreeing with the first, but we now feel the plural form as more natural: And now *abideth* faith, hope, charity, these three (I. Corinthians, XIII. 13).

When the subjects precede, the verb sometimes stands in the singular agreeing with the last, usually, however, only when this part of the subject serves as a climax to the whole of the subject, or summarizes the different subjects: Your interest, your honor, God himself *bids* you do it. Her knights and dames — her court *is* there (Byron, *Parisina*).

In older English, the singular form of the verb was often used with a plural subject. This older usage still occasionally occurs in the literary language, especially in set expressions, *there is, there exists*, etc.: Here there *does seem* to be, if not certainties, at least a few probabilities, that, etc. (H. G. Wells).

b. In case several coördinate singular subjects represent the same person, the verb is in the singular, often also when they are felt as forming a distinct collective idea, a close union, or a oneness of idea: My colleague and friend (one person) *is* near death's door. A cart and horse (felt as a unit) *was* seen at a distance.

Plural nouns, or two or more singular or plural nouns, often convey the idea of oneness, so that the verb is in the singular: The fifty miles *was* (or *were*) covered by the winner in four hours and fifteen minutes. Bread and milk *is* excellent food. In the following mathematical expressions the singular of the verb is more logical since we are dealing with abstract ideas, not with concrete objects; but the present tendency is to use the plural since we are influenced in a mere formal way by the conception of different numbers: Two and two *are* (or *is*) four, or *make* (or *makes*) four. Three times three *are* (or *is*) nine.

On the other hand, when each of a number of singular noun subjects is considered separately, the verb is in the singular: A fever, a mutilation, a cruel disappointment, a loss of wealth, a loss of friends, *seems* at the moment untold loss.

c. Nouns that are plural in form but singular in meaning, such as *gallows, news, mumps*, etc., usually take a verb in the singular: This sad news *was* brought to him at once. Compare § 94.A.2.

Some nouns, such as *means* and *pains*, are sometimes used as plurals, sometimes as singulars: Great pains *have* (or *has*) been taken, or Much pains *has* been taken. "All possible means *have*, or every means *has*, been tried."

Alms, *eaves*, and *riches* (from Old French *richesse*), though, in older English, singular forms, are now felt and treated as plurals: Where *riches are*, some *alms are* due. The *eaves are* not yet finished.

d. If the subject of the sentence is the name of a book, drama, newspaper, country, or in general any title or proper name, the verb is usually in the singular: *The Times* reports, etc.

e. In connection with the conjunctions *not — but*, *not only — but* (*also*), *either — or*, *neither — nor*, *partly — partly*, etc., the different subjects are considered singly, and hence the verb agrees with one of them — the next one to it — and is understood with the others: Not John but his two brothers *are* to blame. Either the mayor or the aldermen *are* to blame. Neither the girls nor William *is* to blame.

After *neither — nor* we now often find the plural verb after singular subjects since there is a growing tendency to give formal expression to the plural idea which often lies in the negative form of statement: Neither Leopardi nor Wordsworth *are* of the same order with the great poets who made such verses as . . . (Matthew Arnold). Compare 1.e above.

We sometimes find the plural with *or* since the speaker or writer feels that the statement, though at any one time applicable to only one of two or more things, holds good for them all: What *are* honor or dishonor to her? (Henry James).

3. The verb is in the plural *where a singular abstract subject is modified by two or more adjectives connected by "and"* which indicate that two or more things are meant: Sacred and profane wisdom *agree* in declaring that pride goeth before a fall. The abstract subject here retains its singular form since as an abstract noun it cannot take a plural.

4. *After the group "more than"* there is a difference of usage according to the meaning. The usual form of expression is the singular verb since *more than* is felt as an adverb, as equivalent

to *not merely;* but others feel *more* as a plural indefinite pronoun and employ the plural verb: More than one *has,* or *have,* found it so. Of course, the plural is used when the words are separated: More *have* found it so than just he. Compare § 34.C (3rd par.).

5. *Where there are an affirmative and a negative subject,* the verb agrees with the affirmative: Virtue, not rolling suns, the mind *matures* (Young, *Night Thoughts*).

6. *Where there is a clear plural idea present,* the predicate noun agrees with the subject in number: The Puritans were the King's most exasperated *enemies.*

7. The verb is in the singular *if the subject is a clause or a group of words* containing a single thought or picture: Early to bed and early to rise *makes* a man healthy, wealthy, and wise.

B. PERSON.

1. *When two or more subjects of different persons are in apposition,* the verb agrees with the first of them, since it is felt as containing the leading idea: I, your master, *command* you.

2. *Where there are subjects of different persons connected by "nor" or "or,"* the verb agrees with the nearest subject, or each subject has the verb after it: Neither he nor I *am* in the wrong, or He is not in the wrong, nor *am* I. Either he or I *am* in the wrong, or Either he *is* in the wrong, or I *am.* The second form, though less terse, is now the favorite, since by repeating the verb with each subject we avoid the annoying necessity of making a choice between the two persons. In popular speech, the annoying necessity of making a choice between the two persons is avoided in a more simple manner, namely by placing the subjects together and employing a plural verb; which, though often incorrect, always avoids the clash of the different persons: Either he or I *are* in the wrong. After *nor,* however, the plural occurs not infrequently also in the literary language; for here it is logical, as often elsewhere after *neither* or *neither — nor:* Neither you nor I *are* ever going to say a word about it (Marion Crawford, *Katherine Lauderdale,* I, Ch. XV). Compare A.1.e and A.2.e above.

In a number of cases the force of *or* is not disjunctive, so that we must be guided by the sense: "There *are* one or two irregularities to be noted." In "The Scriptures, or Bible, *are* the only authentic source" (Bishop Tomline) the words "or Bible" is a mere explanation of "Scriptures."

3. *Where there are an affirmative and a negative subject*, the verb agrees with the affirmative: "I, not you, *am* to blame," or "I *am* to blame, not you."

4. For the person and the number of the *verb in a relative clause* see § 80.E.

C. GENDER. The predicative complement agrees with the subject in gender where it has especial forms to denote sex: *She* is a *countess*. Compare § 95.A.1,2.

D. CASE. The predicate complement agrees with its subject in case: *It* (subject nominative) is *he* (predicate nominative). They supposed *us* (subject accusative) to be *them* (predicate accusative). However, if the complement is predicated of the genitive subject of a gerund, it is in the nominative. For an example see § 54.A.1.a (3rd par.).

SUBORDINATE ELEMENTS OF A SENTENCE

The subordinate elements of a sentence are called modifiers. They are divided into the following general classes:

1) *Adjective modifiers*, which modify a noun or a pronoun.

2) *Objective* and *adverbial modifiers*, which modify a verb, adjective, or adverb. This division into objective and adverbial modifiers is made only for practical purposes. There is no fundamental difference between the two classes. In this book the word object is used where the relation of the word seems necessary or close. The expression adverbial modifier is employed to indicate a less close relation. It is often impossible to observe this distinction and free use is made of the one or the other of these terms according to practical considerations.

Attributive Adjective Modifiers

An attributive adjective modifier is one that stands in direct attachment to its governing noun, thus differing from predicate words which are separated from their subject by a verb: a *little* boy; a man *kind* to everybody.

Originally before the introduction of the verb into the sentence the attributive elements were predicates, the old appositional type of sentence described in § 53.B.*a*, the adjective element lying alongside of the noun as an explanatory appositive predicating something of it, as still often used: A *beautiful* sight! *Poor* Tom! A man *overboard!* Everything *in good order?* When such an attributive adjective element modifies the subject of a sentence, it still often has the force of an old predicate appositive and hence, as described in § 53.C, has the force of an adverbial clause: This poor *friendless* man (or man, *without friends;* or man, *who is without friends*) is to be pitied = This poor man is to be pitied *because he is without friends* (causal clause). This *old* woman still dolls herself up like a young lady = This woman still dolls herself up like a young lady *although she is old* (concessive clause).

Attributive adjective modifiers are treated below in detail.

56. Attributive Adjectives and Participles.

A. FORMS. Attributive adjectives and participles fall into two classes — the *adherent* adjective or participle, which stands before the governing noun, and the *appositive* adjective or participle, which stands after it: (adherent adjective) a *kind* man; (appositive adjective) a man *kind* to everybody. Of the two classes the adherent adjective or participle stands in a closer relation to the noun.

Both the adherent and the appositive adjective or participle are in a logical sense predicative adjectives, since they predicate something of the noun. They differ however in a grammatical sense from predicate adjectives, since they have a different place in the structure of the sentence and have a somewhat different rôle to play, as we shall see below. The appositive adjective or participle is much nearer the nature of the predicate adjective than is the adherent adjective or participle. A predi-

121

cate adjective predicates something of the whole subject, not of
a particular noun or nouns as in the case of attributive adjectives; and besides, standing after the copula, it concludes the
statement.

B. POSITION AND STRESS. The adherent adjective or participle, when stressed less than the noun, describes; when stressed
more than the noun, it distinguishes or classifies: this lìttle
bóy (descriptive stress); the líttle bòy, not the bíg one (distinguishing stress); líttle minds, góod deeds (classifying stress).
The general principle involved here is: In descriptive stress
the heavier stress follows, while in distinguishing and classifying stress it precedes.

In a descriptive group we often stress the adherent adjective
strongly, but we should not make the stress quite as strong as
that upon the noun, if we desire to preserve the descriptive
force: This is bláck ingrátitude! (emphatic descriptive stress).

A participle usually follows the governing noun as an appositive when its verbal force is marked, but of course stands before
the noun when it is felt as an adherent adjective: "a poor
neglècted bóy," but "Bòys neglécted were boys lost" (Kipling)
= Boys who were neglected were boys who were lost. The
appositive participle has the force of an abridged attributive
clause. It is more heavily stressed than the preceding noun,
so that the force is descriptive.

Appositive adjectives are often used with the same force as
appositive participles: Calculàtions quíck and ánxious passed
through the young wife's brain (Mrs. H. Ward).

In contrast to English appositive adjectives and participles
with descriptive stress, are appositive adjectives and participles
formed under French and Latin influence, which in spite of
their descriptive stress have distinguishing or classifying force:
The Prèsident eléct, còurt mártial, Pòet Láureate, sùm tótal,
Àsia Mínor.

C. NOUNS, ADVERBS, PHRASES, SENTENCES USED AS ADJEC-
TIVES. One of the marked features in English is the great
freedom with which nouns, adverbs, phrases, and sentences
can stand before a noun in adjective function: a *stone* bridge,
a *baby* boy, a *bird's-eye* view, *foreign language* instruction, the

United States government, a *parrot and monkey* time, a *cat and dog* (compare next par.) life, the *down* stroke, in *after* years, the *above* argument; an *out-and-out* failure; the *quarter-past-seven* train; a *good-for-nothing* fellow; the *most stay-at-home* person I ever met.

The plural of a noun is often used as an adjective: a lively *good roads* agitation, a *ten-foot* (§ 24.A.4) pole, a *ten-minute* (§ 24.A.4) talk, etc. The descriptive genitive (§ 57.C.6) is often used as an adjective, as can be seen by the fact that there is often an adjective before it which does not modify it but the following governing noun: her *woman's* instinct, a sudden *fool's* paroxysm of despair, a new *beginner's* Latin book, a *printer's* error, obvious *printer's* errors, a *cat and dog's* life, an interesting *ten minutes'* talk, a new *old men's* home, etc. The possessive adjectives, *my*, *her*, etc., were once genitives. Compare § 103.C.

D. Repetition of Limiting Adjective. If the limiting adjective modifies two nouns both representing the same person or thing, or parts of a whole, it should be used only once; while, on the other hand, if the nouns represent different persons or things that it is desired to contrast or to mark as distinct and separate, the limiting adjective should be repeated before each noun: "He is the guardian and natural protector (one person) of the lad," but "*The* teacher and *the* guardian (two persons) of the lad were discussing his case together." "A German and English dictionary" (one book), but "*a* German and *an* English dictionary" (two books); "the red and white rose" (one rose with two colors), but "*the* red and *the* white rose" (two roses, each with only one color); (felt as belonging together) a knife and fork, the King and Queen, a horse and cart, my coat and vest, my watch and chain.

For convenience' sake, however, the second limiting adjective is often dropped even where the reference is to different individuals, provided the thought would not in any way be impaired: "*the* first and *the* second verse," or "the first and second verses"; "*the* English and *the* German language," or "the English and German languages"; "the boys and girls of our school," but "In some towns there are separate schools for *the* boys and *the* girls." A doctor and nurse were provided for them.

Even where the reference is to *one* person or to things that belong together, we repeat the limiting adjective if we desire to present distinct conceptions or to emphasize each object: He was *the* orator and *the* statesman of his age. I broke *my* watch and *my* chain. I bought *a* watch and *a* chain.

57. Attributive Genitive.

A. FORMS. There are four distinct forms:

1. *The* S-*Genitive*. The ending of this genitive is now always written 's and is pronounced as a simple *s* except after sibilants (*s*, *ss*, *c*, *sh*, *tch*, *ch*, *g*, *dg*, *x*, *z*), where it is pronounced *es*, i.e. with a pronounced *e* followed by an *s*-sound: *John's* (with simple *s*), but *Jones's* (with *es*). The *-es* after sibilants is the survival of a once universal usage to pronounce *es* in the genitive ending. As this survival was not understood, it was supposed to be a reduced form of *his* and was written *'s: Jones's son*, wrongly felt as a contraction of *Jones his son*. The genitive ending is now always written 's without regard to the pronunciation.

English once had genitives that had no distinctive ending, so that it became common to suppress elsewhere the genitive ending. This older usage survives in a few words after a sibilant: for *conscience'* sake, for *goodness'* sake, *Jesus'*, *Xerxes'*, *Socrates'*. Some writers still suppress the *-s* in general after a sibilant: *Cards'* pride (Hugh Walpole), more commonly *Cards's* pride.

In the plural genitive, 's is added only in the case of nouns whose plurals are not formed by adding *-s: men, men's; women, women's; mice, mice's*. Wherever the noun ends in the plural in *-s* or *-es*, the genitive takes no additional ending, but in the written language an apostrophe is added to indicate the genitive relation: the Browns' cottage, the Adamses' cottage.

The *s*-genitive is the favorite with names of living beings, so that it has become associated with the idea of life in a literal or figurative sense: the ocean's roar, truth's victory, the mind's peace, duty's call, at death's door. This idea of life is entirely absent when the name of a thing is used as the subject of the gerund: There is no further danger of the *house's* settling. As a survival of older usage it is used also elsewhere with a number of names of lifeless things: a *day's* journey, a *stone's* throw, etc.

This genitive always precedes the governing noun.

2. *The* Of-*Genitive.* This is the usual form with nouns representing lifeless things, but it is also much used with names of living beings: the leg *of the table*, the author *of the book*, the father *of the boy*, etc. This genitive always follows the governing noun.

3. *The Double Genitive.* The simple *s*-genitive cannot be used after the governing noun, for in talking it would be taken for a plural. As it is often desirable to employ after the governing noun the *s*-genitive with its lively conception of personality, we place the genitive sign *of* before the simple *s*-genitive, thus clearly marking it as a genitive: that fine suggestion *of Father's;* "a picture *of the King's*," a picture belonging to the King, but "a picture *of the King*," a likeness of the King; the charming wife *of Smith's;* that ugly nose *of his* (old double gen.); that dear little girl *of yours* (old double gen.). This old form is still common. See § 28.

This genitive can be used only of a definite individual: "that angry outbreak *of Father's*"; but not "a heart *of a father's*," for the reference is general and indefinite. Here we must say "a heart *of a father*."

4. *The Uninflected Genitive.* Originally there was no inflected form to indicate the genitive relation. This was shown by the word-order, the genitive always preceding the governing noun. This old usage survives in genitive compounds: *sun*-rise = the rising of the sun; *earth*-quake = the quaking of the earth.

B. STRESS. The laws for stressing the genitive are the same as those observed in stressing adjectives, as described in § 56.B: (descriptive stress) the ròar of the ócean, the stòrming of the fórtress; (distinguishing stress) Jóhn's hàt, not Wílliam's; the táble-lèg, not the cháir-lèg; (classifying stress) a chíld's vòice, stéam-pòwer. We can also indicate distinguishing and classifying force by stressing the second member more strongly than for descriptive stress: "the lànguage of this chíld" (descriptive stress), but "the lànguage of a chíld" (classifying stress).

C. The Categories of the Attributive Genitive. The central idea of the genitive is that of *sphere*, indicating that a person or thing belongs to the sphere of another, having close relations to it or forming an integral part of it. We may distinguish the following categories of the attributive genitive:

1. *Genitive of Origin*, representing a person or thing as associated with another person or thing in the relation of source, cause, authorship: the son *of the king, the king's* son; the devastations *of the war; this warrior's* deeds, or the deeds *of this warrior; Shakespeare's* works, the works *of Shakespeare*.

a. If two names are connected by *and* and represent persons that are joined together in authorship, business, or a common activity, the second name alone assumes the genitive ending: *Stevens and Malone's* Shakespeare, in *William and Mary's* reign, but of course "*Steele's and Addison's* works" when we are speaking of the separate sets of two different authors.

2. *Possessive Genitive*, expressing possession, sphere, a belonging to, association with, inherence: *the master's* dog (dog owned by the master), the dog *of the master; the dog's* master (not the master owned by the dog, but the master in the sphere of the dog), the master *of the dog; the sheep's* skin, the skin *of the sheep*, the *sheep*-skin (= diploma), the last form now differentiated in meaning from the other two; *the hero's* courage, the courage *of the hero; Marshall Field and Company's* retail store.

a. Adverbs or adverbial expressions are now often inflected like nouns: *yesterday's* mail, *yesterday evening's* newspaper.

b. If two or more names connected by *and* represent persons who are joined together in possession, the second or last name alone takes the genitive ending: *John and William's* uncle; *John, William, and Mary's* uncle.

c. Omission of Governing Noun. The word for house or place of business is often omitted: I was at *Smith's* [house or place of business]. Go to the *baker's*.

d. Group-Genitive. If the genitive itself is followed by a modifying *of*-genitive forming a group with it, the genitive 's must be added to the end of the group, not to the genitive proper, for an *s*-genitive can only stand immediately before its governing noun, since it would otherwise be taken for a plural: *the King of England's* portrait.

3. *Subjective Genitive*, which represents a living being as associated with an act in the relation of author: *a mother's* love for her children, the love *of a mother* for her children; *duty's* call, the call *of duty; your* (old gen.) death, the death *of you* (that will be the death *of you*); often the old uninflected genitive (A.4 above): a *snake*-bite, *heart*-throb.

4. *Objective Genitive*, which denotes the object toward which the activity is directed: [She is devoting much time to] *her children's* education, or the education *of her children; Caesar's* murderers, or the murderers *of Caesar;* often the old uninflected genitive (A.4 above): the *gate*-keeper, *money*-maker, *woman*-hater, etc.

As the possessive adjectives are derived from the genitive of personal pronouns, they still often have various meanings of the genitive, hence also sometimes the force of an objective genitive: my (= gen. of origin) son; my (= possessive gen.) book; my (= subjective gen.) love of God; my (= objective gen.) punishment.

5. *Genitive of Material or Composition*, denoting that of which something consists: a crown *of thorns*, a swarm *of bees*, a group *of children;* sometimes the old uninflected genitive (§ 57.A.4): a *thórn*-hèdge, a *sánd*-pìle, etc., once also a *stóne*-brìdge, etc., but now "a stòne brídge," since the first component has been construed as an adjective, or we can employ an *of*-genitive, a brìdge *of stóne*.

6. *Descriptive Genitive.* There are two groups:

a. Genitive of Characteristic: a màn of áction; a spìrit of háte; a wóman's vòice, mén's shòes. She is worth tén of her dàughter.

b. Genitive of Measure: an *hòur's* deláy, the delày of *an hóur;* an hòur or so's deláy, the delày *of an hóur or so*. We often employ a compound adjective instead of the genitive, usually with classifying force: a *thrée-hour* delày, a *tén-pound* bàby, a *tén-foot* pòle, etc. Compare § 56.C (2nd par.).

Also the possessive and the objective genitive are used in units of measurement: a bóat's lèngth, two shíp's lèngths; a stóne's thròw, within two stónes' throw.

7. *Appositive Genitive*, explaining the preceding governing noun, now usually with the *of*-form, but still with the old *s*-form in poetic expression: the vice *of intemperance*, the art *of printing*, the city *of London*, the island *of Great Britain; treason's* charge (Scott's *Marmion*), *Katrine's* lake and isle (id.); innocent sleep . . . Chief nourisher in *life's* feast (Shakespeare). The old *s*-genitive is still common in certain proper names, often in elliptical construction: *St. James's* [Park], *St. Paul's* [Cathedral], *St. James's* [Theater], etc.

The appositional genitive is often replaced by another appositional construction: The appositive is placed after the governing noun agreeing with it in case: the bìrd *héron*, the màmmal *whále*, the prèposition *with*, Càrdinal *Mánning*, Làke *Michigan*. In older English the appositive preceded: *Témese* strèam (Bede), now often *the rìver Thámes* to conform to the new descriptive stress, as described in §§ 56.B and 58.B. The old word-order, however, is still often used here, but the stress is the new descriptive: *the Thàmes Ríver*. The older word-order has thus survived in a number of words since the appositive was construed as an adherent (§ 56.A) adjective and was consequently left before the governing noun: the *Hùdson* Ríver, the *St. Gòthard* Túnnel, etc.

a. There is another type of appositive that has come from the French: a jewel *of a cup*, a beast *of a night*, a frail slip *of a woman*, etc.

8. *Partitive Genitive*, denoting the whole of which only a part is taken: a piece *of bread*, one *of my friends*, a friend *of John's* (double genitive; see § 57.A.3), a friend *of mine* (§ 57.A.3). He is the soul *of the enterprise*. That will be the last *of it*.

a. Genitive of Gradation. This is only a variety of the partitive genitive: the King *of kings* and Lord *of lords*, the book *of books.* I am looking for the word *of words* that will express my disgust.

b. Blending. There still lingers on from older English a tendency to blend the partitive genitive with some other construction — a usage which in general is now avoided in good English: His versification is by far the most perfect of any English poet (Saintsbury), a blending of "His versification is the most perfect of all English poets" and "His versification is more perfect than that of any English poet." The omission of the word *other* after *any* in the last example is a form of blending still common. In comparisons where there is present the idea of a group or class, the superlative represents the group as complete, while the comparative represents a separation of one or more from all the others in the group. Hence we should say: "Smith is the ablest *of all the* boys in his class," but "Smith is abler than *any other* boy in his class"; but the two forms are sometimes blended: "Smith is the ablest of *all* the *other* boys in his class" and "Smith is abler than *any* boy in his class." The word *other* is incorrectly used here after the superlative and is omitted after the comparative where it is necessary. It should follow *any.*

58. An Appositive as Modifier of a Noun. A noun which explains or characterizes another is placed alongside of it, and from its position is accordingly called an appositive (i.e. placed alongside of): Smith, *the banker.*

There are two groups:

A. LOOSE APPOSITION.

1. *Appositive Nouns.* Where the appositive noun follows the governing noun in a rather loose connection with the force of an explanatory relative clause, it agrees, if possible, with the governing noun in number and gender, but not always in case: the Smiths, *the friends* of my youth; Mary, *the belle* of the village. The appositives *friends* and *belle* may here be regarded as agreeing with their governing word in number, gender, and case.

Often, however, the appositive does not agree with its governing noun in case since it is felt as a nominative, the predicate of an abridged relative clause: There was only one closed carriage in the place, and that was old Mr. Landor's. [who was] *the banker* (G. Eliot). The appositive here indicates the identity of a person, but where it indicates the identity of a place, a shop or a residence expressed by a genitive, it too is in the genitive to make clear that the reference is to a place, not to a person: I bought the book *at Smith's, the bookseller's* (= *at Smith's store, the bookseller's store*). But if we feel the reference is to a person, we may use the nominative, though it is not so common as in older English: I bought the book at Smith's, *the bookseller.* The nominative, however, is the usual form here where the appositive consists of parts connected by a conjunction, or is a noun modified by a prepositional phrase: at Smith's, *the bookseller and stationer*, at Smith's, *the bookseller on Main Street.* On the other hand, the governing noun and the appositive sometimes form a compound, as described in the next paragraph, and as a compound take the genitive sign at the end: I bought the book at Smith *the bookseller's.*

When an appositional group modifies a noun and stands before it, the group is usually treated as a compound noun, the appositive at the end taking the genitive ending: at *Mr. Barton the clergyman's* house; or at the house *of Mr. Barton, the clergyman.* The form with *of* must be used if the appositional group is long: at the house of Smith, the bookseller on Main Street.

The appositive is often introduced by *as:* I have thought of you as your sister might think and spoken to you *as my brother.* The governing word here is often a possessive adjective, which originally was the genitive of a personal pronoun and still implies a personal pronoun in the genitive: Guilford now found himself restricted to his business *as a judge* in equity (Macaulay). The appositive is here regularly in the nominative, never in the genitive.

An appositive noun often stands in rather close relation to a preceding pronoun, but the connection, though close, is not quite so close as in B below. We *boys* like him. One *Smith* came to see us.

2. *Pronouns as Appositives.* An appositive pronoun in choice English usually agrees with its governing noun or pronoun in

case: Mother, who should go, John or *I?* Mother, whom do you want, John or *me?*

3. *Appositive to a Sentence or Clause.* An appositive in the form of an explanatory remark often belongs to a whole sentence or clause: I, like many another, am apt to judge my fellow-man in comparison with myself, *a wrong and a foolish and a natural thing to do.* God, I thank thee that I am not as other men are, *extortioners, unjust, adulterers,* or even as this publican (Luke, XVIII.11).

B. CLOSE APPOSITION: Kìng *Géorge,* Jòhn *Smíth,* my frìend *Smíth,* Profèssor *Bròwn,* the stèamer *Ocean Brìde,* the fìgure *5',* the prèposition *wíth.* The stress is here descriptive as in §§ 56.B and 57.B.

The relation here between the appositive and its governing word is so close that they are in many cases felt as a compound. When this group modifies another noun and stands before it, the appositive takes the ending: at *my friend Smith's* house, or at the house *of my friend Smith.*

59. A Prepositional Phrase as Modifier of a Noun.

A noun or pronoun may be modified by a prepositional phrase: joy *over the victory,* skill *in hand work,* care *for the needy.*

In the early stage of language development there were no prepositions. The modifier was simply placed before the governing noun, the word-order alone indicating that the one noun was dependent upon the other: This primitive type of expression is still widely used in compounds: a *rat*-trap = a trap *for rats; tooth*-brush = a brush *for the teeth.*

a) Attributive Prepositional Clause. In attributive elements the preposition may stand not only before a noun but also in the case of *after, before, since,* before a clause: The day *after I came* (= *after my coming*) was very beautiful. The day *before he came* (= *before his coming*) was very beautiful. The long lonesome period *since we last met* (= *since our last meeting*) has depressed me very much. Compare § 80.B (next to last par.).

60. An Infinitive as Modifier of a Noun. A noun may be modified by a prepositional infinitive. There are different categories:

A. THE INFINITIVE HAS ITS ORIGINAL FORCE, i.e. is still a prepositional phrase with the literal meaning of the preposition *to:* a strong impulse *to do it*, lit. *toward doing it*.

B. THE ATTRIBUTIVE INFINITIVE OFTEN HAS THE FORCE OF A RELATIVE CLAUSE: He was the first man *to come* = *who came*. Compare § 80.G.

C. THE ATTRIBUTIVE INFINITIVE OFTEN HAS THE FORCE OF AN APPOSITIVE: He didn't even do me the honor *to come in*, or *of coming in*, thus competing here with the appositive genitive of the gerund.

61. An Adverb as Modifier of a Noun. An adverb often modifies a noun or pronoun: (adherent adverb) the *above* remark; (appositive adverb) the tree *yonder*, this book *here*, these trees and those *yonder*.

62. A Clause as Modifier of a Noun. A clause may modify a noun: The thought *that we shall help him* gives him courage. Compare §§ 79 and 80.A.

Objective Modifiers

63. Accusative Object.

A. FORM AND POSITION. As the accusative and the dative have lost the concrete forms which they once had, we must now indicate the accusative and the dative relations by the word-order.

If there is only one object, it is in most cases an accusative and stands in the position after the verb: John struck *his dog*. If it becomes necessary to employ a dative object after the verb, we must usually employ the modern dative form with *to*, for otherwise it would be construed as an accusative: Robin Hood robbed the rich to give *to the poor*. Where the thought is clear, however, the older simple form is still often employed: Wire, write, *me* at once. He had already told *me*.

If there are two objects, the dative, or indirect object, stands immediately after the verb; then comes the accusative, or direct object: He gave *her* (dat.) *a book* (acc.). He gave *the house* (dat.) *a new coat* (acc.) of paint.

If for any reason we desire to put the dative after the accusative, we must use its modern *to*-form to make the dative relation clear: He has given some books *to the friend* who is visiting him. We have, however, a great fondness for the old simple dative, so that we are inclined to use it wherever we feel that the situation makes the thought clear: What will you give *me* for it? As we here feel that *what* is an accusative, we do not hesitate to employ the simple dative *me*, thinking that it must be clear that if one object is an accusative the other must be a dative.

B. MEANING AND USE OF ACCUSATIVE WITH VERBS. In an early stage of our language the accusative could be used after intransitive verbs of motion to indicate a concrete goal. This old usage survives in the case of *home*: He went *home*. The old idea of goal developed in different directions. It could indicate a concrete goal of any kind: He struck *his dog*, shot *a bird*. On the other hand, it could indicate a goal in an abstract, figurative sense: Go *lie down* (the goal, i.e. the end, purpose of the going). She wept *tears* (the final goal, outcome, result of the activity). He built *a boat* (the final goal, result of the activity).

1. *Noun and Pronoun as Object.* As the idea of the abstract goal became more and more abstract, the conception arose that the accusative is the proper case form of a noun or pronoun employed to complete the meaning of the verb. Especially common as complement of an intransitive verb is the *cognate* accusative, i.e. an accusative of a meaning cognate or similar to that of the verb, repeating and explaining more fully the idea expressed by the verb: to sleep *the sleep* of the righteous, fight *a good fight*, live *a sad and lonely life*, sing *a song*, play *cards*, etc.

In modern times the list of transitive verbs has been greatly increased by the addition of a large number of originally intransitives which took a prepositional object, as to *depend upon* a man, *laugh at* a person, *talk over* a matter. In course of time the preposition has become attached to the verb as an integral part of it, so that the object is no longer a prepositional object, but a direct object of the compound verb. This becomes apparent in the passive, where the object becomes subject and the preposition remains with the verb: He was *laughed at* by everybody.

The object, however, is often, not a noun or pronoun, but a full or an abridged clause: I hope *that I may accomplish it* or *to accomplish it*. Compare § 82.A, B.

2. *Metonymic Object.* The object is often metonymic, i.e. indicating not the real object but something which stands in close relation to it: "He wiped off *the dust*" (real object) and "He wiped off *the table*" (metonymic object).

3. *"It" and "So" as Object.* In a large number of expressions the accusative object is *it*, which originally was in many instances a concrete reference to a definite thing or a definite situation, but is now also often a convenient complement of the verb without definite reference, leaving it to the situation to make the thought clear: You will catch *it* (reproach, punishment). He footed *it*. I will have *it* out with him. Often as a cognate object after intransitives: I will fight *it* out on this line if it takes all summer.

Where the construction is more or less complicated, *it* is often used as an anticipatory object, pointing forward to a following full object clause, or an abridged infinitival or gerundial object clause: I soon brought *it* about that he thought better of it. I found *it* difficult to refuse him his request. I suppose you think *it* odd my having gone to church.

On the other hand, *it* often points backward to a preceding dependent clause or an independent proposition: If I get home by eight o'clock, I call *it* good luck. "He spoke quite sharply to me. I shall not forget *it* soon."

The adverb *so* is often used as a pronoun pointing backward, referring to the contents of a preceding proposition, especially after verbs of saying, thinking, hearing, fearing, hoping, etc.: "Did your brother receive the letter?" — "I think *so*."

C. PASSIVE FORM OF STATEMENT. In changing a sentence from the active to the passive, the accusative becomes nominative and the nominative is put into the accusative after *by*, in older English *of*: "*The boy* is beating *his dog*" (active), but in the passive "*The dog* is being beaten *by the boy*." *Ye* shall be hated *of all men* (Bible).

D. OBJECT OF AN ADJECTIVE. The object treated above is in all instances the object of a verb. *Worth* is the only adjective that now always governs the accusative: This book is worth *reading*. In "He sat opposite [*to*] *me*" *me* is a dative as indicated by the suppressed *to* given in brackets. Similarly in "He is like *his father*" the object is a dative as can be seen in poetry and older English: Sweet sleep, were death like *to thee* (Shelley). Likewise the seeming accusative after *near*, as in "near *me*" is in fact a dative, for we say, "nearer *to me*," "next *to me*."

Adjectives usually take a dative or prepositional object. Compare §§ 64.A (2nd par.); 66.

64. Dative Object. The dative, like the accusative, represents a person or thing as an object, but differs from the accusative in that it indicates that the activity results in some advantage or disadvantage to the person or thing affected. We may distinguish three groups:

A. DATIVE AS SOLE OBJECT. In the category of single object the dative is not so common as in older English, since we now feel that the accusative is the proper case form to complete the meaning of the verb when there is only one object. However, we not infrequently still employ the modern *to*-dative when the idea of advantage or disadvantage is prominent in our feeling: He yielded, bowed, submitted, surrendered, cringed, got down on his knees, *to me*. Much misfortune has come *to us* recently. The property has fallen *to his son*.

On the other hand, after adjectives and nouns the dative is still as common as it ever was: We no longer say "He helps *to me*," but we always say "He is helpful, or a great help, *to me*." Not "The frost injures *to plants*," but "The frost is injurious, or an injury, *to plants*."

B. DATIVE AS INDIRECT OBJECT. As indirect object in connection with the accusative as direct object, the dative is still as common as it ever was. Its form and position is discussed in § 63.A. Compare C below and § 67.A.

C. DATIVE AS SENTENCE OBJECT. The dative is also common where it is used in a little looser relation to the verb than in its function as indirect object: "She reached *her son* (indirect object) his coat," but "She made *her son* (sentence dative) a new coat." In the indirect object the idea of the direction of an activity toward a person or thing is prominent, while in the sentence dative all that is expressed by the verb and its modifiers is represented as resulting in the advantage or disadvantage of someone.

There are three groups:

1. *Dative of Interest.* This dative denotes the person to whose advantage or disadvantage the action results, sometimes in simple form, sometimes with *to* (in older English also *unto*) or *for:* He lent *me* some money. Inasmuch as you have done it *unto* (now *to* or *for*) one of the least of these my brethren, ye have done it *unto me* (Matthew, XXV.40). I shall do all I can *for you.* I'll break his head *for him.* He's setting a trap *for you.*

Other prepositions are coming into use here, originally with more concrete meaning, but now more and more developing into real dative signs: He stole a watch *from me.* While I was reading, he turned the light out *on me.*

This dative is now for the most part used only where there are two objects — an accusative and a dative. In older English it was also employed where it was not accompanied by an accusative: Haste *thee*, Nymph (Milton, *L'Allegro*). Occasionally still: She looked *him* tenderly in the eyes. In poetic and comic style: He sat *himself* (or as in older English *him*) down under a shady tree.

2. *Dative of Reference.* In this dative the idea of advantage or disadvantage is not so prominent as in the dative of interest. It denotes the person to whom the statement seems true, or with reference to whom it holds good: *To me* she is pretty. What is that *to me?* The dress is too long *for me.* He never made *me* such excuses. The hat cost *me* five dollars (adverbial accusative; § 68.B). It took *him* twenty years to

do it. I bet *you* five dollars (adv. acc.) that you can't do it (acc. clause).

3. *Ethical Dative.* In older English and sometimes still, a simple dative is employed to denote the person who has, or is expected to have, an emotional or sympathetic interest in the statement: Whip *me* such honest knaves (Shakespeare, *Othello*, I,i,49). We now often use the *for*-form here: There's a fine fellow *for you!*

65. Genitive Object. In older English, the simple genitive was much used with verbs and adjectives as an object to indicate the sphere in which the activity or quality played. The simple genitive is no longer employed here, but the modern *of*-genitive not infrequently occurs: A man ever mindful *of his duty* (i.e. in the sphere of his duty). She reminded him *of his duty.* Since people give *of their time* (i.e. in the sphere of their time, some time), will they not also give *of their money?*

As we no longer feel the genitive object as a distinct grammatical category but now construe it as a prepositional object, it is not discussed here. Compare § 66.

66. Prepositional Object. The prepositional object is the natural complement of many adjectives and intransitive verbs: He was angry *at me*, pleased *with me*, worried *about me.* He is shooting *at a mark.* He is striving *for the first place* in his class.

The prepositional object is also often used after transitive verbs in connection with an accusative object: He threw a stone *at me.*

There is a strong tendency for a preposition after an intransitive verb to enter into a compound with the verb, verb and preposition forming a transitive verb, as described in § 63.B.1 (2nd par.).

The object, however, is often, not a noun or pronoun, but a full or an abridged clause: I am thinking of *what I should answer* or *what to answer.* Compare § 83.A,B.

A. INFLECTIONAL PREPOSITIONS. For many centuries there has been a trend toward the prepositional object. Verbs and adjectives which once required a simple genitive or dative object now take a prepositional object. Although we today make a liberal use of prepositions, our tongue is not by any means entirely a prepositional language. The seemingly prepositional element *of*, so often used in the attributive genitive categories described in § 57.C.1–8, is in fact at present not a preposition, but a case sign, and this new *of*-genitive is just as much a case form as the older case forms. The preposition *of* in its new function lost its original concrete force and developed into an inflectional form to indicate definite case relations, once expressed by a genitive ending. Likewise, the *to* of the modern dative form is not a preposition, but the dative case sign. On account of the loss of the inflections in English it became necessary to find other means of expressing these relations. *Of* and *to* proved to be the best available forms to make a clear genitive and a clear dative. We often employ also the prepositions *for*, *on*, *upon*, *from* as dative signs, as described in § 64.C.1–3.

67. Double Object or Object with Its Objective Predicate. An accusative, dative, or prepositional object may not only each be used singly after a verb, but two objects may be employed, one an accusative to denote the direct object of the verb and one a dative, accusative, objective predicate, or prepositional object to express some additional limitation.

There are four groups:

A. DATIVE AND ACCUSATIVE. This construction is found after many verbs, especially those with the general meaning of giving, sending, handing, throwing, telling, teaching, saying, writing, selling, paying, etc.: My uncle gave *me a gold watch*. Suffering has taught *me patience*.

The form and the position of the dative in this construction are discussed in § 63. The use and the meaning of the dative here are treated in § 64.C.1–2.

The accusative object may be a full or an abridged clause: He told me *that I should do it*, or *to do it*.

1. *Passive Form of Statement*. There are here two forms, the first a favorite in the literary language, the second, in colloquial speech, but often also preferred in choice expression.

The accusative of the active becomes in the passive a nominative and the dative is retained, either in its old simple or its modern prepositional form, the latter regularly when the dative is stressed: Active: I gave *them ample warning*. Passive: "*Ample warning* was given *them*," but "*Ample warning* was given *to thém*, but not *to mé*."

Or the dative becomes nominative, and the accusative or the full or the abridged clause is retained: *They* were given *ample warning*. *I* was told *that I should do it*, or *to do it*. Only the simple dative, not the *to-* or *for*-dative, becomes nominative, so that we do not say: "*I* was suggested *this*," for in the active we say "He suggested *this to me*."

B. Accusative of the Person and Accusative of the Thing. This construction is now reduced to two verbs, *ask* and *lead*: I asked *him his name*, or *the price*, or *the reason*, or *the way*. Ask *the cabman the fare*. He led *them a lively dance*, or *chase*. She leads *him* a dog's *life*. Passive form: *He* was asked *his name, the price*, etc. *He* is led *a lively dance*, or *chase*.

C. Accusative of the Direct Object and an Objective Predicate. This construction differs from the double object in B above in that the two accusatives together form logically a sentence in which the first accusative performs the office of subject and the second accusative the office of predicate: The President made *him the head* of the navy (= *He* is *the head* of the navy through appointment by the President).

For the absence of the copula here between the accusative subject and the objective predicate see § 53.B.*a*. The copula is now sometimes used here, especially when the objective predicate is a pronoun: I deem him *an honest man*, or *to be an honest man*. "He thought Richard *to be me*," but "He thought us *a parcel* of fools."

1. *Form of Objective Predicate*. There are two groups:

a. The objective predicate is a noun or a pronoun in the accusative or the genitive of characteristic, or an adjective, participle, adverb, or prepositional phrase: The king dubbed his son *a knight*. He showed himself *of noble spirit* (§ 54.A.5).

139

I thought it *just*. I painted the door *green*, or *a green color* (§ 54.A.5). *What color* (§ 54.A.5) shall I paint the door? He kept us *waiting*. I consider the matter *settled*. I found him *there*. I found everything *in good condition*. The copula is now often expressed here: I have often found him *to be reliable*. The objective predicate participle is widely used in terse expression: They reported picketing *going* (or *as going*) *forward in an orderly manner*.

Instead of the simple predicate accusative we still often as in older English employ a phrase, placing *for* or *to* before the predicate noun: He took me *for my brother*. I got the machine *to running*. The *to* represents the new state as the result of a development. We often use *into* and other prepositions to express this idea: His presence will melt her resolution *into thin air*.

As, though not a new form, has in modern English been crowding the older forms back. It is now widely used here: I regard him *as very skilful*, *as a very skilful man*. They chose him *as their king*, or *to be their king*. I regard this *as of great importance*. It is always used after the new prepositional compounds (§ 20, last par.) and after verbal nouns: All of them look upon him *as a discreet man*. The selection of Smith (objective genitive; § 57.C.4) *as chairman* pleases everybody. Notice the difference of meaning between *as*, denoting complete identity, and the preposition *like*, denoting mere similarity: "Large minds treat little things *as* little things and big things *as* big things," but "He treats his wife *like* a child."

(i) Passive Form. In the passive, the first accusative becomes nominative and the predicate word or phrase is retained as in the active with the exception that the predicate accusative becomes nominative: He was elected *president*. It was at first thought *to be he*. I have often been taken *for my brother*. Picketing was reported *going* (or *as going*) *forward in an orderly manner*.

b. An Infinitive as Objective Predicate. After the verbs *let, bid, make, have, see, behold, notice, observe, perceive, feel, watch, find, hear, know*, the objective predicate may be an infinitive, usually the simple form, but the *to*-infinitive is also used after most of them: Bid him *come* in. I felt something *touch* my head. You will never find him *neglect*, or *to neglect*, his work. The modal idea requires *to:* I find much *to do* (§ 54.D.2).

The present infinitive here states a fact, the present participle describes: I saw him *do* it (a fact). I saw him *working* in the field (descriptive).

To give the infinitive passive force we give it passive form after *let:* He wouldn't let her wound *be dressed*. After other verbs, the past participle, with the force of an elliptical present passive infinitive with the infinitive *be* suppressed, is used here instead of the regular full present passive infinitive: He will have a new coat *made*. I saw the net *hauled in* (fact), or *being hauled in* (descriptive). Instead of the present passive infinitive or participle the active form is sometimes used, as in older English, which used the active form for both the active and the passive: I have never heard *tell* (now usually *it said*) that we were put here to get pleasure out of life (Conan Doyle). Annie seemed to hear her own death-scaffold *raising* (Tennyson, *Enoch Arden*, 175).

(i) Passive Form. In the passive statement, the direct object becomes nominative and the infinitive or participle is retained, the infinitive now usually with the *to*-form: (fact) "I saw him *do* it" (active), but "He was seen *to do* it" (passive); (descriptive) "I saw him *doing* it" (active), "He was seen *doing* it" (passive). The participle itself may be passive: In the picture the archbishops are shown *being met by Col. Bosch* (*New York Sun*, 1946).

D. ACCUSATIVE AND PREPOSITIONAL PHRASE. This is a very common type: He laid *the book upon the table*. She laid *the child on the bed*.

1. *Passive Form*. The accusative becomes nominative and the prepositional phrase is retained: The child was laid on the bed.

E. DATIVE AND PREPOSITIONAL PHRASE. This type is less common than the one in D: He telegraphed *me* (or *to me*) *for help*. He wrote *me about his experiences in the war*.

1. *Passive Form*. *I* was telegraphed to *for help*.

Adverbial Modifiers

As illustrated in § 17, an adverb may modify a verb, adjective, or another adverb. An adverb, however, modifies not only thus a single word, but often also a prepositional phrase, a subordinate clause, or an independent statement as a whole: He has traveled *entirely* around the world (prepositional phrase). He is *almost* across the river. He lives *a mile* (adverbial accusative; see § 68.B) beyond our house. An example of an adverb modifying a subordinate clause is given in § 70.B.1. Examples of adverbial elements modifying independent statements are given in § 70 (1st par.).

The different classes of adverbs are described in § 18.

68. Form of the Positive. The adverbial element itself may have the form of a word, prepositional phrase, or subordinate clause: He did it *easily*. He did it *with ease*. He did it *as soon as he could*. We treat here only the form of simple adverbs. For the adverbial prepositional phrase see §§ 19; 86.A.1, C.1, E.2.a; 87.A.1.c.i; 88.C; 89.B; 90.B; 91.B. The adverbial clause is presented on pp. 176–199.

There are different groups of simple adverbs:

A. ADVERBS WITHOUT DISTINCTIVE FORM. Adverbs have in part no distinctive form, as in *here, there, then, where, when, why, long, slow, fast, quick*, etc.; in part they have the distinctive suffix *-ly*, as in *rapidly, diligently*, etc., also often in case of some of the words in the first group, which now have a more common form in *-ly* alongside of their simple form, as in *slowly, quickly*, etc. Sometimes the two forms are differentiated in meaning: "He aimed *higher*," but "We ought to value our privileges *more highly*." "He sits up *late*," but "He died *lately*." "He works *hard*," but "I could *hardly* hear him." "He lives *near* us, *nearer* to us," but "It is *nearly* done." "He is *real* (colloquial for *very*) good," but "He is *really* (sentence adverb; see § 70) good."

In Old English, many adverbs had the suffix *-e*, which distinguished them from the corresponding adjectives. In the fifteenth century, after this ending had disappeared, many adjectives and adverbs had the same form. For a long while

142

there has been a tendency to distinguish the adverb from the adjective by giving it the suffix *-ly*. The old simple form, though often replaced by the new form in *-ly*, often remains firm before an adjective or participle: "*wide*-open," but "He advertises *widely*"; "*tight*-fitting," but "He clasped his hands *tightly* together." Here before adjective or participle we feel the adverb as the modifying component of a compound and leave it in its simple form, while after the verb we feel it as an ordinary adverb and add *-ly*. Under the influence of these compounds a real adverb often in colloquial speech keeps its simple form before an adjective: *pretty* cold, *mighty* slow, *precious* sorry. On the other hand, we often feel such adverbs with their full adverbial force and add *-ly*: "*new*-laid eggs," but "a *newly* opened street."

We should distinguish between "a *góod*-nàtured boy," where the group *gòod náture* has been converted into a derivative adjective by means of the suffix *-ed*, and "a *wéll*-behàved boy," where *behaved* is an adjective participle and *well* a modifying adverb. In the first construction the stress shifts to the second component in the predicate: "He is gòod-nátured," but "He is *wéll-behàved*."

B. SURVIVALS OF OLD ENGLISH FORMS. In Old English, nouns and pronouns in the genitive, accusative, and instrumental were often used adverbially.

The old genitive survives in a few words and has spread analogically to other forms, so that today it is found in many words, especially in loose colloquial and popular speech, which at this point is gradually influencing the literary language: *nowadays, unawares, needs* (= of necessity), *once* (i.e. *ones,* from *one*), *twice* (formerly *twyes*), *afterward* or *afterwards, backward* or *backwards, forward* or *forwards, sideways, always,* etc.; in popular speech: *anywheres, somewheres, nowheres,* etc. instead of literary *anywhere, somewhere, nowhere,* etc. Where the old *s*-genitive is preserved we now often feel it as an accusative plural: He could see the plow at work before he got out of bed *mornings.*

The modern *of*-genitive is still used in a few expressions: We like to sit on the porch *of rainy afternoons,* or now also *on rainy*

143

afternoons. Of late years we see very little of each other. He would often drop in *of an evening*.

The old adverbial accusative is very common. Accusative of extent, amount, degree, number: The lake is *three miles* long. The snow is *ankle* deep. The waves are *mountain* high. The book is *six inches* wide. It is *a long way* (sometimes genitive, *ways*) off. He went *the full length*. This hat cost *five dollars*. There is no doubt *whatever*. "He is *all* (§ 34.C) the better for it," or "He is *none* (§ 34.C) the worse for it." "Is he *any* (§ 34.C) better this morning?" — "He is *much* (§ 34.C), or *some* (colloquial for the literary adverb *somewhat*) better." "Isn't it *any* later than that?", or in American colloquial speech also "Is that *all* the later it is?" *Nothing* daunted, he began again. I have met him *many times*. Accusative of time: I paid him *the following morning*. In colloquial speech, there is a strong tendency to employ the adverbial accusative in the category of place instead of older adverbs: *some place* instead of *somewhere* (§ 9.E, 2nd par.).

The, the old instrumental case of the demonstrative *that*, is still much used as an adverb although we no longer feel its original force: This stone gets *the* harder *the* longer it is exposed to the weather. He was made *the* bolder by his failures.

On the other hand, adverbs are often used as nouns: till *now*, for *ever*, from *here*, since *then*. Compare § 19 (next to last par.).

C. "That" and "This" Used as Adverbs. In our colloquial speech the adjectives *that* and *this* on account of their greater accuracy of expression are widely used instead of the adverb *so*: I am not *that* foolish. I never expect to come *this* far again. I'm *that* hungry, I could eat a dog (Hall Caine, *The Woman Thou Gavest Me*).

D. Adverbs Often Occur as the First Component of Compounds: *up*root, *over*turn, *under*done, *out*lying, *mis*judge, *re*turn, *co*öperate; *tight*-fitting, *long*-suffering; etc. The form of the adverb here has been treated in A above. The adverb *not* is here usually replaced by *un-*: *un*able, *un*fit, *un*opened, etc. In many foreign words the negative adverb here is *in-* (or *im-*) or *dis-*: *in*convenient, *im*possible, *dis*obey. Some of these adverbs, *mis, un, re, co,* etc., which are not now used outside of compounds, are called prefixes. Compare § 16.A.

69. Comparison of Adverbs.

A. RELATIVE COMPARISON. Adverbs are compared much as adjectives, as described in § 104. There are two forms:

1. *Normal Form.* A few monosyllabic adverbs add *-er* in the comparative and *-est* in the superlative: *fast, faster, fastest.* He climbed *higher.* He lives *nearer* us. I can do that *better.* Also the dissyllabic adverb *early* is compared by means of endings: *early, earlier, earliest.* But, in general, terminational comparison is much less common with adverbs than with adjectives, although common in older English.

Most adverbs are compared by means of *more, most, less, least; rapidly, more rapidly, most rapidly; rapidly, less rapidly, least rapidly.*

A few irregularities occur, corresponding closely to those found in adjectives:

well	better	best
ill, badly	worse	worst
much	more	most
little	less	least
near, nigh (§ 104.G)	nearer, nigher	nearest, next, nighest
far	farther, further	farthest, furthest
late	later	latest, last
	rather (compar. of obsolete rathe = *soon*)	

2. *Newer Form.* Instead of the normal adverbial form we now sometimes employ the adverbial accusative (§ 68.B) of the noun (§ 108) made from the adjective comparative or superlative preceded by the definite article: He runs *fast, the faster, the fastest.* Where we compare by means of *more* and *most* the adverbial suffix *-ly* is added to the adjective comparative or superlative preceded by the definite article: It was difficult to say which of the two men seemed to regard her *the more tenderly* (which of the men seemed to regard her *the most tenderly*).

In the relation of sentence adverb (§ 70) the preposition *at* is often placed before the corresponding adjective noun preceded by the definite article: I can't hear from John *at the earliest* before Tuesday.

When it is not the actions of different persons that are compared, but the actions of one and the same person at different times and under different circumstances, we employ the accusative of the adjective noun preceded by a possessive adjective: Smith smiled *his pleasantest*. Two women shrieked *their loudest*. In the relation of sentence adverb the preposition *at* is often placed before this same form: Nature *at her most unadorned* never takes that air of nakedness which a great open, unabashed window throws upon the landscape.

B. Absolute Superlative. This superlative is formed by adding *-ly* to the absolute superlative (§ 104.D.1) of the adjective: "Mary's mother is a *most béautiful woman*" and "Mary's mother sings *most béautifully*."

Instead of this form we often use a prepositional phrase containing a simple superlative of an adjective in attributive or noun form: The letter was written *in the kindest spirit*. That does not concern me *in the least*.

Instead of a superlative here we more commonly use a positive modified by *very, exceedingly*, etc.: She sings *very beautifully*.

a) To express an absolutely high degree of activity in connection with a verb, we place *very* before an adverb of degree, such as *much, greatly*, etc.: He is suffering *very much*. To express an absolutely high degree of a quality we place *very* before the positive of the adjective: *very rich, very pleasing, a very distressed look*. But instead of saying "I was *very greatly distressed, very much pleased*," many incorrectly say "I was *very distressed, very pleased*," feeling *distressed* and *pleased* as adjectives rather than as verbal forms, which they are.

70. Sentence Adverbs. An adverbial element, i.e. a simple adverb, adverbial phrase, or complete sentence, often modifies the statement as a whole rather than the verb or predicate complement alone: He *apparently* thinks so. I *frankly* confess it. I *undoubtedly* believe it. He is *without doubt* an able man. *I think* (or *in my judgment*) he is trustworthy. Compare § 53.C.4.

A. Negatives "Not" and "No." One of the most common sentence adverbs is the negative *not:* It is *not* my fault. There is an older negative, *no,* which we still regularly use in an answer with the force of a complete negative sentence and which consequently is not an adverb: "Are you going tomorrow?" — "*No.*" This form is often used as a regular adverb, instead of *not,* before a comparative and sometimes elsewhere: He is *no* more to be trusted than you are. This *no* should be distinguished from the limiting adjective *no: no* money, *no* time.

1. *Double Negation.* In older literary English, as in current popular speech, two or three negatives were felt as stronger than a single negative on the same principle that we drive in two or three nails instead of one, feeling that they hold better than one: I can'*t* see *no* wit in her (Lamb in a letter to Coleridge in 1797). Under Latin influence this older usage has disappeared in literary English.

B. Position and Stress of Sentence Adverbs. An adverbial element is often more heavily stressed than a verb and then usually follows it: He *àcted prómptly.* In many cases, however, the adverbial element does not modify the verb directly but the sentence as a whole or the verbal phrase (i.e. verb with its modifiers). In this case, the adverbial element sometimes precedes and sometimes follows the sentence: "*Of course,* John came late," or "John came late, *of course.*" Usually, however, the sentence adverb precedes the verb and has a weaker stress, for in English when we in any way call attention to the thought as a whole, the verb or the verbal phrase is strongly stressed, since it is felt as the basal element of the sentence: He *evidently thóught* so. He not only belíeves in such books, but he *even* réads them to his children. We *at last, fortunately, cáme to a túrn* in the road and could see beyond.

When we desire to convey unusual emphasis, we stress both sentence adverb and verb: I did *nót dó* it. I *útterly forgót* the matter.

The tendency for the sentence adverb to stand before the verb explains the use of *do* in the negative form of statement:

He does *not know*. In older English, *not* followed the verb, the part with the personal ending: He knows *not*. By employing *do* before the real verb we can attach *not* to *do* and thus bring *not* before the real verb in accordance with our modern feeling that the sentence adverb should stand immediately before the verb: He does *not know*.

Similarly, we often put the sentence adverb between *to* and the infinitive, i.e. we split the infinitive, in order that the sentence adverb may stand immediately before the infinitive, just as it elsewhere stands immediately before the verb: "She desired to *útterly forgét* her past" (Henry James), just as we say "She desired that she might *útterly forgét* her past." Thus the split infinitive is in full accord with the spirit of modern English and is now widely used by our best writers. Compare § 123.C.

1. *Distinguishing Adverbs*. *Not, also, even, only, at least*, etc. have the peculiarity that as sentence adverbs they can direct attention not only to the verb and thus to the sentence as a whole, but also to any person or thing that becomes prominent in the situation as a whole, standing either immediately before or after the noun or pronoun, except *not*, which must precede: He hit mé, *not* hím. John passed *only* in Látin (or in Látin *only*). John has passed *only* ónce in Latin. *Only* Jóhn (or Jóhn *only*) passed in Latin. John *only* (= barely) pássed in Latin. They stand before a subordinate clause: I did it *only* (or *simply*) *because I felt it to be my duty*.

2. *Contractions of "Not."* The weak stress of *not* often leads in colloquial speech to its contraction and fusion with the preceding auxiliary: I, we, you, he, they, *can't* and after the analogy of this simplicity: I, we, you, he, they, *don't*. But the literary language rejects this simplicity in the case of *don't* and prescribes as contractions: I, we, you, they *don't*, but he *doesn't*. In popular speech *ain't*, like *don't*, is used in the different persons and numbers: I, we, you, he, they *ain't; ain't* I, we, you, he, they? The literary language requires here: I'*m* not, we, you, they *aren't*, he *isn't; am* I *not?* (or in England *aren't* I in collo-quial speech), *aren't* we, you, they? *isn't* he? In the literary language there is still in choice expression a tendency to avoid contractions and employ the old uncontracted forms. All

these contractions are of modern origin. They first began to appear about 1660 and soon came into wide use.

INDEPENDENT ELEMENTS OF A SENTENCE

Independent elements are words, phrases, or clauses, which are not related grammatically to other parts of the sentence, or stand all alone without having any grammatical relation to another word expressed or understood. As we shall see below, however, these elements all play a useful part in the expression of our thought and feeling.

71. Interjections. The simplest interjections, such as *Oh!* (usually *O* when not followed by a punctuation mark), *Ouch!*, *Pooh!*, belong to the oldest form of spoken language and represent the most primitive type of sentence. Although they are often used alone as independent sentences, they are often embodied in modern sentences without any grammatical relations to the other words, but expressing here, as elsewhere, emotion of various kinds: *O* for a breathing-space! *Oh*, what a fool I've been! *Oh*, when will they come? Why, *oh*, why did I grumble at these trifles? Compare § 23.

72. Direct Address. The name of a person who is addressed is often inserted in a sentence without grammatical relations to the other words, but serving the useful purpose of attracting the attention of the person addressed: *John*, I have brought something home for you. We now put such words into the nominative, the nominative of address.

73. Absolute Nominative. There are two classes of nominatives which go under this name:

A. ABSOLUTE NOMINATIVE IN ADVERBIAL CLAUSES: Off we started, *he remaining behind* (= *while he remained behind*). *This disposed* (or *having been disposed*) *of* (= *after this had been disposed of*), I turned to something else. *Conditions being favorable* (= *if conditions are favorable*), we shall surely succeed. *He being absent* (= *since he was absent*), nothing could be done. The nominative here forms with the words with which it is connected a clause, in which it serves as logical subject. There is no finite

149

verb in the clause, but the nominative is in reality always the subject, the rest of the clause predicate, so that the nominative is actually not an absolute nominative. The predicate may be a noun, adjective, participle, adverb, or prepositional phrase. Such clauses always have the force of a full adverbial clause, as can be seen by the above examples.

When the predicate is a participle, as in the first and second examples, the clause is always of the old appositional type described in § 53.B.*a*, the predicate participle lying alongside of its subject without a connecting word, i.e. without a copula.

When the predicate is an adjective, noun, adverb, or prepositional phrase, it is now usually linked to the subject by a copula, as in the last two of the above examples. In older English the copula was lacking here, the subject and the predicate lying side by side without any connecting word: *Thou away*, the very birds are mute (Shakespeare). This is the old appositional type of clause described in § 53.B.*a*. This older usage is here still common where the clause has the force of an adverbial clause of manner proper (§ 86.A) or attendant circumstance (§ 86.C): He put on his socks *wrong side out* (manner proper). He lay on his back, *his knees in the air*, *his hands behind his head* (attendant circumstance). They met *face to face*. Tom, *his dog at his heels*, entered.

The predicate here follows the subject, but in older English it could precede. This older usage survives in poetry:

> *All loose her negligent attire,*
> *All loose her golden hair,*
> Hung Margaret o'er her slaughtered sire.
>
> — Scott, *Last Minstrel*, I. 10.

This usage survives elsewhere, but we no longer understand it: *Granted this is true*, you are still in the wrong. Here the sentence *this is true* is the subject of the clause and *granted* (a past participle) the predicate. As we do not now feel the old construction, we construe *granted* as a subordinating conjunction introducing a concessive clause.

In Old English the dative was the usual case of the subject in the absolute construction. It was used in imitation of the Latin ablative absolute. Later, when the dative lost its distinctive form the case was quite generally construed as the nominative. In the literary language under foreign influence the accusative case was here and there used as a nearer approach to the original construction than the nominative: *Him* destroyed for whom all this was made, all this will soon follow (Milton, *Paradise Lost*, IX, 130). In colloquial and popular speech the accusative is still often found here, but it is of different origin, being the accusative used instead of a nominative, as found so often in colloquial and popular speech in constructions without a finite verb: You wouldn't expect anything else, would you, *me* (instead of the choicer *I*) being here like this, so suddenly, and talking face to face with you? (Arnold Bennett, *Sacred and Profane Love*, Act I).

1. *Absolute Nominative Replaced by Prepositional Phrase.* In this old absolute construction in the categories of manner proper, attendant circumstance, cause, and condition, the nominative is often replaced by a prepositional phrase, the preposition serving both as a preposition and as a conjunction linking the clause to the principal proposition: He put on his socks *with the wrong side out* (manner proper). He lay on his back *with his knees in the air and his hands behind his head* (attendant circumstance). She is lonesome *with her husband so much away* (cause). *With conditions in every way favorable*, he might succeed (condition). The clause here is usually of the old appositional type, the predicate lying alongside of its subject without a connecting word; but sometimes a copula is employed: She is lonesome with her husband *being* so much away.

B. Absolute Nominative in Subject Clauses: *Three such rascals hanged in one day* is good work for society. Here the subject of the clause is *three such rascals*, the predicate *hanged in one day*, a clause without a copula, the old appositional type of clause described in § 53.B.*a.* The whole clause is the subject of the sentence, a subject clause. Compare § 77.B.

In older English the predicate here was often an infinitive: I *to bear* this is some burden (Shakespeare, *Timon*, IV, iii, 266). Compare § 77.B.

74. Absolute Participles. In "*Taking* (= *if one should take*) *all things into consideration*, his lot is a happy one" *taking* is a dangling participle, having no word that can serve as its subject. In such sentences we feel no deficiency, for the reference is general and indefinite, so that we expect no definite mention of a subject. This is the only place where the dangling participle is common in the literary language (§ 89.B).

In a few expressions the dangling participle has become established also elsewhere: *Including* today, they have been here a week. *Beginning* with the July number, it is intended to widen the scope of this Quarterly. This service is to be performed *standing*. In general, the dangling participle is slovenly English and can easily become ridiculous: *Being* not yet fully grown, his trousers were too long.

II. CLASSES OF SENTENCES

SENTENCES are divided according to their structure into three classes — simple, compound, and complex. A simple sentence contains but one independent proposition. A compound sentence contains two or more independent propositions. A complex sentence contains one independent proposition and one or more subordinate clauses.

THE COMPOUND SENTENCE

75. Structure and Connectives. The compound sentence consists of different independent propositions or members. These members may be two or more simple sentences, or one member may be a simple sentence and the others complex sentences, or there may be any combination of simple and complex sentences.

These members are usually connected or arranged in the following ways:

A. Coördinating Conjunctions. The members are connected by coördinating conjunctions. The commonest are *and*, *or*, *but*, *for*: John is in the garden working *and* Mary is sitting at the window reading. The members of a compound sentence, however, are not always thus complete, each with subject and finite verb, for a natural feeling for the economy of time and effort prompts us, wherever it is possible, to contract by employing a common verb for all members, so that the conjunctions connect only parts of like rank: not "John is writing and Mary is writing," but "John and Mary are writing."

Sentences containing these conjunctions, however, are often not an abridgment of two or more sentences, but a simple sentence with elements of like rank connected by a conjunction: The king *and* queen are an amiable pair.

Coördinating conjunctions also link together subordinate clauses of like rank: The judge said that the case was a difficult one *and* that he would reconsider his decision.

Besides the pure connectives mentioned above there are many adverbs which not only perform the function of an adverb but also the function of a conjunction. Coördinating conjunctions and conjunctive adverbs may be divided into the following classes:

1. *Copulative*, connecting two members and their meaning, the second member indicating an addition of equal importance, or, on the other hand, an advance in time or space, or an intensification, often coming in pairs, then called correlatives: *and; both — and; as well as; not — nor; not — not* (or *nor*); in elliptical sentences where the subject or finite verb is expressed in only one member and understood elsewhere, *no* (or *not* or *never*) *— or* (or often *nor* when it is desired to call especial attention to what follows and thus emphasize); *neither — nor; neither — nor — nor* (with three or more members instead of two); *nor — nor* (in poetry or older English, now replaced by *neither — nor*); *not only — but* (or *but also* or *but . . . too*); *too; moreover; besides; likewise; further, furthermore; even; let alone; in the first place; first; secondly*, etc.; *finally; then; first — then; now — now; sometimes — sometimes; partly — partly; what with — and what with*, literally *somewhat* (i.e. *in part*) *on account of and somewhat* (= *in part*) *on account of*, often with elliptical form *what with — and;* etc.

EXAMPLES:

He can. *both* sing *and* dance.
I can get *no* rest by night *or* by day.

153

He is *not* brilliant *or* attractive.

I want *no* promises, *nor* notes (more emphatic than *or* notes); I want money.

The house is uninhabitable in summer, *let alone* in winter.

What with his drinking and *what with* his jealousy, or *what with* his drinking *and* his jealousy, he wore himself out.

2. *Disjunctive*, connecting two members but disconnecting their meaning, the meaning in the second member excluding that in the first: *either — or; either — or — or* (with three or more members instead of two); *or — or* (in poetry or older English): *Either* he *or* I must go.

3. *Adversative*, connecting two members but contrasting their meaning: *but* (§ 89.C.4.e), *but then, only* (= *but, but then, it must however be added that;* § 89.C.4.e), *still, yet, and yet, however, on the other hand, on the contrary, rather, notwithstanding, nevertheless, none the less, all the same, though, after all, for all that, at the same time, in the meantime,* etc.

EXAMPLES:

This is not winter, *but* it is almost as cold. He is small *but* strong.

He makes good resolutions, *only* he never keeps them.

"The sheep which we saw behind the house were small and lean; in the next field *though* (coördinating) there were some fine cows" — but *though* is a subordinating conjunction in "*Though* it never put a cent of money into my pocket, I believe it did me good."

4. *Causal*, adding an independent proposition explaining the preceding statement, represented only by the single conjunction *for:* The brook was very high, *for* a great deal of rain had fallen overnight.

5. *Illative*, introducing an inference, conclusion, consequence, result: *for that reason, on that account, consequently, therefore, then, hence, so, thus,* etc.: There was no one there, *so* I went away. I am here, you see, young and sound and hearty; *then* don't let us despair.

6. *Explanatory*, connecting words, phrases, or sentences and introducing an explanation or a particularization: *namely, to wit, viz.* (short for Latin *videlicet*, the *z* indicating a contraction,

as in *oz.* for *ounce*), *that is* (when it precedes, often written *i.e.*, for Latin *id. est*), *that is to say, or, such as* (or in less formal speech *like*), *as, for example* (often written *e.g.*, which is for Latin *exempli gratia*), *for instance*, etc.

EXAMPLES:

There were only two girls there, *namely* Mary and Ann.

He has an enemy, *to wit* his own brother.

There are four elementary qualities of taste sensation, *i.e.* sour, salt, sweet, and bitter.

A commander, *like* (or in more formal language *such as*) Mansfield, who could not pay his soldiers, must, of necessity, plunder wherever he was. — Gardiner, *Thirty Years' War.*

Starch is found in cereals, potatoes, and in lesser amounts also in many kinds of fruits and vegetables, *as* (or *such as*) bananas, peas, beans, nuts.

We designate odors by the objects from which they come, *e.g.* violet, orange, leather, etc.

B. PRONOUNS AND ADVERBS AS CONJUNCTIONS. The connection between the members may be made by placing at the beginning of the sentence a stressed personal pronoun, possessive adjective, or demonstrative pronoun or adverb referring back to the preceding proposition: "In this crisis I have often thought of the old home, of Father, of Mother. *That* was a good place to start out in life from. *Their* life has always been an inspiration to me. *There* at least in memory I shall still often tarry. *Them* I shall still often consult."

C. PARATAXIS. Sometimes there is no formal link binding the sentences together since the logical connection forms a sufficient tie. Upon close investigation, however, it will become clear that such apparently independent propositions are not absolutely independent. One of the propositions often stands in some grammatical relation to the other, such as that of subject or object, or in an adverbial relation, such as that of cause, purpose, result, concession, condition: The best way is *you ask the man himself* (subject clause). "*We should do something to stop this*" (object clause), he remarked. Hurry up; *it is getting late* (causal clause).

Similarly, propositions connected by coördinating conjunctions are often not absolutely independent: Come *and see us* = *to see us* (an abridged infinitive clause of purpose). It is *nice and warm* = *nicely warm*.

There were originally no conjunctions. *Parataxis* reigned supreme, i.e. sentences simply lay side by side, a still common construction, as illustrated above. Later, coördination arose, a still common construction as illustrated above. Later, *hypotaxis*, i.e. formal subordination, a clause with a formal sign of subordination, gradually developed and is still ever developing, introducing finer shades of expression. Hypotaxis will be treated below in considerable detail.

Although hypotaxis is more precise and absolutely necessary in scientific language and practical intercourse, parataxis is more direct and lively and hence still often preferred in lively style: I came, I saw, I conquered.   On the other hand, coördination is in place where different objects are presented for the sake of making the picture more impressive, or different activities are described separately in their natural sequence in order to depict the march of events in a stately or impressive way: We have ships, *and* men, *and* money, *and* stores (Webster). *And* the rain descended, *and* the floods came, *and* the winds blew, *and* beat upon that house; *and* it fell; *and* great was the fall of it (Matthew, VII. 27).

THE COMPLEX SENTENCE: SUBORDINATE CLAUSES

76. Classification by Form and Function. If a sentence is made up of a principal and a subordinate statement, each statement is called a clause — the principal and the subordinate clause. Subordinate clauses are of different fullness of form and are of different kinds, performing different functions, thus forming different classes:

A. FULL AND ABRIDGED CLAUSE. Every subordinate clause usually has a full form with a finite (p. 52) verb and a subject in the nominative: It is stupid of you *that you should say it*.

Alongside of the full form with a finite verb are often two abridged forms, one with a *to*-infinitive, another with a gerund, both forms now often, as in the following example, more natural and common than the full form with the finite verb: It is stupid of you *to say it*, or *saying it*. The subject of the infinitive or gerund is usually not expressed but implied in some word in the principal proposition, as here in the pronoun *you*.

When the subject of the infinitive or gerund is general or indefinite, it is never expressed, but merely implied in the situation: It is wholesome *to be cheerful*, or *being cheerful*.

When there is in the principal clause no word that can serve as the subject of the infinitive or the gerund, and it thus becomes necessary for the infinitive or the gerund to have a subject of its own, the two constructions differ in the form of their subject: The infinitive requires *for* before its subject and the gerund requires as subject a genitive of a noun or pronoun, or a possessive adjective, which was originally a genitive of a personal pronoun: It is of no use *for John*, or *for you*, *to say anything*, or *John's*, or *your*, *saying anything*. As explained in § 124.B, it is often necessary for the gerund to have an accusative subject: There is no use in *John's brother* (acc. subject of gerund) *saying anything*.

The *for* before the subject of the infinitive indicates an old sentence dative of reference (§ 64.C.2), out of which the present form has developed: It is necessary *for me* (originally a dative of reference, now felt as the subject of the infinitive) *to go*, i.e. It is necessary *that I go*. Compare § 123.B.

The full clause can often be abridged to a predicate appositive (§ 53.C) clause: She makes the first advances, *dear kind soul as* (relative pronoun = *that*) *she is* (= *since she is a dear kind soul*). *Tired and discouraged* (= *since I was tired and discouraged*), I went to bed. *Going down town* (= *while I was going down town*), I met an old friend. The subject of the predicate appositive is not expressed but merely implied in some word in the principal proposition, usually the subject.

Sometimes the conjunction employed in the full subordinate clause is also used in the abridged clause to indicate more clearly the different adverbial relations, such as time, cause, condition, etc. — an improvement introduced in the sixteenth century: John, don't speak *until* spoken to. The sophists were hated by some *because* powerful, by others *because* shallow (Lewes). He will do it for you, *if* properly approached.

The inquiry *so far as* showing that I have favored my own interests, has failed. For Lovers' hours are long, *though* seeming short (Shakespeare, *Venus and Adonis*, 842). *Where* having nothing, nothing can he lose (id., *Henry VI*, Third Part, III, iii, 152). Such clauses are the result of the blending of the full and the abridged clause. Compare § 122.B (last par.).

There are two other types of abridged clauses, which are described in § 73.A–B.

All these abridged clauses are of the old appositional type of clause described in § 53.B.*a*, the predicate infinitive, gerund, participle, adjective, adverb, or prepositional phrase simply lying alongside of its subject.

1. *An abridged clause differs from an elliptical clause* in this, that the former never has a finite verb, expressed or understood, while in the latter there is a finite verb understood: "There was nothing left for me to do *but to* withdraw" (abridged clause), but "There was no one there *but* [*that*] *I*" [*was there*] (elliptical clause).

B. CLASSIFICATION BY FUNCTION. A clause is a unit, and, like a single word, it performs a definite function in the sentence. Upon the basis of function clauses may be divided into subject, predicate, adjective, object, adverbial clauses. These clauses may be reduced to three if we divide them according to the parts of speech which they represent: (1) substantive clauses, which represent a noun, including subject, predicate, object clauses, and such adjective clauses as represent a noun in the attributive relation of appositive, prepositional phrase, or genitive, as described in § 79.A–C; (2) adjective clauses; (3) adverbial clauses.

Subject and Predicate Clauses

77. Subject Clause.

A. CONJUNCTIONS: *that;* after verbs of saying, telling, relating sometimes *how* instead of *that; lest* after nouns expressing fear, sometimes still as in older English used instead of *that; but, but that,* or in colloquial speech *but what* instead of the more common *that* after *not improbable, not impossible, cannot be doubted.*

there is no question; indefinite relative pronouns (§ 9.D.2), adjectives (§ 13.E), and adverbs (§ 18.A.3), *who, what* (pronoun and adjective), *whoever, whatever, which, where, whither* (in a choice literary style, usually replaced in plain prose by *where*), *when, why, how; whether* or *if; whether — or whether; whether — or,* used when the second member has its subject, or its verb, or both, suppressed; in direct and indirect (§ 9.F) questions introduced by interrogative pronouns, adjectives, and adverbs, *who, what, which, where, when, whither, whether,* etc., developments out of the indefinite pronouns, adjectives, adverbs, and still closely related in meaning to them; in indirect exclamations introduced by *what a, how.*

A conjunction or conjunctive pronoun, adjective, or adverb usually introduces the clause to show the oneness of the words in the clause, but the conjunction is sometimes omitted when the connection makes the thought clear: It (§ 51.C) was natural ⌈*that*⌉ *they should like each other.*

EXAMPLES:

"It (§ 51.C) is best *that he go,* or more commonly *that he should go,*" but originally "The best (predicate) is *that: he should go,*" the subject *that* pointing to the following explanatory clause.

My only terror was *lest my father should follow me.*

It could not be doubted *that* (or now less commonly *but, but that,* or *but what*) *his life would be aimed at.*

On the merits of the case, there (§ 51.C) is no question (or doubt) *but that* (or simple *that*) *he is wholly right.*

It is ten to one, or It is odds, *but,* or now more commonly *that he will recover,* or The odds are *that he will recover.*

It (§ 51.C) is not known *who* (indefinite relative pronoun) *did it.*

Handsome is *that* (or *as,* both rel. pronouns = *who*) *handsome does* (proverb).

It has often been asked *who* (interrogative pronoun) *did it* (indirect question; § 9.F).

It is not known *what* (indef. rel. adj.), or *which* (indef. rel. adj.), *way was taken.*

The most important question now is *when* (indef. rel. adv.) *he will return,* or more graphically in the form of a rhetorical question, *when will he return?*

It has often been asked *when* (interrog.) *he intends to return* (indirect question).

It has often been asked *whether* (interrog. adv.) *he will come himself, or whether he will send a substitute* (indirect question).

It is not yet known *whether* (or *if;* indef. rel. adv.) *he has arrived.*

It has just been asked *whether* (or *if;* interrog. adv.) *he has arrived* (indirect question).

It is not yet known *whether* (indef. rel. adv.) *he did it or not.*

The test of public officials and public policies alike must be *whether they will serve,* or *whether they will exploit, the common need,* or more graphically in the form of the rhetorical question, *will they serve* or *will they exploit, the common need?*

In this sore trial it has become evident *what a fine fellow he is.*

a) Emphasis and Attraction. When it is desired to make any word or phrase in the sentence emphatic, we may place it at the beginning after *it* (or *that*) *is,* construing it as a predicate and placing the rest of the sentence after it in the form of a subject clause, *it* serving as anticipatory (§ 51.C) subject and the subject clause as the real subject: "It wasn't *this mórning,* it was *yésterday,* that I saw him," instead of "I didn't see him *this mórning,* I saw him *yésterday.*" "It was *toward thése quéstions* that my thought turned," instead of "My thought turned toward *thése quéstions.*"

Similarly, we can make the subject emphatic by making it predicate: Instead of "*I* am not wrong," "*Yóu* are not wrong," we often say "It is not *Í* that *am* wrong," "It is not *yóu* that *are* wrong." Notice that in such sentences the subject clause is construed as a relative clause, so that the verb is attracted into the person and number of the false antecedent, the preceding predicate. The relative pronoun is often omitted: *Whó* was that [who] just came in?   It was *thát* [which] decided him.

b) Repeated Subject. When a compound subject consisting of two or more full or abridged clauses introduces the sentence, it is usual to place a *that* at the beginning of the principal proposition to point back to the compound subject as a unit: To know how others stand, that we may know how we ourselves stand; to know how we ourselves stand, that we may correct our mistakes and achieve our deliverance — *thát* is our problem (Matthew Arnold).

B. ABRIDGMENT OF SUBJECT CLAUSE. The usual (§ 76.A) infinitival and gerundial abridgments are common here: It was thoughtful of you *to do that*, or *doing that*. *For me to back out now* would be to acknowledge that I am afraid. In older English the nominative was often used as subject of the infinitive instead of *for* + noun or pronoun (§ 76.A): *I to bear this* is some burden (Shakespeare, *Timon of Athens*, IV, iii, 266). This is the absolute nominative construction described in § 73.B. The absolute nominative is still in common use where the predicate is a participle: It is vilely unjust, *men closing two thirds of the respectable careers to women* (Sir Harry Johnston). Where the subject of the participle is in the singular, this construction is liable to be ambiguous, so that it sometimes becomes necessary to replace it by the gerundial construction. The *writer's* (not *writer*) *being a scholar* is not doubted.

We render the abridged subject clause emphatic by making it predicate, as described in A.*a* above: It is *men closing two thirds of the respectable careers to women* that is unjust.

78. Predicate Clause.

A. CONNECTIVES. This clause is introduced by the indefinite relative pronouns (§ 9.D.2) *who* and *what*, sometimes by *why*, *as*, *where*, *that*.

EXAMPLES:

"He was not *who* (now more commonly *the man*) *he seemed to be*," but regularly in the accusative relation "He was not *the man I took him to be*."

We are not *what we ought to be*.

These wares come from Russia. That is *why they cost so much*.

Things are not *as they seem to be*.

This is *where he lives* (= *his dwelling*).

The *that*-clause here is introduced by *so*, which serves as the formal predicate, followed by the *that*-clause, the real predicate: Yet *so* it is, *that people can bear any quality better than beauty* (Steele, *Spectator*).

In all the preceding examples, the predicate clause is a nominative clause, predicated of a subject; but as it can be predicated of an accusative object, it can also be an accusative clause: I found it to be *what I wanted*.

Adjective Clause

There are two classes:

79. Attributive Substantive Clause.

A. THIS CLAUSE MAY BE AN APPOSITIVE TO A NOUN, with the force of an attributive appositive noun, or substantive: The hope *that he may recover* is faint. A conjunction, or a conjunctive indefinite relative pronoun or adverb or an interrogative pronoun or adverb, usually introduces the clause, but the conjunction is sometimes omitted where the connection makes the thought clear.

EXAMPLES:

There was in his eye a look *as if he would annihilate me*.

I was in mortal fear *lest* (or now more commonly *that*) *he should see me*.

The good people of the place had no doubt *that*, or *but*, or *but that*, *the end had really come*.

"They had no fear *that he would do it*," but "They had no fear *but that he would not do it*" reverses the meaning as it is a clause of exception (§ 89).

His fear [*that*] *he might never accomplish anything* is torturing him a good deal.

We now come to the main question (or problem), *what* (indefinite relative pronoun) *the cause of the disturbance is and who* (indefinite relative pronoun) *the proper person would be to remove it*, or more graphically in the form of a rhetorical question (§ 9.F), *what* (interrog. pronoun) *is the cause of the disturbance, and who* (interrog. pronoun) *would be the proper person to remove it?*

I now put the question to you plainly, *Will you come or not?* (direct question).

I insisted upon an answer to my question *whether* (interrogative adverb) *he was coming or not* (indirect question, § 9.F).

We must now decide the difficult question *whether* (indefinite relative adverb) *we shall go*.

162

We are trying to solve the vexing problems *why* (indefinite relative adverb) *John got so angry and how* (indefinite relative adverb) *we can put him into a good humor again.*

I insisted upon an answer to my question *why* (interrogative adverb) *he had done it* (indirect question, § 9.F).

It is difficult to answer your question *how* (interrog. adv.) *I did it* (indirect question).

I should like to say to you one important thing, *Go slowly in this matter* (or more modestly *You should go slowly in this matter*).

1. *Abridgment.* The usual (§ 76.A) infinitival and gerundial abridgments are common: Your plan *to go yourself* (or *of going yourself*) doesn't please me. I am in doubt *whether to buy or sell.*

B. THE CLAUSE MAY HAVE THE FORCE OF AN ATTRIBUTIVE PREPOSITIONAL PHRASE: I have little insight *into what* (indefinite relative pronoun) *he is doing.* Do you have any insight *into what* (indefinite relative pronoun) *he is doing?* The preposition is sometimes suppressed: Jones and I had a bet [*as to*] *who would stick out the longer.*

1. *Abridgment:* I haven't a clear insight *into how to proceed.* I was at a loss *about what to do.*

C. THE CLAUSE MAY HAVE THE FORCE OF THE GENITIVE OF A NOUN, OR SUBSTANTIVE: I shall make a note *of to whom* (indefinite relative pronoun) *the circulars are to be sent.* Then came his explanation *of why* (indefinite relative adverb) *he had done it.* His description *of how* (indefinite relative adverb) *he did it* is very interesting. I heard little *of what* (indefinite relative pronoun) *he said.*

1. *Abridgment:* Then came his description *of how to do it.*

80. Attributive Adjective Clause. This clause has the force of an attributive adjective.

A. CLASSIFICATION: There are two classes:

1. *Asyndetic Relative Clause.* There is an old type of relative clause, which follows the antecedent, like other relative clauses, but is not linked to it by a relative pronoun, so that we often

say that the relative pronoun is omitted and call the clause *asyndetic*, i.e. without a connective: Here is the book *you lent me*.

In fact, however, such clauses are not without a connective. In this sentence the definite article before book is a determinative, i.e. a demonstrative adjective that points to a following explanatory clause. Thus the determinative *the* stands in the principal proposition and points, like an index finger, to the following relative clause, binding it to the principal proposition.

We also use *this* (*one*), *these*, *that* (*one*), *those*, *the one*(*s*) as determinatives: this book and that one *you hold in your hand;* this book and that pen *you have;* these books and those *you have;* this book and the one *you hold in your hand.*

In all these cases the determinatives are definite, but there are also a large number of indefinite determinatives: *a, any, which, whichever, what* (more indefinite than *which*), *whatever* (more indefinite than *whichever*), *every, each, all,* etc.: this book and any other *you select;* every book *I have;* whatever course *you take.*

If we desire to use a preposition, we place it at the end of the clause: This is the pen *I write with* [*it*]. There is often as here a personal pronoun suppressed, which brings the preposition into the last place. The close connection in thought with the preceding antecedent suggests the meaning, so that we are not conscious of an omission.

If we should insert a relative pronoun in any of the above examples, it would be in the accusative. But the dative relation is also common, the prepositional dative sign *to* or *for* standing at the end of the clause after the analogy of true prepositions: the man *I gave it to;* the boy *I told the story to.* The nominative relation, though common here in older English, is now in general avoided as unclear, but in many expressions where the situation makes the thought clear it is still common: I lent Mrs. Jones what butter *there was in the house.* My children have had every complaint *there is to be had.* There isn't one of us *really knows* (W. D. Howells). There is a man at the door *wants to see you.*

The asyndetic construction is still often used instead of employing *where, when, why:* This is the place *we met yesterday.* He was quite sick the day *I visited him*. That is the reason *I did it*. Often also to express manner: That is the way *I do it*.

The usual custom of saying that the relative pronoun is omitted, suggests carelessness and has brought this construction into bad repute with many who are wont to attach value to form. A careful study of the true nature of this favorite old construction will show at once that it is a good natural English expression, not a mutilated grammatical member, but perfect and neatly fitted into the structure of the sentence, performing its function tersely, yet clearly and forcefully, often even with elegant simplicity.

2. *Relative Clause with Expressed Relative*. We now have a number of relative pronouns, but they are developments out of old determinatives, so that our present relative clause with an expressed relative pronoun is historically related to the old determinative type described in 1 above.

In the concrete expression of older English, there was often not only a determinative before the antecedent but also another after it to make the reference doubly clear: "Here is *the* book you lent me," or with a double determinative "Here is *the* book *that* you lent me," the two determinatives *the* and *that* pointing as with two index fingers to the following explanatory clause *you lent me*.

Later, *that* developed into a relative pronoun, pointing not forward, but backward, linking the relative clause to the antecedent. But features of its former nature still cling to *that*. It cannot take a preposition before it, but the preposition still stands at the end of the clause, as in the old determinative construction: This is the pen *that* I write *with*.

Similarly, the old determinatives *as, who, which* have developed into relative pronouns. *As*, like *that*, has retained so much of its old determinative nature that a preposition cannot stand before it but keeps its old place at the end of the clause: Let us discuss only such things *as* we can talk *of* freely. In the case of *who* and *which* we can put the preposition before the relative or at the end of the clause: I should like to introduce to you the gentleman *of whom I spoke* (or sometimes *whom I spoke of*). I'll lend you the pen *with which I write*, or *which I write with*.

B. LIST OF RELATIVE PRONOUNS. There has developed in the English relative clause a rich variety of expression, as attested by the following list of relative pronouns: *that,* for persons and things, except after *that,* where we now say *that which,* thus avoiding the repetition of *that,* although *that that* was once common; *who* for persons; *which* for things, in older English also for persons; sometimes as in older English *the which = which;* after a negative or a question *but* or also, especially in colloquial speech, *but what,* both forms with the meaning of *that not, which not, who not; as,* the usual relative after *such,* also after *the same* in elliptical clauses without a finite verb, while in the full clause with finite verb we may employ *that, which, who,* or *as; as,* quite frequently in older English, where there is no preceding *such* or *same; as,* still common in the predicate relation where the reference is to some preceding noun; moreover a number of adverbs or conjunctions, *where* (= *in which*), *whence* or sometimes *from whence* (both restricted to poetry or choice prose, elsewhere replaced by *from which*), *whither* (in poetry or choice prose, elsewhere replaced by *to which*), *while* (= *during which*), *when* (= *on which*), *why* (= *on account of which*), also a large number of others, once common but now little used except in exact, especially legal, language, such as *whereby, wherein, whereof,* etc.

After, before, since are often seemingly used as relative pronouns. Like relative pronouns, they link a clause to a preceding noun; but in reality they still, as originally, have the full force of prepositions, so that in fact preposition and clause form an attributive prepositional clause: The day *after I came* (= *after my coming*) was very beautiful. Compare § 59.*a*

Illustrative examples of the relative pronouns enumerated above are given in the following list and in C and D below.

EXAMPLES OF RELATIVE CLAUSES WITH EXPLANATORY REMARKS:

The boy *who just entered.*

The boy *whose father died yesterday.*

The bed *that the ball rolled under.*

Dumas the Elder *than whom* (an incorrect form now thoroughly established in good usage, instead of *than who*) there never was a kinder heart.

She that, or *he that* (in choice style), or (in plainer language) *she who* or *he who*, or (in colloquial speech) *a girl who, a woman who, a boy who, a man who*, would do such a thing.

They that (in older English), now *they who* or more commonly *those who*, would do such a thing.

No leader worthy of the name ever existed, or Was there ever a leader worthy of the name, *who was not an optimist*, or *but* (or *but what*) *was an optimist?*

There is not a touch of Vandyck's pencil *but* (used as a rel. pronoun in the object relation) *he seemed to have reveled on* (Ruskin).

It was such a scarlet *as* (subject) *makes the eyes ache.*

But those *as* (now *who*) *sleep and think not of their sins* . . . — Shakespeare, *The Merry Wives of Windsor*, V, v, 57.

Such men *as* (predicate) *he* (subject) *[is]* are rare.

You should associate with such men *as he [is]*.

The children get the same food *as I [get]*.

He sits in the same row *as* (or *that*) *we do*.

The city *whither* (in plain prose *to which*) *they were going* was far distant.

The boy stood on the burning deck *whence* (in plain prose *from which*) *all but he had fled.* — Mrs. Hemans, *Casabianca.*

This is the spot *where I lost it.*

The pauses *while we are thinking of the right word* are often quite awkward.

I remember well the day *that* (or *when*) *he came.*

That is the reason *that* (or *why*) *I did it.*

C. Descriptive and Restrictive Relative Clauses. Descriptive clauses stand in a loose relation to the antecedent and hence are separated by a pause, indicated in print by a comma; while restrictive clauses are quite closely linked to the antecedent in thought, so that they follow immediately without a pause, and hence are not usually set off by a comma: "I like to chat with John, *who is a clever fellow*." "We went on to Paris, *where we stayed a week*." "We traveled together as far as Paris, *at which* (relative adjective; see § 13.E.1) *place we parted*." But: "What is the name of the boy *who brought us the letter?*" "This is the spot *where I lost it*." The descriptive relative clause is in a formal sense a dependent clause, but it does not in any way modify the antecedent and is logically an independent proposition.

Who, *that*, and *which* have long been used with either restrictive or descriptive clauses, but in our time there is a strong tendency to limit *that* to restrictive clauses.

In descriptive clauses that refer to a thought as a whole, whether contained in a proposition or a single word, *which*, or sometimes *as*, is used with reference to a preceding statement or word; while with reference to a following statement or word we now usually employ *what:* We talked a long while about our boyhood days, *after which we had a good dinner.* I am getting gray and wrinkled, *which is not particularly cheering.* You behave like a madman, *as* (or *which* or *that*) *you are.* He praised the apples of the country and, *what was more to the purpose,* gave us the opportunity of tasting them.

Also the adverbs *when*, *whence* (§ 86.E.2.b.ii), *whereupon*, and *whereat* are used here as relative pronouns: The whole nation was jubilant, *when, like a bolt from the blue, news arrived of a serious reverse.* I saw him a month ago, *since when I haven't seen anything of him.*

D. PERSONALITY AND FORM. Current English stresses the idea of personality much more than older English. Even a little earlier in the period *who* was used of animals, while we today usually employ *that* or *which*, since we feel the absence of personality.

The relative is always near the antecedent; hence the incongruity of placing a personifying form alongside of a noun designating a being without personality is more keenly felt than in the case of personal pronouns, which stand farther away: "We have one cow *that* (or *which*) we highly prize. *She* is a Jersey."

Our strong desire to express personality is leading us to prefer more and more *who* to *that*, which we still freely use of animals but which we often avoid using of a person, since it does not express clearly enough the idea of personality.

With children the idea of personality increases with their age: "the last child *which* was born," but "our only child, *who* is now in college."

The idea of personality varies considerably with collective

nouns denoting persons: "He instructed crowds *which* surrounded him," but "People *who* have enjoyed good educational opportunities ought to show it in their conduct and language."

When the relative refers to both persons and things we cannot, of course, in one word indicate both personality and lack of it; hence we here must use *that* or *which:* He spoke largely of the men and the things *that,* or *which,* he had seen. We can use only *which* after prepositions: The company had, indeed, to procure in the main for themselves the money and the men *by which* India was conquered. Once *which,* like *that,* could refer to persons as well as things. This older usage survives here.

On the other hand, we often find *which* after a single noun denoting a person, but it here expresses the idea of estate, rank, dignity, not the lack of personality: He is not the man *which* (or *that*) his father wants him to be. In the predicate relation we can use also *as* here provided there is no definite article immediately before the antecedent: I will do my best to stop you, madman *as* (or *that* or *which*) you are.

In sharp contrast to the principle of indicating personality or the lack of it, which now prevails in the nominative and the objective cases of the relative, as described above, is the employment of the genitive *whose* for reference to persons, animals, and living and lifeless things: the man *whose* watch was stolen; the dog *whose* name is Carlo; the tree *whose* top is broken; the house *whose* windows are overgrown with creepers.

In the case of lifeless things we use also the *of*-genitive: the house in the shade *of which* we sit. As *that* has no genitive, it disappears at this point entirely.

E. CASE OF RELATIVE AND ITS AGREEMENT WITH ITS ANTECEDENT. The relative pronoun performs a double function: it is a pronoun in the clause in which it stands, and it is a connective joining the clause in which it stands to the antecedent.

As a pronoun it has the case required by its function in the relative clause, i.e. is subject, direct or indirect object, or a genitive modifying some noun in the clause: The boy *who* (subject) was sick is now well. The boy *whom* (object of the verb of the clause) I trusted proved worthy of my confidence. The boy *with whom* (object of the preposition *with*) I play lives next door.

The boy *to whom* (indirect object) I gave a knife has lost it. The boy *whose* (genitive limiting *knife*) knife was lost has bought another.

As a connective or conjunctive pronoun, the relative has relations to its antecedent, with which it agrees in *gender*, *number*, and *person*: "The boy *who* is standing by the gate is my brother," but "The book *which* lies upon the table is a history." As relative pronouns have the same form for both numbers and all three persons, their number and person can be gathered only from the number and person of the antecedent. This becomes important wherever the relative is the subject of the clause, for it then controls the number and person of the verb: "*I, who am* your friend, tell you so," where *am* is in the first person singular agreeing with its subject *who*, which agrees with its antecedent *I*. For help I look up to *thee who art* all-powerful and able to help. The *roads that lead* to the shore are sandy. An antecedent which is in the case of direct address is felt as being in the second person: Dark *anthracite, which reddenest* on my hearth!

1. *Form of the Antecedent*. The antecedent is usually a noun or a pronoun in the principal proposition, but it is sometimes, especially in older English or in poetry, a possessive adjective, which is explained by the fact that the possessive adjective was originally the genitive of a personal pronoun:

> Would you have me . . .
> Put my sick cause into *his hand that* (now usually *into the hand of him who*) hates me.
>
> — Shakespeare.

2. *False Agreement*. A speaker or writer sometimes carelessly puts the verb into agreement with the governing pronoun *one* instead of its dependent genitive, the real antecedent: Tyranny is one of *those evils* which *tends* (instead of the correct *tend*) to perpetuate *itself* (instead of *themselves*) (Bryce, *American Commonwealth*, 2nd Ed. II, 344).

3. *False Attraction*. Writers and speakers not infrequently place the relative pronoun in the accusative under the false impression that it is the object of the following verb, while in

reality its grammatical function demands the nominative: Instinctively apprehensive of her father, *whom* she supposed it was, she stopped in the dark (Dickens). Here *whom* is incorrectly used for *who*, the predicate of the relative clause *who it was*, which is the object of the verb *supposed*.

F. POSITION AND REPETITION OF THE RELATIVE. To avoid ambiguity the relative should be put as near as possible to the antecedent: "The *figs which* we ate were in wooden boxes," not "The figs were in wooden boxes *which* we ate." If this cannot be done, the sentence must be altered, so that the thought becomes clear: not "*Solomon*, the son of David, *who* built the temple," but "David's son *Solomon*, *who* built the temple."

Though, in general, the relative pronoun introduces the clause, we sometimes for emphasis put some other word into the first place: A deeply interesting book is this ancestor of the modern dictionary, to *describe* which adequately would take far more time than the limits of this lecture afford (Sir J. Murray).

Where the construction in two or more successive relative clauses is the same and there is no particular reason to contrast them or emphasize each statement, the relative need not be repeated: John Jones, *who* was born and buried in New York. The relative, however, should be repeated if the case or government is changed: Nor do I, either in or out of Cambridge, know any one *with whom* I can converse more pleasantly, or *whom* I should prefer as a companion. As in this example we should always use the same relative pronoun when we repeat a relative.

On the other hand, if there are two relative clauses in the sentence, and one of them is subordinate to the other, a change of relative is helpful to keep the grammatical relations clear: He enjoyed a lucrative practice, *which* enabled him to educate his family with all the advantages *that* money can give.

G. ABRIDGMENT OF RELATIVE CLAUSE. The contracted form is that of an appositive noun, adjective, participle, or a *to*-infinitive. In such clauses the noun, adjective, participle, or infinitive is the logical predicate and the antecedent the logical subject, the copula always being understood: The English, [*who are*] *a practical and energetic people*, have spread beyond their islands and now hold territory in all parts of the world. Pride [*which is*] *joined with many virtues* chokes them all. The sights [*which are*] *to be seen*, i.e. *which can be seen*, are not impressive. We have not an instant *to lose* (= *which we can afford to lose*). He is building for all time *to come* (= *which must yet come*). John is the boy *to send* (= *whom you should send*). This predicate infinitive has the usual modal force of the predicate infinitive described in § 54.D.2.

As in § 54.D.2, we can also predicate the infinitive of an object: It is the glory of Trinity that she has an abundance of famous men *from whom to select* (= *from whom she can select*), or in simpler form *to select from*.

When the reference is general or indefinite, the infinitive has no subject: It is not a night *to turn a dog from the door* (= *in which one should turn a dog from the door*).

Where the subject of the infinitive is not indefinite, or is not implied in some word in the principal proposition, it is now introduced by *for*, as explained in § 76.A: The thing *for you to do* is to go to bed.

Object Clauses

81. Dative Clause. The dative clause performs the function of a noun which is in the dative after a verb or adjective: He told the story *to whoever would listen*. He told the story *to whomever he met*. He was unkind *to whoever opposed him*. This is like *what we saw yesterday*. The explosion took place near *where we were playing*.

A. ABRIDGMENT. The full clause is sometimes replaced by the participial construction: He is unkind *to all opposing him*, instead of *to whoever opposes him*. If is often abridged to a gerundial clause (§ 124.C.3.b).

82. Accusative Clause after Verbs.

A. CONJUNCTIONS: *that; lest*, sometimes still as in older English used after verbs of fearing instead of *that; but, but that*, or in colloquial speech *but what*, often used instead of *that not* after a negative or interrogative proposition containing a verb of knowing, thinking, believing, fearing, or saying; an illogical *but, but that*, or in colloquial speech *but what*, sometimes used instead of the more common *that* after a negative or interrogative proposition containing a verb of doubting, wondering, in both cases verbs which though positive in form are negative in meaning; after verbs of remembering, recalling, thinking, knowing, learning, perceiving, hearing, and relating often *how* instead of *that;* often introduced by the indefinite relative pronouns (§ 9.D.2), adjectives (§ 13.E), and adverbs (§ 18.A.3), and by interrogative pronouns, adjectives, and adverbs, as in § 77.A; in indirect exclamations introduced by *what a.*

A conjunction or conjunctive pronoun, adjective, or adverb usually introduces the clause to show the oneness of the words in the clause, but the conjunction is sometimes omitted when the connection makes the thought clear: He always answers us *he is well.* This always takes place when the principal proposition is embedded in the subordinate clause: *God himself,* they devoutly trusted, *would shelter his servants in the day of battle against the impious men who were less their enemies than his* (Gardiner).

In colloquial speech and sometimes in the literary language an indirect question often has, aside from a change of person and tense, the form of a direct question, i.e. is without the interrogative adverb *whether* and has the word-order of a question — a blending of direct and indirect discourse: He spoke of Pen's triumph as an orator at Oxbridge, and asked *was he coming into Parliament* (Thackeray, *Pendennis*), instead of *whether he was,* etc. My sister asked me *what was the matter* (Doyle, *Sherlock Holmes*), instead of *what the matter was.*

EXAMPLES:

"I know *that he has come,*" originally "I know *that: he has come,*" the object *that* pointing to the following explanatory clause.

I feared *that it might anger him,* or *lest it should* (or *might*) *anger him.*

I don't know *that it isn't all true,* or *but,* or *but that,* or *but what, it is all true.*

Who knows *that it isn't all true,* or *but,* or *but that,* or *but what, it is all true.*

Take the money — there is no saying *but* (or *but that,* or colloquially *but what*) *you will need it.*

I do not doubt, or Who doubts *that,* or now less commonly *but,* or *but that,* or *but what, he will win.*

I saw *how* (= *that*) *he was gradually falling behind in the race.*

I do not know *who* (indefinite relative pronoun) *did it.*

I asked him *who* (interrogative pronoun) *did it,* (indirect question; § 9.F).

It is fair to ask not only, "What did the world gain from the First World War?" but "Was the gain in any way commensurate with the loss?" (direct questions).

I asked *where* (interrog.) *she came from,* (indirect question; § 9.F).

I do not know *where* (indefinite relative adverb) *she came from.*

I'll ask him *whether* (or *if;* interrogatives) *he is going.*

I do not know *whether* (or *if;* indef. relative adverbs) *he is going.*

I do not know *whether he will come himself, or whether he will send a substitute.*

I doubt *whether* (or *if*) *he will win.*

Who did he say *took it?*

1. There is often an anticipatory word such as *this, it, one thing,* in the principal proposition pointing to the following object clause: I know *this,* or *one thing, that he will never do that again.*

If the principal proposition is placed at the end for emphasis, it often contains a pronominal object which points back to the object clause: What the light of your mind pronounces incredible, *thát* in God's name leave uncredited (Carlyle).

B. ABRIDGMENT OF ACCUSATIVE CLAUSE AFTER VERBS. The usual (§ 76.A) infinitival and gerundial abridgments are common here: "My convictions do not permit me *to take part in this,*" or "My convictions do not permit *my taking part in this.*" I planned *to go myself.* I begged him (acc.) *to go.* I told him (dat.) *how to do it.*

When the subject is expressed in the principal proposition the *to*-infinitive is usually employed, as in the preceding examples, but with the group of verbs in § 67.C.1.b the simple infinitive is the usual form: I saw him *come.*

After the negative form of *help* in the meanings *avoid, prevent* the abridged form is now much more common than the full form with *that* or *but.* We may now use here the gerund or the simple infinitive: I could not help *laughing,* or *but laugh.* The

174

older regular *to*-infinitive is now only rarely used here: He could not help *to weep and sigh* (Kingsley).

Wherever there is no word in the principal proposition that can serve as the subject of the infinitive, so that the infinitive must have a subject of its own, it is usual, according to § 76.A, to introduce the subject by *for*. This rule holds in part for the accusative clause: I'll arrange *for you to see it*. After the following common verbs, however, *want, wish, desire, order, request, know, think, believe, suppose, take* (= *suppose*)*. expect, report, represent, cause, get, enable*, etc., it has become usual to put the subject of the infinitive into the simple accusative instead of introducing it by *for:* I desire *the rubbish to be removed*. I know *him to be an honest man*. I supposed *it to be him* (§ 54.A.1.a), or more commonly with a clause with a finite verb "I supposed *it was he*" I took *him to be nearer sixty than fifty*. We often omit *to be* of the passive infinitive, since this construction is influenced by the objective predicate construction described in § 67.C.1.b: I want *these letters* [*to be*] *stamped and mailed at once*. Compare § 123.B.

83. Accusative Clause after Prepositions.

A. CONJUNCTIONS: *that;* the indefinite relative pronouns (§ 9.D.2), adjectives (§ 13.E), and adverbs (§ 18.A.3), as in § 77.A.

EXAMPLES:

I insist upon *it that he go, should go, must go*, or *shall go*.

He is worrying about *what we shall do next*.

I am not informed as to *who did it, what he said, whether he went, why he went, when he went, where he went, where he came from*.

The preposition that should stand before the conjunction that introduces the clause is often suppressed: I am not certain *that he did it*, or in the gerundial construction with the preposition expressed: I am not certain *of his having done it*. I am much pleased *that he has gained such a great victory over himself* = *over his great victory over himself*. The idea of cause is often prominent in such clauses, as in the last example, often leading to the use of *because* as conjunction instead of *that*.

When the preposition is expressed, it is often placed before some formal word, such as *it* or *this*, which points to the following subordinate clause, the real object of the preposition: I am counting on *it that you come*. It has come to *this, that he can't support his family any more*.

B. ABRIDGMENT OF ACCUSATIVE CLAUSE AFTER PREPOSITIONS. Abridgment to a gerundial clause as described in § 76.A is very common after most prepositions: She was worried over her little *boy's* (or more clearly *boy*) *having to cross the railroad on the way to school*.

After the preposition *to* the simple infinitive is the usual form: Something impelled me *to do it* (i.e. *toward the doing of it*). The Moscow announcement goes far *to reëstablish an atmosphere of public confidence* (*New York Herald Tribune*, 1945).

The *to*-infinitive is used after most prepositions if the clause is introduced by an indefinite relative pronoun, adjective or adverb: I am thinking of *what to say, whom to select, what course to pursue, how to do it*.

Adverbial Clauses

Adverbial clauses are divided into classes corresponding to those of adverbial elements — clauses of place, time, manner, degree, cause, condition and exception, concession, purpose or end, and means. As will be described below, clauses of manner and degree are subdivided into other classes.

Thus adverbial clauses indicate many different shades of thought. The conjunctions introducing the clause express these meanings, so that they play an important part. The force of these conjunctions was once more concrete than now. A glimpse into the older structure of the clause throws light upon their present abstract meaning.

In oldest English, a liberal use was made of determinatives, i.e. words that point to a following explanatory remark. It was especially common to place the determinative *so* or *all so* (i.e. *quite so*, now contracted to *as*) in the principal proposition pointing to a following explanatory remark: "I met him *so: he was coming out of his house*," now "I met him *as he was coming out of his house*." "I am going to bed, *so* (= it is thus): *I am very tired,"* now "I am going to bed *as I am very tired."* "He hurried *so: he wouldn't be late,"* now "He hurried *so,* or *so that, he wouldn't be late."* In this explanatory clause lay the ideas of time, cause, purpose, etc. These ideas did not lie in *so* or *as.* Now these ideas are largely associated with *so* and *as.* The old *so* standing immediately before the explanatory remark became very closely associated with it, forming with it a subordinate clause and serving as its connective, binding it to the principal proposition and thus becoming a subordinating conjunction.

Instead of the single determinative *so* there was often in older English a double *so,* i.e. *so so,* pointing as with two index fingers to the following explanatory remark: He went to bed *so soon so: he came home,* now "He went to bed *as soon as he came home."* The group of words *so soon so* early fused into a unit and became a part of the subordinate clause, serving as its conjunction.

The old determinative *so* has developed not only into adverbial conjunctions but also into the relative pronoun *as:* Such experiences *as* this [*is*] are rare. Compare § 80.A.2.

84. Clause of Place.

A. Conjunctions: *where; whereas,* in older English = *where,* now with adversative meaning with the force of *while on the other hand* (§ 85.A.1) and with causal meaning with the force of *seeing that* (§ 88); *as,* in older English = *where,* now used here in only a few expressions; *whence* or sometimes *from whence,* in poetry and choice prose, now in plainer language replaced by *where — from,* or *from where; whither,* in poetry or choice prose, now usually *where; wherever, everywhere, everywhere that,* or the less common but more emphatic *wheresoever; whithersoever,* now usually replaced by *wherever.*

Examples:

We live *where the road crosses the river.*

> My Lord Protector, 'tis his Highness' pleasure
> You do prepare to ride unto Saint Alban's,
> *Where as* (= simple *where*) the King and Queen do mean to hawk.
> — Shakespeare. *Henry VI*, Second Part, I, ii, 56.

Here, *as* (now *where*) *I point my sword*, the sun arises.

— Id., *Julius Cæsar*, II, i, 106.

He now lives *where I came from*.

For *whither* (now *where*) *thou goest*, I will go. — Ruth, I. 16.

She is the belle and the spirit of the company *wherever*, or *everywhere (that), she goes*.

B. ABRIDGMENT OF CLAUSE OF PLACE. The full clause of place is sometimes abridged to a predicate appositive (§ 53.C) clause, in which the subject of the principal proposition is the subject and a participle is the predicate: *Where having nothing, nothing can he lose* (Shakespeare, *Henry VI*, Third Part, III, iii, 152). But in "*Wherever* [it has been] *feasible*, the illustrations have been taken from standard literature" we have to do with an ellipsis.

85. Clause of Time.

A. CONJUNCTIONS: *as* (or *so*) *soon as, as* (or *so*) *long as, as often as; whenever*, or the less common but more emphatic *whensoever* or *so surely as; if* (= *whenever*); *as; when*, or in older English *when as* or *when that; the time* (*that*), *by the time* (*that*); *the year* (*that*), *the month* (*that*), *the moment* (*that*), etc.; *every time* (*that*), *the next time* (*that*), *any time* (*that*); *while* or *whilst; once, directly, immediately, instantly; since; after, against* (now usually replaced by *by the time that*), *ere* (archaic, poetic, or choice prose), *before, till, until*, all earlier in the period followed by *that; no sooner — than, scarcely* (or *hardly*) — *when*, or earlier in the period instead of both *scarcely — but*.

1. *Adversative Conjunctions*. In *while, when*, and *at the same time that* the original temporal force is often overshadowed by the derived adversative force, just as in *whereas* the original local meaning is often overshadowed by the derived adversative force: *Whereas* (or *while* or *at the same time that*) in applied physics we hold our own, in applied chemistry we have lost much ground. I am really very cross with you for sticking to your work *when* (or *while* or *whereas*) you ought to be away having a change and a good rest. Compare § 90.

178

EXAMPLES:

I came *as soon as I heard of it.*

Whenever, or *if, I feel any doubt,* I inquire.

So surely as she came into the room, however, Martin feigned to fall asleep. — Dickens, *Martin Chuzzlewit,* Ch. IV.

I bought it *the year (that) I was in Europe.*

Once (= after once) a beast of prey has licked blood, it longs for it forever.

Once (= as soon as) he hesitates we have him.

Directly I uttered these words there was a dead silence.

Immediately, or *instantly, the button is pressed,* the mine explodes.

I had no sooner done it *than* (§ 87.A.2) *I regretted it.*

I had scarcely done it *when I regretted it.*

Scarce had I left my father, *but I met him borne on the shields of his surviving soldiers* (Addison, *Cato*).

B. ABRIDGMENT OF CLAUSE OF TIME. The full clause of time is often abridged to a predicate appositive (§ 53.C) clause, in which the subject of the principal proposition is subject and an adjective, noun, or participle is predicate: *When young,* or *when a boy,* I looked at such things differently. She always sings *when doing her work.* John, don't speak *until spoken to.* Do not read *while eating.* Compare § 76.A (7th par.), § 122.B (last par.).

After a preposition we may employ the gerund: I must write my exercise *before going to bed.* The gerund competes with the simple appositive participle after the prepositions *in* and *after:* *In going down town,* or *going down town,* I met an old friend. *After having finished my work,* or *having finished my work,* I went to bed. The participle is a favorite in lively language since it is more concrete and impressive. The gerund, on the other hand, is more precise, hence in scientific style more suitable.

Also the absolute nominative (§ 73.A) construction may be used: *This disposed of,* I turned to something else.

Sometimes the infinitive construction can be employed: He was surprised *to see this* = *when he saw this.* The idea of time here mingles with that of cause.

86. Clause of Manner. There are different classes:

A. MANNER PROPER: I interpret the telegram *so:,* or *in this way:, he is coming tomorrow, not today,* or *that he is coming tomorrow,*

179

not today. They strove to escape *in what manner they might.* Do it *how,* or *in what manner,* or *in whatever manner, you can.* Do *as you like, as you think best, as I told you to do.* They trim the roses *as their mother used to trim them.* He differed from his colleagues *in that he spent his spare time in reading.*

1. *Abridgment:* She came into the house *singing, crying,* etc. I must go *dressed in these clothes.* He spent the day *roaming* (or *in roaming*) *through the woods.*

B. COMPARISON: Do at Rome *as the Romans do.* You do not act *as you speak.* She plays with him *as a cat* [*plays*] *with a mouse.* He looks *as* [*he would look*] *if* (or *though*) *he were sick.* It looks as [*it would look*] *if* (or *though*) *we should lose the game.* He was so strong-willed that he always tried to drag, *as* [*if*] *it were* [so], everybody to his point of view. *Like as* (now usually simple *as*) *a father pitieth his children,* so the Lord pitieth them that fear him (Psalms, CIII. 13).

Older literary *like as* has been simplified to *like.* Since Shakespeare's time simple *like* has been gaining ground in colloquial speech as a clearer exprcssion than the literary form *as: Like* an arrow shot from a well-experienc'd archer hits the mark (Shakespeare, *Pericles,* I, i, 163). They don't marry *like* we do (A. Marshall, *Abington Abbey,* Ch. XIII). Though the use of *like* here as a conjunction has become very common in colloquial speech, our literary language still requires the colorless, less expressive *as.* If, however, there is no finite verb expressed and none is understood, *like,* not *as,* is the usual expression wherever there is a noun or pronoun present which can be construed as the object of the preposition *like:* He acts *like his father.* He speaks *like her.* He treats his wife *like a child.* But "Men here *as* [*they are*] *elsewhere* are inclined to seek their own interest," since the force of the verb *are* [*inclined*] is here distinctly felt.

In colloquial speech *like* is much used with the force of *as if* or *as though:* It looks *like it would rain.* It looks *like he is afraid.*

1. *Abridgment:* She hurriedly left the room *as though angry.* He raised his hand *as though to command silence.*

C. ATTENDANT CIRCUMSTANCE: The enemy devastated the country *as they retreated*. He never passed anybody on the street *that he didn't greet him*, or *but*, *but that*, or in colloquial speech *without*, *but what*, he greeted him. It never rains *but it pours*.

The once widely used *but* means *without*. As this meaning is today not vividly associated with *but* we often find modern *without* here instead of older *but*, regularly so in the abridged clause, not infrequently also in the principal clause in colloquial speech. The *but*-clause can be used only after a negative statement or a question. After a positive statement we must use a *without*-clause, usually in abridged-clause form: A large company can often raise wages *without raising the prices of its products* (*The New York Times*, 1945).

1. *Abridgment: Retreating*, or *in retreating*, the enemy devastated the country. I shall do it, *regardless of the consequences*, or *without regard to the consequences*, or *without regard to what he may advise*. He never passed anybody on the street *without greeting him*. He did it himself *instead of getting a man to do it*.

The absolute nominative construction (§ 73.A) is much used here: The ruffian approached, *dagger in hand*. As described in § 73.A.1, the nominative here is often replaced by a prepositional phrase: The ruffian approached *with his dagger in his hand*. She sang *with the window open*.

D. CLAUSE OF ALTERNATIVE AGREEMENT: Things are often good or bad for us *according as we look at them*. This idea can also be expressed by a prepositional clause (§ 83.A): They were praised or scolded *according to how they had done their work*.

E. MANNER CLAUSE OF RESULT. There are two classes:

1. *Manner Clause of Modal Result:*

He has always lived súch a life *that he cannot expect sympathy now*.
He is not súch a fool *that he is not able to see that*.
He has always lived só *that he cannot expect sympathy now*.
He placed his chair só *he could see her go by*.

I gained a son,
And súch a son *as* (now *that*) *all men hailed me happy*.

—Milton, *Samson*, 353.

181

In older English *as* was often used instead of *that*. This older usage survives in the abridged clause (a below).

a. Abridgment: This is not súch weather *as to encourage out-door sports*. He is not súch a fool *as not to be able to see that*. He lays out his work each day só *as to be able to finish it by six o'clock*.

b. Adverbial Clause Replaced by Relative Clause: That's a sight *that would make the angels rejoice* = That is such a sight that it would make the angels rejoice.

2. *Manner Clause of Pure Result:* She sat directly before me, *so that* (or in colloquial speech simple *so*) *I could not see the expression on her face*. He no longer has any backing, *why should you fear him?*, or *so that there is no need of your fearing him*. Something is wrong, *that he hasn't come before this*. I must have been blind, *that I didn't see that post*, or Where were my eyes, *that I didn't see that post?* The children never played together *that they didn't quarrel*, or *but* or *but that*, or in colloquial speech *without*, *but what*, they quarreled. Compare C above.

In older English *so as* was often used instead of *so that*. This older usage survives in the abridged clause (a below). In popular speech it survives also in the full clause: P-pay anything, *so's* (*so as* = literary *so that*) you get it (Winston Churchill, *Coniston*, Ch. VII).

a. Abridgment: Put on your gloves *so as to be ready*. What is he *to give himself such airs?* When his old friend John Street's son volunteered for special service, he shook his head querulously and wondered what John Street was about *to allow it*. A catbird sang *to split its throat*. He did not see Stenning again *to speak to* (A. Marshall, *Anthony Dare*, Ch. III), or more commonly *to speak to him*. The children *never* (or *usually*) played together *without quarreling*.

The full clause can often be abridged to a participial clause: He mistook me for a friend, *so that he caused me some embarrassment*, or *causing me some embarrassment*, or with a formal expression of the idea of result *thus causing me some embarrassment*. The use of *thus* here has been unjustly criticized on the ground that a coördinating conjunction should not link a subordinate clause to the principal proposition. But a clause of pure result is logically in most cases a principal proposition, for in most cases it does not in any way modify the meaning of the principal proposition. It often, like a descriptive (§ 80.C) relative clause, is in a mere formal sense a subordinate clause, but it may just as properly have the regular form of a principal proposition, as described in *b.ii* below.

The idea of result is often expressed by a prepositional phrase: The garrison was starved *into surrender*. He worked himself *into a frenzy*.

The result in all the above cases is represented as the effect of the activity or state indicated in the principal proposition. The *to*-infinitive is often employed to express an entirely different kind of result, namely a result which is the natural outcome of events or plans which are independent of the action described in the principal proposition: They parted *never to see each other again*. He awoke *to find all this a dream*.

b. Adverbial Clause Replaced by Other Constructions. Instead of an adverbial clause of pure result we often employ:

(i) An independent proposition linked to the preceding independent proposition by the conjunctions *and, and so, so, thus, and thus*, etc.: It began to rain, *and só* (adverb) *we went home*, or *só* (coördinating conjunction = *consequently;* see § 75.A.5) *we went home* (coördinated independent propositions); or *so* (unstressed old simple form, now only colloquial) *we went home*, or now in the literary language usually with distinctive form, *so that we went home* (subordinate clauses of pure result).

(ii) A relative clause, introduced by *whence, wherefore, which:* This bird (shrike) has a strong bill toothed at the end, and feeds on small birds and insects, *whence* (or *on account of which*) it *is known as the butcher bird*. He mistook me for a friend, *which caused me some embarrassment*.

87. Clause of Degree. There are different classes:

A. DEGREE CLAUSE OF COMPARISON:

1. *Signifying a Degree Equal to That of the Principal Proposition:*

a. Expressing a Simple Comparison: "*Quick as thought* he seized the oars," but more commonly with *as — as* in positive sentences to express complete equality and *so — as* in negative statements and questions with negative force to indicate inequality: I am *as* tall *as she* [*is*]. Is she *as* tall *as I* [*am*]? (question simply inquiring whether there is an equality). She is *not so* tall *as I* [*am*] (inequality). But are you *so* tall *as she* [*is*]? (question with negative force). "I am always *as* busy *as I am now*," but "I am not always *so* busy *as I am now*."

This differentiation between *as — as* and *so — as*, though recommended by grammarians, has not become established in the language. There is a strong trend to employ *as — as* in both positive and negative statements, following the simple principle that *as — as* expresses equality and *not . . . as — as* denies the existence of an equality: "I am *as* tall *as she*" and "I am *not as* tall *as she*."

(i) Abridgment: To go ahead resolutely and fail, or going ahead resolutely and failing, is not so bad *as not to try at all*, or *as not trying at all*. Nothing could be so unwise *as for him to attempt that*, or *his attempting that*.

b. Proportionate Agreement: One advances in modesty *as one advances in knowledge*. We can earn more or less *according as we work*, or in the form of a prepositional clause (§ 83.A) *according to how we work*. His humid eyes seemed to look within *in degree as*, or *in proportion as*, *they grew dim to things without*. The (§ 68.B) *more money* (*that*) *he makes* the more he wants. The stone gets the harder *the longer* (*that*) *it is exposed to the weather*. *In what degree we get self under foot* in that degree we get a larger view of life, or *By how much more we get self under foot* by so much we get a larger view of life, or much more simply *The more we get self under foot* the larger view of life we get.

A primitive form of this clause is preserved in old saws, as in "*The more* the merrier," where we still find the old verbless type of sentence described in § 53.B.*a*.

c. Restriction or Extent.

(i) Restriction: *So far as* (or *as far as*) *I could see*, they were all satisfied. The outlines of the proposal, *in so far as* (or *so far as*) *they interest the general public*, are well known. Mr. Carlton is not a prudent man *as* (§ 52.C) *regards money matters*. He recognized it for a fact, *as* (§ 52.C) *regarded the past* no more was to be said. Why, Hal, thou know'st *as* (now *so far as*) *thou art but man*, I dare; but *as* (now *so far as*) *thou art prince*, I fear thee as (= as much as) I fear the roaring of the lion's whelp (Shakespeare, *Henry IV*, First Part, III, iii, 165).

A restriction is often contained in a substantive relative clause: It has never been done before *that I ever heard of*.

A restriction is also often expressed by a prepositional phrase consisting of *for* and a pronoun (*aught, anything,* or now more commonly *all* or *what*) or noun modified by a relative clause, or instead of this construction we may employ a subordinate clause introduced by *so far as*, especially after a negative proposition: He may be dead for *aught (that)*, or *anything (that)*, or *all (that)*, or *what, I know*, but "He isn't dead *so far as I know*." After a personal pronoun the relative clause is omitted, as unnecessary. "She's got a pretty waist and a brown eye, Davy, and she's seventeen." — "She may *for me*" (= *for all I care*). Similarly after possessive adjectives, for possessive adjectives have developed out of personal pronouns: The boy is clever *for his age*.

The full clause of restriction is often abridged to a participial clause: The inquiry, *so far as showing that I favored my own interests*, has failed.

We still sometimes find here the old verbless type of sentence described in § 53.B.*a* : *So far so good*.

(ii) Extent, Degree, Amount, Number: I followed him with my eyes *as far as I could*. I know these people about here, fathers and mothers, and children and grandchildren, *so as* (or *to such an extent as*, or simple *as*) *all the science of the world can't know them*. I had as much *as I could bear*. Bring me as many flowers *as you can find*.

Extent is often expressed by the adverbial accusative (§ 68.B) of a noun which is made from the superlative of an adjective and is modified by a relative clause: She sang *the best (that) she could*.

2. *Following a Comparative:* He is taller *than* (older form of *then*) *I am* (subordinate clause, but originally coördinate with temporal force: He is taller, *then I come*). She eats less *than*

185

a bird [*eats*]. I do not desire my children other *than they are*. I cannot do otherwise *than that I give my full consent*. "I regard her more highly *than he* [*does*]," but "I regard her more highly *than* [*I do*] *him*." The personal part of the verb is often necessary to make the thought clear: "Tom likes me better *than he does Harry*," but "Tom likes me better *than Harry does*." I had no sooner done it *than* (still with temporal force as originally) *I regretted it*. He is taller *than me* (§ 89.A, 2nd par.).

Other as a comparative formation takes *than* after it, as illustrated in the preceding paragraph. Since *different* has the same meaning as *other*, many improperly employ *than* after it instead of the preposition *from*, the proper construction: Your idea is different *than* (instead of the correct *from*) mine. On the other hand, *different* often improperly influences *other*, so that many often use *from* after *other* instead of *than:* I hope to live to be another man *from what I was* (Dickens, *Christmas Carol*), instead of *than I was*.

a. Abridgment: I knew better *than to mention it*. Nothing is more foolish *than to waste time*. Nothing could be more unwise *than for you to do that*. I cannot do otherwise *than give my full consent*, or we may say: I cannot *but give my full consent*.

B. Degree Clause of Modal Result:

He is speaking so loud *that I hear him even from here* (actual result).

He is so badly injured *that he must die* (inevitable result).

He is so badly injured *that he will probably die* (probable result).

He is so badly injured *that he may die* (possible result).

He is so badly injured *that he might die* (a result faintly possible).

I am not in that collected mood at present *that I could listen to them quietly* (Coleridge, *The Piccolomini*, III, i, 47) (a result under other conditions possible).

He is so badly injured *that he shall be taken to the hospital at once* (a result determined upon by the speaker).

John is not old enough, or sufficiently old, *that we can send him with this message*.

I feel such a sharp dissension in my breast,
. . . .
As (now *that*) *I am sick*.

                                         — Shakespeare, *Henry VI*, First Part, V, v, 84.

Your informant seems to have given you no very clear idea of what you wish to hear, if he thinks these discussions took place *so* lately *as that* (now simple *that*) *I could have been of the party.* — Shelley.

I shall never be so busy *but that,* or *but what, I shall find time to answer your letters,* or *that I shall not find time to answer your letters.* Between spelling and pronunciation there is a mutual attraction, *insomuch that* (or *to such an extent that*) when spelling no longer follows pronunciation but is hardened into orthography *the pronunciation begins to move toward spelling.* — Earle.

Aldons silently assented, *so much so that Hallin repented.* — Mrs. H. Ward, *Marcella.*

As can be seen by the example from Shakespeare, *as* could once be used as a conjunction instead of *that.* This older use of *as* survives in the abridged clause (*a* below).

In colloquial speech simple *that* is often lacking: It is so dark *I can't see my hand before me.*

a) Abridgment: He was so kind *as to help me.* I was too near *to avoid him.* He was not near enough *for me to distinguish his features.*

88. Clause of Cause.

A. CONJUNCTIONS: *that; as; because; not that* — *but because* (or less clearly simple *but*); *not that not* — *but because* (or less clearly simple *but*); *not that not* (or *not but that,* or *not but what*) — *but because; since; now* or *now that; for the reason that,* or *by reason that; on the ground that; seeing* or *seeing that; considering* or *considering that; when; after; as long as; whereas* (§ 84.A); *inasmuch as; for fear* (*that*) or *lest; in that; for* or *for that,* in older English introducing either a subordinate clause with the meaning *because,* or, on the other hand, an independent explanatory remark, in the former function now only found in archaic style, while in the latter function simple *for* is still widely used, as described in § 75.A.4.

EXAMPLES:

I am sorry *that he is going.*

⸾ saw that I had said something wrong *as they all laughed.*

As you are not ready, we must go without you.

The Englishman is peculiarly proud of his country's naval achieve-ments, *not that he undervalues its military exploits, but simply because England is essentially maritime.*

He rarely ever saw the squire and then only on business. *Not that the squire had purposely quarreled with him, but* (or better *but because*) *Dr. Thorne himself had chosen that it should be so.* — Trollope.

Not a word had been said between them about Mary beyond what the merest courtesy had required. *Not that each did not love the other sufficiently to make a full confidence between them desirable to both, but* (or better *but because*) *neither had the courage to speak out* (id.).

I am provoked at your children, *not that they didn't behave well* (or *not but that,* or *but what, they behaved well*), *but because they left us too early.*

Now that this burden is rolled off, I can get my mind on my work again.

Your harshness to him is strange, *considering* (or *seeing*) *that you have always been good friends.*

How convince him *when he will not listen?*

I don't think much of John *after he has treated me in that way.*

Once (or *after*) *you have made a promise* you should keep it.

As long as you act so mean, you can't expect anybody to do anything for you.

Whereas the Royal Kennel Club of Great Britain has stopped the exhibiting of dogs with cut ears, be it resolved that the American Humane Associa-tion ask the American Kennel Club to take like action.

I regret the seeming harshness of my procedure the more, *inasmuch as I am deeply indebted to him and am truly desirous of showing my gratitude.*

He was afraid to stir *for fear* (or *lest*) *he should be discovered.*

He made a great mistake *in that he didn't act promptly.*

B. CLAUSE OF CAUSE REPLACED BY AN INDEPENDENT PROP-OSITION. Instead of a causal clause we often employ a principal proposition, placing it after the preceding statement to explain it, to give a reason for it: "I'll stay at home tonight; *I am very tired.*" Habits to young men are like threads of silk, *so lightly are they worn, so soon broken.* Instead of parataxis (§ 75.C) here, the second proposition may be introduced by the coördinating conjunction *for:* I'll stay home tonight, *for I am very tired.* Com-pare §75.A.4.

C. ABRIDGMENT OF CAUSAL CLAUSE: *Being poor*, he could not afford to buy books. You ought to be ashamed *stealing from a poor widow*. *Having run for an hour*, we were almost exhausted. *Like* (predicate appositive adjective) *a fool*, I cried most bitterly. She makes the first advances, *dear kind soul as* (relative pronoun = *that*) *she is*. He was shunned *as* (introducing the predicate appositive according to §53.C.3, a vigorously growing construction in English) *a man of doubtful character*. Our remaining horse was utterly useless, *as* (used here as in the preceding sentence) *wanting an eye*. They criticized the boy *as* (used as in the two preceding sentences) *showing no interest in his work*. The sophists were hated by some *because* (causal conjunc.) *powerful*, by others *because* (causal conjunc.) *shallow* (Lewes). For the use of causal conjunctions here see § 76.A (7th par.).

As explained on p. 121, the idea of cause is often expressed by an attributive element: This poor *friendless* man is to be pitied = This poor man is to be pitied *because he is friendless*.

The absolute nominative construction (§ 73.A) is common here: *It being very stormy*, she stayed at home. *There being no expense connected with the plan*, it was quickly adopted. As described in § 73.A.1, the absolute nominative here is often replaced by a prepositional phrase: She is a bit lonesome *with her husband so much away*.

The gerundial construction is common here after a preposition: I can't do anything *for thinking of her*. We feel kindly toward him *for*, or *because of his*, *waiting so patiently*.

The *to*-infinitive occurs not infrequently: Fool! *to have looked* for common sense on such an earth as this! I know how deeply she must have offended you *for you to speak like that*.

89. Clause of Condition or Exception.

A. CONJUNCTIONS OF CONDITION: *if*, *on condition* (*that*), *if not*; *were it not that*; *except for the fact that*; *only that* (= *were it not that*, *except for the fact that*); *unless*, *without* (in colloquial or popular speech = *unless*), *saving* (in higher literary style = *unless*); *except* (in archaic language = *if not* or *unless*); *but* (in colloquial and archaic language = *if not* or *unless*); *but that* (= *were it not that*, *except for the fact that*); *provided* (*that*), *provided only*; *providing* (*that*); *so that*, or in older English *so as*, in older English

189

and often still simple *so*, now also *so only; so long as*, or some-times *while in case that* or *in the event that; suppose, supposing*, or *say; once;* in older English *and* or *an* (= *if*).

CONJUNCTIONS IN CLAUSES OF EXCEPTION. In clauses of ex-ception: *but* or more commonly *but that; except that, except for the fact that*, or, after a negative proposition or a question, often also *beyond that; save that, saving that; only that;* in elliptical clauses the simple forms *but, except, save*, also *than* after a comparative. In elliptical clauses where there is no finite verb, it is common to employ here an accusative instead of a nominative in the subject relation, as so often elsewhere the accusative is fre-quently used instead of the nominative: Nobody was there *but me*, instead of *but* [*that*] *I* [*was there*]. He is taller *than me* (§ 87.A.2). This usage has become accepted for the reason that *but, save, except*, and in colloquial speech, *than* are con-sidered prepositions here. But in older language these forms were conjunctions and are still treated as such by some writers, so that they use the nominative form.

In colloquial speech the *that* after *except, only*, etc. in clauses of exception is often lacking in the full clause: I don't know any-thing, *only he hasn't any folks, and he's poor* (Louisa Alcott, *Little Men*, VI).

EXAMPLES OF CONDITIONAL SENTENCES:

I'll not go *if it rains*.

I would go *only that I am engaged*.

I'd burn the house down *but I'd find it* (= *if I could not find it without doing so*).

All would have done the like *but that they lacked courage*.

I would have told you the story *but that it is a sad one and contains another's secret*.

I should never have repeated these remarks *but that they are in truth complimentary to the young lady whom they concern*.

I will come *provided*, or *provided that*, or *providing*, or *providing that*, *I have time*.

You may go where you like *so that*, or simple *so, you are back by dinner time*.

Let him go, *so only he come home with glory*.

I do not care *so long as* (or *while*) *you are happy.*

The government is determined to dissolve parliament *in case* (or *in the event that*) *the oppositional forces fail to grant it the required majority.*

Suppose (or *supposing*, or *say*) *you were in his place*, would you do it?

There's no dealing with him *once* (= *if once* or *when once*) *he's got a notion in his head.*

An (= *if*) I could climb and lay my hand upon it,

Then were I wealthier than a leash of kings.

— Tennyson, *Gareth and Lynette*, 1. 50.

For the use of the indicative and subjunctive here see § 115.B.3.

EXAMPLES OF CLAUSES OF EXCEPTION:

I don't believe that God wants anything *but that we should be happy.*

Nothing would content him *but that I must come.*

My boy is quite as naughty as yours, *except that he always begs my pardon when he has done wrong.*

I can say no more *beyond that you have made me inexpressibly unhappy.*

I know almost nothing about him, *only that he is a young lawyer.*

Who is glad *but he?* — Chaucer.

Nobody knew her *but I.* — Pinero.

Everybody is to know him *except I* (Meredith, *Tragic Comedians*).

None heard *save I.* — Bridges, *Demeter*, Act II.

All save *he* and Murray pleaded guilty. — *Chicago Tribune*, Nov. 12, 1924.

I knew nobody there *but* [*that I knew*] *him.*

Nothing but a miracle, or *nothing else than a miracle*, or sometimes a blending of the two constructions *nothing else but a miracle*, can save us.

No one *but* (conjunction) *he*, or *but* (as preposition) *him*, or *else than he*, or *other than he*, could have done it, or sometimes a blending of two constructions: No one *else but he*, or *else besides him*, could have done it. Who *but he*, or *else than he*, or *other than he*, could have done it?

B. ABRIDGMENT OF CLAUSE OF CONDITION OR EXCEPTION

A full clause introduced by *if* or *unless* is often abridged to a predicate appositive (§ 53.C) clause, in which the subject of the principal proposition is subject and a participle or an adjective is predicate: *Born in better times*, he would have been a credit to the profession of letters. He will do it *if properly approached*. The child is never peevish *unless sick*. Situation *it* (§51.A) understood may be subject: Come tomorrow *if [it is] possible* (an elliptical, not an abridged, clause). The dangling (§ 74) participle is common here: *Taking all things into consideration*, my life has been a happy one. *Strictly speaking*, that is not true.

The usual (§76.A) infinitival abridgments are common: I should be glad *to go*. *To judge by his outward circumstances*, he must be rich. There is now nothing to do *but to go home*. I see no way *but for you to go in his stead*. Often in exlamations: *Oh, to be in England* now that April's there! (Browning) = Oh, how happy I should be *if I were*, etc. *O for a friend to help and advise us!* = Oh, how happy we should be, *if only a friend could help and advise us!*

The absolute nominative construction described in § 73.A is often used instead of a full clause: *Conditions being favorable*, he might succeed. *Present company excepted*, no one did his full share. As described in §73.A.1, the nominative here is often replaced by a prepositional phrase: *With conditions in every way favorable*, he might succeed.

Sometimes the full clause can be replaced by an attributive adjective: A *true* friend would have acted differently = A friend would have acted differently *if he had been true*. Compare p. 121.

A prepositional phrase often takes the place of a conditional clause: *Without him* I should be helpless. In negative form we often find *but for*, *except for*, *save for*, or *only for* here: I should never have guessed that he gave the matter a thought *but for* (or *except for*, *save for*, or *only for*) *that last remark of his*.

The gerund is common after prepositions: How many critics would be able, *on being shown this drawing*, to say from whose pencil it had emanated?

The old verbless appositional type of sentence described in § 53.B.a is common here: *Forewarned*, forearmed. *Small pains*, small gains. *No song*, no supper. Better *dead!* (Galsworthy, *The First and the Last*, Scene III) = It would be better *if we were dead!*

C. "If"-Clause Replaced by Other Constructions. The *if*-clause can be replaced by:

1. *A Relative Clause:* Any boy *who would do that* would be laughed at.

192

2. *A Clause with Question Order*, originally an independent question: *Is any among you afflicted?* let him pray (James, V.13). *Would space allow*, I should like to quote the notice in full.

3. *A Wish* felt as impossible or difficult of fulfilment: *Could I see her once more*, all my desires would be fulfilled.

4. *Two Independent Sentences* linked by a conjunction or unlinked.

a. Two sentences linked by *and* or unlinked, the first of which is an expression of will containing an imperative or a volitive (§ 114.A.1) subjunctive: *Give him an inch* and he'll take a mile. [*go*] *One step farther* and you are lost. *But enter a Frenchman or two* and a transformation effected itself immediately (DuMaurier, *Trilby*). *Do it at once*, you will never regret it! For use of coördination and parataxis see § 75.C.

b. Two sentences linked by *or, otherwise, else, or else*, the first of which is an expression of will: *Do that at once, or* (or *otherwise, or else, or or else*) you will be punished. For use of coördination here see § 75.C.

c. Two unlinked expressions of will: *Love me*, love my dog; *Sow nothing*, reap nothing; *bear no burden of others*, be crushed under your own. Compare § 75.C.

d. Two independent declarative sentences linked by *or, or else, or otherwise: He cannot be in his right mind, or*, or *else*, or *otherwise*, he would not make such wild statements = *If he were in his right mind*, he would not, etc.

e. *In Conditional Sentences* the subordinate clause is often, in colloquial speech, replaced by an independent sentence introduced by adversative (§ 75.A.3) *but* or *only: The airship would have made a safe landing, but the metal nose came* (= *if the metal nose had not come*) *up against an electric wire and set fire to the gas. We'd have done better, only we struck* (= *if we had not struck*) *a hard wind against us about two miles up in the air.*

90. Clause of Concession.

A. CONJUNCTIONS: *if, though, although;* the adversatives (§ 85.A.1) *while, when, whereas*, in older English also *where; as* (as in *bad as he is*, in older English *as — as* or *so — as: as bad as he is*, or *so bad as he is*); *in spite of the fact that, despite that, notwithstanding (that);* relative pronoun or adverb + *ever* or *soever; for all that, for as little as; granting* or *granted (that); admitting that, assuming that;* in older or archaic English *albeit* (= *all be it* = *be it entirely so*), *and* or *an* (= *if*).

A pair of concessive clauses is usually connected by *whether — or whether, whether — or, if — or,* in older English *or whether — or.*

EXAMPLES:

"I don't care *if I do lose,*" or in rather choice English "I don't care *though I lose.*"

I couldn't be angry with him *if* (or stronger *even if*) *I tried.*

Though, or *although, he promised not to do it,* he did it.

Though they worked never (once common here, now usually replaced by *ever*) *so hard,* it was all in vain.

Her mother, *while she laughed,* was not sure that it was good to encourage the pert little one.

We sometimes expect gratitude *when we are not entitled to it.*

You are free *whereas I am handicapped.*

Stupid as he is, he never loses his profit out of sight.

The world, *as censorious as it is,* hath been so kind. — Swift.

Foolish though she may be, she is kind of heart.

He's a scoundrel *whoever he may be.*

I shall go, *whatever he may say.*

She is always cheerful *in whatever condition her health is.*

However bad the weather may be, or *bad as the weather may be,* we shall have to confront it.

For all that (or simply *for all*) *he seems to dislike me,* I still like him.

"They spoke in tones so low that Francis could catch no more than a word or two on an occasion. *For as little as he heard* (or *although he heard little*), he was convinced that the conversation turned upon himself and his own career. — R. L. Stevenson.

Granted, or *granting, that he had the best intentions,* his conduct was productive of much mischief.

If I have broke anything, I'll pay for't, *an* (= *if*) *it cost a pound.* — Congreve.

Whether he succeed(s) or fail(s), we shall have to do our part.

Whether I go alone, or whether he goes (or *go*) *with me*, the result will be the same.

B. ABRIDGMENT OF CONCESSIVE CLAUSE. Abridgment often occurs in the form of a predicate appositive (§ 53.C) adjective, participle, or noun: *Well or sick, calm or worried*, or *whether well or sick, calm or worried*, she is always restrained in her feeling. *Though sick*, she went to school. *Vagabond or no vagabond*, he is a human being and deserves pity. *Whig as* (relative pronoun = *that*) *he was and rather a rancorous one at that*, Creevy was a welcome person even to the Duke of Wellington. *Strong man that he is*, he has been severely put to the test during the last few weeks.

The participle is sometimes in apposition with a possessive adjective, which is explained by the fact that the possessive adjective was originally the genitive case of a personal pronoun: *Waking or sleeping*, this subject is always in *my* mind.

The adjective here sometimes appears as an adherent (§ 56.A) adjective instead of a predicate appositive: With a dogged perseverance and a keen, *if narrow*, insight into affairs President Kruger has worked with a single object. This *old* woman dolls herself up like a young lady = This woman dolls herself up like a young lady, *although she is old*. Compare p. 121.

The abridged form is often that of a prepositional phrase, especially one containing the word *all:* His wife clung to him *with all his faults*. *For all his learning* he is a mean man. Often in the prepositional construction described in § 73.A.1: *Even with conditions quite unfavorable*, he would suceed. Often in connection with a gerund: But we haven't got any wind *for all the barometer falling* (Joseph Conrad).

The abridged clause sometimes has the infinitive construction: You couldn't do that *to save your life*.

We sometimes employ here the old verbless type of sentence described in § 53.B.*a: Right or wrong* — my country.

C. CONCESSIVE CLAUSE REPLACED BY OTHER CONSTRUCTIONS. The concessive clause is often replaced by the following constructions:

1. *The concessive adverbial clause is often replaced by a principal proposition which may be:*

a. An expression of will in the form of an imperative sentence, which, though independent in form, is logically dependent: *Laugh as much as you like*, I shall stick to my plan to the bitter end. This is parataxis (§ 75.C). We often employ coördination here with two sentences linked by *and*, the first of which is a command: *Take any form but that* and my firm nerves shall never tremble.

The different personal forms of the imperative are common here: *Let him be the greatest villain in the world*, I would not keep from wishing to do some little thing to benefit him. The old simple subjunctive, a mild volitive (§ 114.A.1) subjunctive, frequently serves here as a mild imperative, often with suppressed subject. First person: There is no task to bring me; no one will be vexed or uneasy, *linger I ever so late* (Gissing). *Sink [I] or swim [I]*, I shall undertake it. *Argue [we] as we like, dogmatize [we] as we please, experiment [we] up to the extinction of the canine race*, no fellow can ever understand the mysteries and vagaries of idiosyncrasy. Third person: Home is home, *be it ever so homely*. There are certain great books that have for me no charm, *charm they ever so many others whose opinions I respect and accept*. I shall go *rain [it] or shine [it]*. I shall buy it *cost [it] what it may*.

b. As in primitive speech the concessive idea is still often expressed by declarative parataxis or coördination (§ 75.C): The meat is good; *it is a little tough, though* (§ 75.A.3). I cannot keep these plants alive; *I have watered them well too* (or *and I have watered them well too*). *No matter* (= *it is of no importance*) *what he says* (or *it doesn't matter what he says*), I am going.

c. A clause in question order, originally an unreal wish, first employed in unreal conditional sentences, as described in § 89.C.3, where it had a meaning, but later transferred to use in concessive clauses: *Were the danger even greater*, I should feel compelled to go. Some adverb, as *even* in this example, differentiates the concessive clause from the conditional.

2. *The concessive idea sometimes finds expression in a relative clause:* Many American boys *who* (= *although they*) *have had few advantages in their youth* have worked their way into prominence.

91. Clause of Purpose.

A. CONJUNCTIONS: *that*, old but still often used, more commonly, however, now replaced by the more expressive forms *in order that* (i.e. with the purpose that), *so that*, or in colloquial speech simple *so; for the purpose that, to the end that; in the hope that;* after a negative or a question *but that* or more commonly *unless that;* three forms to express apprehension, *that — not, for fear that*, and sometimes *lest;* in older English with the force of *in order that* the conjunctions *because, for that*, and *so as*. Though *so as* has disappeared in the literary language from the full clause, it survives in the abridged clause described below, in popular speech also in the full clause.

The conjunctions *that, so that*, and *so* are used also in the closely related clause of result. These two clauses are not differentiated by their conjunctions but by the use of different moods. The indicative in the clause of result represents the statement as an actual result, while in the clause of purpose *may, might, shall, should*, or sometimes the simple subjunctive form of the verb, represents the result as only planned or desired: "I am going to the lecture early *so that I may get a good seat*" (clause of purpose), but "I went to the lecture early *so that I got a good seat*" (clause of result). We often employ the indicative also in the clause of purpose, especially the future indicative, since we desire to express our confidence that the result will surely follow, or in the case of *can* the present tense, since the present tense here usually has future force: He is going early *so that* (or simply *so*) *he'll get a seat*. I'm giving my boy a good education *so that* (or simply *so*) *he can more easily cope with life's difficulties.*

EXAMPLES:

They are climbing higher *that* (or *so that*, or *in order that*) *they may get a better view.*

They climbed higher *that* (*so that*, or *in order that*) *they might get a better view.*

Let us be silent — *so we may hear the whisper of the gods.* — Emerson, *Friendship.*

Father has the first one (i.e. first whistle) blown at half-past six, *so's* (*so as* = literary *so that*) the men can have time to get their things ready and start. — Dorothy Canfield, *The Brimming Cup*, Ch. VI.

197

He never comes *but that* (or *unless that*) *he may scold us*.

"He is keeping quiet *that he may not disturb* his father," or *lest* (or *for fear*) *he disturb*, or *shall disturb*, or more commonly *may*, *should*, or *might*, *disturb his father*.

B. ABRIDGMENT OF CLAUSE OF PURPOSE. The usual (§ 76.A) infinitival abridgments are common: The lad has gone *to bring in some coal*. The lad pulled at his mother *for her to take notice of him*. I am going early *so as*, or *in order, to get a good seat*. Often after *on purpose:* He did it *on purpose to provoke me*. Compare § 123.B.

In oldest English, the simple infinitive could be used here instead of the form with *to*, and this older usage survives in a few set expressions: I'll go *see*. Compare § 63.B.

The principal proposition upon which an infinitive clause with *to* depends is often suppressed: *To be sincere*, [I must tell you] you have not done your best.

After the preposition *for* and prepositional phrases the gerundial clause is common: We planted a hedge *for preventing the cattle from straying*. I am not here tonight *for the purpose of making a speech*. I didn't come *with the object* (or *intention*) *of destroying the good feeling prevailing among you*.

We often abridge to a prepositional phrase: He strove *for glory*. He worked *for grades*.

To indicate continued activity, we employ the present participle: He went *hunting, fishing, swimming*. He took me out *riding*.

C. ADVERBIAL CLAUSE OF PURPOSE REPLACED BY OTHER CONSTRUCTIONS. The adverbial clause is the usual form for expressing pure purpose, but it is sometimes expressed by:

1. *An Independent Coördinate Proposition* connected with a preceding independent proposition by *and:* Come *and see*. Go *and ask*. Try *and go*. Won't you come *and see us?* I'll try *and do it*. Compare § 75.C.

2. *An Attributive Relative Clause*, either the full or abridged form: Envoys were sent *who should sue for peace*. The doctor gave me something *to ease my pain*.

92. Clause of Means. In the principal proposition there is always a preposition: You can recognize him *by the fact* (a formal anticipatory word pointing to the following clause) *that he limps badly*, or in abridged form *by his limping badly* or *by his bad limp*. All strove to escape *by what means they might*. In a formal sense such a clause is a prepositional clause and is identical with the prepositional clause discussed in § 83.A. Hence it is not further discussed here.

A. ABRIDGMENT. Abridgment to a gerundial clause is very common here:

By holding on to the rope firmly, or *holding* (pres. participle) *on to the rope firmly*, I came safe to the shore. *By John's holding the ladder firmly*, I succeeded in climbing onto the roof.

PART FOUR

SYNTAX OF THE PARTS OF SPEECH

SYNTAX OF NOUNS

93. Case
94. Number
    A. Conflict between Form and Meaning
        1. Collective Nouns
        2. Plural Used as Singular
    B. Names of Materials and Abstract Nouns
    C. Nouns without a Singular
    D. Plural of *Kind* and *Manner*
    E. Number in Titles
95. Gender
    A. Natural Gender
        1. Use of Distinctive Terms to Indicate Sex
        2. Use of Prefixes and Suffixes to Indicate Sex
        3. Use of Pronouns and Possessive Adjectives to Indicate Sex
    B. Gender of Animation

SYNTAX OF PRONOUNS

96. Personal Pronouns
    A. Use and Form
    B. Agreement with Antecedent
97. Reflexive Pronouns
98. Reciprocal Pronouns
99. Relative Pronouns
100. Interrogative Pronouns
101. Indefinite Pronouns

SYNTAX OF ADJECTIVES

102. Functions
103. Substantive Form of Adjectives
    A. Substantive Forms of *One* and *No*
    B. Substantive Forms of *Other*
    C. Substantive Forms of Possessive Adjectives
104. Comparison of Adjectives
    A. Degree
    B. Relative Comparison
        1. Terminational Type of Comparison
        2. Analytic Type of Comparison

SYNTAX OF VERBS

Voice

Mood

SYNTAX OF PREPOSITIONS

PART FOUR

SYNTAX OF THE PARTS OF SPEECH

SYNTAX OF NOUNS

93. Case. Case has been treated in § 25 and in Part **III**. Now follows the discussion of number and gender.

94. Number.

A. Conflict between Form and Meaning. A singular form is often plural in meaning and a plural often singular. Some of the more common or more peculiar cases are treated here.

1. *Collective Nouns.* While, in general, the singular denotes one and the plural more than one, in certain cases the opposite is true, namely that one denotes many and many one. A group of persons or things may be felt as a unit, a whole: the gentry, the army, the police, the seaworthiness of the English *craft*, etc. In spite of the singular form here the idea of plurality is so strong that we now not infrequently find before these collective nouns a limiting adjective plural in form and meaning: *these offspring* of her own heart (Hawthorne), 80,000 cattle, etc. Such nouns when used as subject quite commonly require a plural verb (§ 55.A.1.d).

With a number of words there are two forms, a singular to express the idea of oneness, a distinct type, a mass, and a plural to indicate different individuals or varieties within a group or type: "an abundance of good *fruit*," but "the *fruits* of California"; "gentlefolk," "peasant-folk" with the idea of a class, "young folks" with the idea of individuals; "a boat-load of *fish*," but "different kinds of *fishes*"; "the English *people*," but "the *peoples* of Europe." "Why should I expose myself to the *shot* of the enemy?" but "Two *shots* hit the mast." "She washed her *hair*," but "The *hairs* of your head are numbered." "My father is sowing turnip *seed* in the garden," but "There are a hundred *seeds* in this packet."

In the case of certain gregarious animals the idea of separate individuals is not sharply developed and hence does not find expression: One *trout*, two *trout;* flocks of water-*fowl*.

Certain nouns denoting measure have the same form for singular and plural, especially: *brace, yoke, dozen, score, gross, ton, head*, etc., a list now smaller than in older English with a tendency to grow still smaller, now with singular form in plural meaning only after numerals and not always even there: "two *dozen* of the best figs," but "*dozens* of times"; forty *head* of cattle.

2. *Plural Used as Singular.* A number of plural nouns now have the force of the singular: *pains* (§ 55.A.2.c), *means* (§ 55.A.2.c), *news, small-pox* (for *small-pocks*, the singular still preserved in *pockmarks*), *measles, mumps, lazybones, gallows, a bellows* or *a pair of bellows*, a rather uncomfortable *ten minutes, the United States* (felt either as a singular or plural); *mathematics, physics*, etc., usually singulars, *gymnastics, athletics, politics, tactics* more commonly used as plurals, but in the case of *politics* there is considerable fluctuation.

B. NAMES OF MATERIALS AND ABSTRACT NOUNS. From their very nature these nouns do not usually admit of a plural: *wine, gold; silk*, etc.; *beauty, liberty*, etc. But these nouns have a plural when they indicate different kinds, definite individuals, persons or things, distinct actions or manifestations: Rhine *wines;* a fine stock of *linens* (linen goods); the *beauties* of nature; the rustic *beauties* (beautiful women) of our village; the latest *deaths* (cases of death) in our community, etc.

C. NOUNS WITHOUT A SINGULAR. Some words occur only in the plural since the things represented are not simple in their make-up, so that the plural idea is uppermost in our minds: the Alps, the Pyrenees, tongs, trousers, spectacles, etc.

D. PLURAL of "KIND," "MANNER." Instead of saying "an apple *of this kind*," "apples *of this kind*," "*Of what kind* is this apple?" "*Of what kind* are these apples?" many people say "this *kind of* apple," "these *kind of* apples," "What *kind of* apple is this?" "What *kind of* apples are these?" In these expressions *kind of* has developed into an adjective. The absolute proof is found in its wide use in colloquial speech as an adverb in connection with a verb, just as adjectives in general are used as adverbs: I *kind of* expect it. As *kind of* is an attributive adjective when it stands before a noun, the number of the verb is regulated by the number of the governing noun: "*This* kind of *man annoys* me," but "*These* kind of *men annoy* me." The *these* here before *kind of* modifies, not *kind*, but *men*. As many grammarians censure "these *kind of* men" and "these *kind of* apples," falsely concluding that *kind* is a noun here, this expression has gradually come into bad repute and is not felt as good English. The curious thing about this situation is that the other three expressions "this *kind of* apple," "What *kind of* apple is this?" "What *kind of* apples are these?" are widely used even in choice English although they are of the same formation as the censured expression. Similarly, *type of*, *manner of*, *sort of*, are used in the literary language as attributive adjectives: this *type of* house, to show what *manner* of man he was (Macaulay). Under the false impression that *kind*, *type*, *manner*, *sort*, are nouns here many people say "this *kind of an* apple," "this *type of a* house," "what *manner of a* man."

In all the above examples the reference is to only one kind. When the reference is to more kinds than one, the word *kind* is always a noun and the plural form is, of course, always used: There are many *kinds* of apples. In older English, *kind* and *manner* had an indistinctive plural of the same form as the singular. The old indistinctive plural of *manner* survives: They played all *manner* of games.

E. NUMBER IN TITLES. We may say:

1. Messrs. Smith and Brown, the two Mr. Smiths, or the two Messrs. Smith; Mr. Paul [Smith] and Mr. John Smith, or Messrs. Paul [Smith] and John Smith; Master Smith, the two young Master Smiths, or the two young Masters Smith.

In the case of *brother* and *sister* we may say: the Smiths, or the Smith brothers, or the brothers Smith, but on a sign without the article, Smith Brothers; the Smith sisters.

2. We say: the two Mrs. Smiths; the Miss Smiths, or less commonly but in formal language preferably, the Misses Smith; the Miss Smiths' little cottage or the Misses Smith's little cottage; the numerous Mrs. and Miss Grundys.

3. We say: the two Dr. Smiths; Drs. William Smith and Henry Brown; Professors Smith and Brown; the Captains Smith and Brown.

95. Gender. Gender is a distinction in the form of words to indicate sex. There are two kinds of gender in English — natural gender and the gender of animation.

A. NATURAL GENDER. This gender rests upon the conception of sex in nature, hence its name *natural gender*. The name of anything of the male sex is of the masculine gender, as *man, bull, John*. The name of anything of the female sex is of the feminine gender, as *woman, cow, Jane*. The name of anything without sex is of the neuter gender, as *tree, stone, water*. Such words as *dog, mouse, teacher*, which are used for both male and female beings, are said to be of common gender.

The necessities of life require us still in a large number of cases to indicate sex, but in the literary language there is a growing disinclination to do this with reference to man or beast. Sex is shown by nouns, pronouns, and possessive adjectives in the following ways:

1. *Use of Distinctive Terms to Indicate Sex.* The male and the female are in many cases indicated by a different word: *man, woman; salesman, saleswoman; foreman, forewoman; gentleman, lady; Sir, Madam; Lord, Lady; father, mother; papa, mama; grandfather, grandmother; son, daughter; brother, sister; husband, wife; uncle, aunt; nephew, niece; monk, nun; king, queen; earl, countess; bachelor, old maid* or *spinster* (the *-ster* originally a feminine suffix but now usually masculine: young*ster*, team*ster*, etc.); *wizard, witch; boy, girl* or *maid, maiden; milkboy, milkmaid; cash boy, cash girl; lad, lass; tom, tabby; dog, bitch* or *slut; cock* or *rooster, hen; gander, goose; drake, duck; fox, vixen; sire, dam; buck, doe; hart* or *stag, hind; ram* or *wether, ewe; bull, cow; bullock* or *steer, heifer; stallion, mare; colt, filly;* etc.

Some feminine nouns, as *duck, goose*, and some masculine as *dog, horse*, are often used to denote either sex where there is no desire to be accurate.

There are a number of words which apply only to females without a corresponding word for males: *frump, dowd, slattern, shrew, termagant, virago, minx, hussy, prude, dowager*, etc. On the other hand, there are a number of words which apply only to males: *dude, fop, ruffian*, etc.

2. *Use of Prefixes and Suffixes to Indicate Sex.* The male and the female are in many cases distinguished by prefixing a noun or pronoun, or by placing an adjective before the noun: *a woman friend, women friends* (or *lady friend, lady friends*); *man friend, men friends* (or *gentleman friend, gentlemen friends*); *woman doctor* (or *lady doctor*); *girl cashier; hen bird* (or *lady bird*); *cock pheasant, cock robin*, but *guinea cock, peacock, turkey cock; jenny robin, hen sparrow,* but *guinea hen, peahen, turkey hen; buck rabbit, doe rabbit; dog fox; she-bear, he-bear; tom-cat, she-cat; billy goat, she-goat* or *nanny goat; he-ass* or *jackass, jenny ass; bull calf, cow* (or *heifer*) *calf; cow rhinoceros;* the *fair singer, fair readers; female* (or better *woman*) *novelist; female dog; male lamb* or *buck ram, female lamb* or *ewe lamb*, etc.

The female is distinguished in a number of cases by adding the suffix *-ess* to the masculine form: *God, goddess; emperor, empress; prince, princess; marquis, marchioness; baron, baroness; ambassador, ambassadress; mayor, mayoress* (in England); *abbot, abbess; prior, prioress; actor, actress; adventurer, adventuress; benefactor, benefactress; caterer, cateress; enchanter, enchantress; giant, giantess; heir, heiress; host, hostess; hunter, huntress; Jew, Jewess; laundress; leopard, leopardess; lion, lioness; master* (in weakened form appearing as *mister*, written *Mr.*), *mistress* (in abbreviated form *Mrs.*, pronounced Missis); *murderer, murderess; Negro, Negress; ogre, ogress; prophet, prophetess; proprietor, proprietress; protector, protectress; songster, songstress; seamstress; sorcerer, sorceress; servitor, servitress; tiger, tigress; traitor, traitress; typewriter, typewriteress*, or more commonly *woman typewriter* or *typist* with common gender; *waiter, waitress.* Other suffixes are used in a few words: *hero, heroine; administrator, administratrix; executor, executrix* or *executress; testator, testatrix; sultan, sultana; czar, czarina; Joseph, Josephine; Francis, Frances.*

The ending -*ess* was once more widely used. There is a derog-
atory touch in it, which makes it unsuitable when we desire to
show respect, but on the other hand appropriate when we speak
slightingly. Rather than use it we go a roundabout way: wife
of the ambassador, wife of the pastor, woman doctor, etc.
If we stress the idea contained in the stem of the word, we use
the masculine form for females: Dr. Louise Smith. George
Eliot is a great *writer*. She is an able *teacher*. The forms in -*ess*
have become established in certain titles and a few other words
given above, but even some of these are avoided.

Widower is formed by adding -*er* to the feminine word.

3. *Use of Pronouns and Possessive Adjectives to Indicate Sex.*
The male and female are often distinguished by a possessive
adjective or pronoun that refers back to the noun: The
speaker, doctor, teacher, shook *her* head as *she* heard these
words.

It is now usual to treat animals as neuter, since the idea of
personality is not prominent and the idea of sex doesn't seem
important to us, but we not infrequently regard them as masculine, employing masculine pronouns and possessives without
regard to sex: The camel is inestimable for long desert journeys,
for *he* has strong powers of endurance. In contradistinction to
other animal life there is a tendency to regard birds as feminine, especially in case of *dove*, *sparrow*, *lark*, *thrush*, sometimes
other little animals and insects, as *mole*, *bee*, etc., but for the
most part the masculine prevails, if we do not choose to employ
the neuter. Of course, the feminine pronoun is used with reference to all kinds of animal life where the idea of a female
animal naturally suggests itself. Compare § 80.D.

The masculine pronouns and possessives are usually employed for persons without regard to sex wherever the antecedent has a general indefinite meaning and hence doesn't indicate
sex and the situation doesn't require an accurate discrimina-
tion: Everybody is to do just as *he* likes. Often, however, the
natural feeling here that *he* is one-sided prompts us to use both
he and *she*, *his* and *her*: Everybody spoke out plainly just as *he*
or *she* thought. Each of us must lead *his* or *her* own life. In
choice English, however, this accuracy is often quite out of place

211

since the idea of the oneness of man and woman is present to our feeling:

> Breathes there the *man* with soul so dead
> Who never to *himself* hath said,
> This is my own, my native land!

With reference to little children and small insects where the idea of personality is little developed we usually employ the neuter pronoun and the possessive adjective *its:* As soon as the baby saw her, *it* stretched out *its* arms to her. Something flew on to my neck and I soon felt *it* crawling downward. This *it*, thus closely associated with the idea of the lack of personality, is often used disparagingly of persons, similarly also *that:* Would you like to marry Malcolm? Fancy being owned by *that!* Fancy seeing *it* every day!

On the other hand, *it*, like the relative *which* (§ 80.D), is used to indicate estate, rank, dignity: She is a queen and looks *it*. Likewise *itself:* The Englishman in him at last asserted *itself*.

B. GENDER OF ANIMATION. In Old English, many nouns designating lifeless things were masculine or feminine. At this early period, gender did not, as now, rest upon the conception of sex, but often it depended upon the form and inflection of the noun, as in modern German. Not only nouns had gender but also adjectives, which always agreed with their governing noun in gender, number, and case. This agreement was a grammatical device to link the adjective to its governing noun. After the old inflection of noun and adjective with the distinctive endings for gender had disappeared, there was nothing in noun or adjective which could suggest the gender, when it was necessary for a pronoun to refer back to its antecedent. To avoid the confusion which naturally followed, the gender was regulated by the simple device of following the sex or sexlessness of the persons and things represented.

The new order of things, of course, did not come about all at once. The old habit of associating lifeless things with sex continued and in our playful moods with their animated feeling still has strong sway: That helps the blood to draw the wart and pretty soon off *she* comes (*Tom Sawyer*). You are provided

212

with the needful implement — a book, sir? — Bought *him* at a sale, said Boffin (*Our Mutual Friend*).

In colloquial speech, the use of animating gender is very capricious, but in the higher forms of literature certain rules are more or less observed: *the sun, the ocean, rivers, mountains, time, day, death, love, anger, discord, despair, war, murder, law, the vices,* etc., are masculine; *spring, nature, the soul, virtue, night, darkness, cities, countries, arts, sciences, liberty, charity, victory, mercy, religion, ships, the earth, world, moon,* are feminine. This gender does not — as most grammars and rhetorics falsely suppose — rest upon vivid personification, but is merely an animated form to serve as a contrast to the scientific precision of our normal expression, which treats as neuter all living and lifeless things which lack personality. The present literary gender of animation arose after the loss of our old grammatical gender, largely under the influence of Latin and French, which have grammatical gender.

<h3 style="text-align:center">SYNTAX OF PRONOUNS</h3>

96. Personal Pronouns (§ 28).

A. USE AND FORM. Important uses of the personal pronouns are described in §§ 51 and 63.B.3. The development of the forms of address is described in § 51.H.

B. AGREEMENT WITH ANTECEDENT. A personal pronoun as a mere substitute for a noun must agree with its antecedent in gender, number, and person wherever there is a distinctive form to indicate these conceptions; but, of course, it takes a case form in accordance with the grammatical function it performs in the proposition in which it stands: "Your sister borrowed my dictionary yesterday. I met *her* this morning and *she* gave *it* back to me."

Where a pronoun or possessive adjective refers to a word plural in meaning, but in form being an indefinite pronoun in the singular, or a singular noun modified by an indefinite limiting adjective, it was once common to indicate the plural idea by the form of the following pronoun or possessive adjective; but it is now usual to put the pronoun or possessive adjective into the singular in accord with the form of the antecedent: Nobody knows what it is to lose a friend *until he has lost him* (formerly also *until they have lost him*). Everybody is discontented with *his* (formerly also *their*) lot in life. If the part deserves any comment, every considering Christian will make it *himself* (formerly also *themselves*).

Remarks on gender bearing upon the proper use of personal pronouns are given in § 95.A.3.

97. Reflexive Pronouns. The normal forms are given in § 9.B. Instead of these long forms the personal pronouns were often used in older English as reflexive pronouns. This older usage is still the rule after prepositions which express local relations in a literal sense: I have no money with *me*. We see the stars above *us*. "Look about *you!*", but in a figurative sense "Look into *yourself*."

The old short form is still much used in colloquial speech in the first and second persons when employed in the dative relation: I bought *me* (or *myself*) a new hat. Did you buy *you* (or *yourself*) a new hat? We now always use the new long dative in the third person: He bought *himself* a new hat. The short form *him* here is now always felt as a personal pronoun referring to someone other than the subject.

In crisp business style the long forms *himself, herself*, etc. are often contracted to *self:* a ticket admitting *self* and friend Especially in the headings of newspapers: G. W. Howard. Author, Kills *Self* (*Chicago Tribune*, Nov. 21, 1922).

The reflexive *oneself* or *one's self* corresponds to the subject *one*, while *himself* corresponds to *no one, someone, everyone, anyone:* "One cannot interest *oneself* (or *one's self*) in everything," but "No one can interest *himself* in everything." Many often still, however, employ here *himself* instead of *oneself* or *one's self*, as in older English: One might fall and hurt *himself*.

98. Reciprocal Pronouns (§ 9.C). *Each other* and *one another* are often used without any differentiation, but there is a tendency to employ *each other* for reference to two and *one another* for reference to more than two: These two doctors hate *each other*. We at last all understand *one another*.

In older English, the long reflexive pronouns (§ 9.B) were

sometimes used as reciprocal pronouns: The older usage still occurs after the prepositions *among* and *between:* They quarreled *among themselves*, but with *one another*. They resolved *between themselves* to start immediately.

99. Relative Pronouns (§ 9.D.1–2).

Relatives with an antecedent are treated in considerable detail under the head of Relative Clause, § 80.

Indefinite and general relatives (§ 9.D.2) are treated under the head of Subject Clause in § 77, Predicate Clause in § 78, Attributive Substantive Clause in § 79, Dative Clause in § 81, Accusative Clause after Verbs in § 82, Accusative Clause after Prepositions (Prepositional Clause) in § 83.

100. Interrogative Pronouns (§§ 9.F; 33). These pronouns are not only used in direct questions, as illustrated in § 9.F, but often also in indirect questions in substantive clauses, namely subject clause (§ 77), attributive substantive clause (§ 79), accusative clause (§ 82.A). Illustrative sentences are given in the articles referred to in parentheses.

101. Indefinite Pronouns. The nominative, genitive, dative, accusative referring to *one* are now usually *one, one's, one, one* or for reflexive function *oneself* or *one's self*, but the older forms *he, his, him* or *himself* still occur: *One* never realizes *one's* (sometimes *his*) blessings while *one* (sometimes *he*) enjoys them. In life *one* notices only what interests *one* (sometimes *him*). *One* ought not to praise *oneself* or *one's self* (sometimes *himself*). But *he, his, him, himself* correspond to *no one, someone, somebody, anyone, anybody, everyone, everybody*. If *someone*, or *anyone*, loses *his* purse, let *him* apply to the Lost Property Office. *Everybody* should look out for *himself*.

SYNTAX OF ADJECTIVES

102. Functions. Adjectives can be used predicatively, attributively, appositively, and substantively. Some adjectives can also be used as nouns. Certain limiting adjectives are employed as pronouns. The nominative predicate is described in §§ 53.B; 54.B; 73.A,B, the objective predicate in § 67.C.1.

the attributive adjective in § 56.A, the predicate appositive adjective in § 53.C, the adjective in substantive function in § 103, the adjective used as a noun in § 108. The employment of the substantive forms of certain limiting adjectives as pronouns is described in §§ 9.G and 34.

103. Substantive Form of Adjectives. In the attributive and predicate relations the descriptive (§ 11) adjective has lost its inflection entirely, as described in § 35. The older inflection was intended to link the adjective to the governing noun. We now feel that the position of the attributive adjective immediately before or after the noun, as in "a *heavy* burden" or "a burden *hard* to bear," indicates that it belongs to its governing noun.

On the other hand, there is still in the case of certain attributive limiting (§ 11) adjectives something in the form or the meaning of the adjective to indicate a relation to its governing noun: *this* book, *these* books; *that* book, *those* books. *This* and *that* are the only attributive limiting adjectives that thus indicate the plural idea by their form and stand in formal agreement with their governing noun. But many limiting adjectives can indicate the plural idea by their meaning and thus stand in logical agreement with their governing noun: *two* books, *three* books, *many* books, etc. Other limiting adjectives, however, have nothing in form or meaning to indicate the plural: *the* books upon the table, *my* books, *any* books, etc. We have come to feel here, as in the case of descriptive adjectives, that the position before the governing noun is sufficient to indicate that they limit it. Position is a powerful factor in English.

The case is quite different, however, when adjectives stand in the substantive relation, i.e. when they are separated from their governing noun: My brother bought a *white sheep* and I bought a *black one*. My brother bought *two white sheep* and I bought *two black ones*. Here we need something to link the adjective to the governing noun. After the loss of our adjective endings it became necessary in the substantive relation to insert *one* or *ones* after the descriptive adjective, as described more fully in § 35. In the superlative and comparative, *one* is not so thoroughly established (§ 104.C).

216

On the other hand, *one* or *ones* is not employed in the substantive relation so uniformly with limiting (§§ 11; 13) adjectives, since there is often here something in the form, or meaning, or situation which suggests the grammatical relations. We here follow our feeling a good deal, inserting *one* where it seems helpful to the sense, leaving it out where the connection makes the meaning clear: *every one* of these books; *either*, or *either one*, of these two books; *neither*, or *neither one*, of these two books; *either*, *either one*, or more accurately *any one*, of these three books; *either*, *either one*, or much more commonly *any one*, of these twelve books; *each*, or *each one*, of the books I hold in my hand. *Which*, or *which one*, of these books is yours? *Which* of these books are yours? "I do not know *which* (or *which one*) of the books is best," but "*which of* the books are best." "I do not know *which* (or *which one*) of the books I like best," but for reference to more than one the form "*which of the books* I like best" is not clear. We cannot say here "*which ones of the books* I like best." We must say either "*Of these books* I do not know *which ones* I like best," or more simply leaving it to the situation to make the thought clear: I do not know *which ones* I like best.

We avoid the use of *one* where the reference is to something abstract or to an indefinite mass, since *one* from its origin has been associated with the idea of a concrete whole, unit, with definite outlines: "His hat was *the same*, or *the same one*, he wore yesterday," but always "His condition remains *the same*" and "I don't want *any* of your nonsense."

We do not feel it necessary to use *one* where the limiting adjective has a plural form or meaning, since we feel the form or the meaning as a link binding adjective and plural noun together: "this book and *that one* on the table," but "these books and *those* on the table; these books and *the three* on the table."

There are a few special substantive forms:

A. Substantive Forms of "One," "No." *One* is used attributively or substantively without change of form: I have only *one* apple. "How many apples have you? I have only *one*."

The negative of *one* is *no*. Its substantive form is *none*: "Lend me your pencil" — "I have *none*," or "I haven't *any*." "*None* of the books *is*, or *are*, fit to read," usually here with plural meaning and verb, whereas we usually say "*Not óne* of the books is fit to read" with reference to one. *Not óne* is more emphatic than *none*. *Not a one*, *néver a one*, are much used in colloquial speech for emphatic *not óne, néver one:*

> I have received no letters, no, *not a óne.*

> I have sung many songs,
> But *néver a one* so gay.
> — Tennyson, *Poet's Song.*

1. *The One, the Ones*, are much used as determinatives, pointing to a following phrase or clause, with much the same force as *that* except that they can only point to definite individuals, persons or things: this butter and *that* (not *the one*) I bought yesterday; this book and *that one*, or *the one*, upon the table; these books and *those*, or *the ones*, upon the table.

B. SUBSTANTIVE FORMS OF "OTHER." The form remains unchanged in the singular and in the plural takes -*s*, or in accordance with older usage sometimes remains unchanged, especially when followed by the word to which it refers: this book and *the other*, *another*, or *one other;* this book and *the others*, *two others;* these books and *no others; many others*, or sometimes *many other*, of the men and women I met last night.

Other is often used in the predicate as a pure predicate; hence it here, as predicative adjectives in general, remains unchanged: These precepts lighted her to conclusions which were quite *other* than those at which he had arrived himself. I would not have boys *other* (objective predicate) than they are.

C. SUBSTANTIVE FORMS OF POSSESSIVE ADJECTIVES. The substantive forms of the possessive adjectives *my, thy, our, your, his, her, its* (in older English *his* or *it*), and *their* are: *mine, thine, ours, yours, his, hers, its*, two forms, *his* and *its*, remaining unchanged in substantive function.

EXAMPLES:

"*My* wheel is new," but "John's wheel is older than *mine*."

"This is *our* house," but "His house is not so near the school as *ours*."

"*His* wheel is new" and "My wheel is older than *his*."

"The baby has lost *its* rattle" and "The children's health is poor except the baby's and *its* is perfect."

These distinctions of form and function are of comparatively recent date. In older English, *mine* and *thine* are used attributively before a vowel: *mine* arm (Psalms, 89.21).

These forms were originally the genitives of the personal pronouns, *I*, *you*, etc., and their former force can often still be felt. Compare § 57.C.4. In the case of the double (§ 57.A.3) genitive the form is still always a genitive: that patient wife *of yours*. In the predicate where the subject is not a noun but an indefinite pronoun, the form can be only the genitive of the pronoun: I don't want what is *yours* or anybody else's. Where a noun is subject, the predicate may be regarded either as a substantive adjective form or the genitive of a personal pronoun: This hat is *mine*. But in such a sentence as "*Yours* is the greater treason, for *yours* is the treason of friendship" *yours* cannot possibly be construed as the genitive of the pronoun, for it is the subject of the sentence. The fact that we cannot supply a noun after *yours*, *mine*, *hers*, etc. shows plainly that the old possessive genitive in all these cases has become a substantive adjective form. Likewise the possessive genitive of any noun or pronoun which, unaccompanied by a governing noun, points backward or forward to a preceding or following governing noun becomes a substantive possessive adjective, for we do not now place here a noun immediately after it: My hand is larger than *John's*. *Mary's* is a sad fate. But to emphasize the idea of legitimate ownership we put stressed *own* after the short possessive adjective and the genitive of a noun or pronoun: I write with *my own* pen. The pen is *my own*. It is *John's own* pen. It is best to be *one's own* master.

1. *His One.* In modern British English *one* is sometimes used also here in the substantive relation: Leaning back in *his one* of the two Chippendale armchairs in which he sat (Juliana Ewing, *Jackanapes*).

104. Comparison of Adjectives.

A. Degrees. There are three degrees — the positive, the comparative, the superlative. The positive is the simple form of the adjective: a *strong* man. The comparative indicates that the quality is found in the person or thing described in a higher degree than in some other person or thing: the *stronger* of the two men. This tree is *taller* than that. The superlative indicates often that the quality is found in the highest degree in the person or thing described: Mt. Everest is the *highest* mountain in the world. Often, however, the superlative is used in a relative sense, indicating that of the persons or things compared a certain person or thing possesses the quality in the highest degree; which need not be a very high, or the highest degree: John is the *strongest* of these boys.

In general, comparison is characteristic of descriptive adjectives, the comparative and the superlative indicating different degrees of a quality. But a number of limiting adjectives are compared. Here the comparative and the superlative do not indicate different degrees, but point out different individuals: his *former* secretary, the *last* chapter, the *topmost* round, the *southernmost* island of the group.

B. RELATIVE COMPARISON. There are two quite different types of inflection employed in comparing English adjectives — the terminational and the analytic.

1. *Terminational Type of Comparison.* In this type we add to the positive -*er* to form the comparative and -*est* to form the superlative: strong, strong*er*, strong*est*. This way of comparing adjectives was universal in Old English, but it is now confined to words of one syllable and a large number of words of two syllables, especially those in -*er*, -*le*, -*y*, -*ow*, -*some*, such as *tender, bitter, able, idle, holy, narrow, handsome.* Some adjectives which are accented on the last syllable follow this type, as *absurd, remote.* Also others that cannot be easily described, such as *pleasant, cruel, quiet,* etc. But exceptions to these rules occur, such as *eager, proper, docile, fertile, hostile, content, abject, adverse,* etc., which take *more* before them in the comparative and *most* in the superlative. In older English, however, the terminational type was not confined to words with the endings enumerated above, but was often employed where we now use *more* and *most: woefullest* (Shakespeare), *powerfullest* (Milton).

Some adjectives which take -er and -est may also take *more* and *most*, the simple form before the noun with classifying force (§ 56.B), the form with *more* and *most* after the noun with descriptive force (§ 56.B): "There never was a *kinder* and *juster* man" (classifying), but "There never was a man *more kind* and *just*" (descriptive). The simple superlative is the favorite in the position before the noun in emphatic or excited language: It is the *stupidest* nonsense! Our baby is the *blessedest* (§ 42.A.1) little bundle of sunshine Heaven ever sent into this world! Often the choice between the old and the new type depends merely upon the agreeableness of sound, so that there is much variation in expression here.

a. Rules for Spelling when Adding the Ending: (1) Drop *e:* larg*e*, larg*er*, larg*est*. (2) Change *y* to *i* if a consonant precedes, but retain the *y* if a vowel precedes: dr*y*, dr*ier*, dr*iest*, but gray, gray*er*, gray*est*. (3) In monosyllabic words double the final consonant after a short vowel: hot, ho*tter*, ho*ttest*.

2. *Analytic Type of Comparison.* Here we put *more* before the comparative and *most* before the superlative: *beautiful*, *more beautiful*, *most beautiful*. Adjectives and participles with more than two syllables regularly follow this type, also many words with two syllables, especially those in -*full* and -*ish*, and all participles in -*ed* and -*ing:* intrusi*ve;* use*ful*, child*ish*, strain*ed*, charm*ing*. Other parts of speech used as adjectives always take *more* and *most:* John is *more in debt* than I am. Though the youngest among them, she was *more woman* than they. Where we feel a noun more as a noun than as an adjective we say: Charles was *more of a gentleman* than a king and *more of a wit* than a gentleman.

a. Advantages of the Analytic Type. In the old terminational form the sign of the degree is intimately associated with the stem, so that it is a mere suffix and can never be stressed. On the other hand, in the analytic form the sign of the degree, *more* and *most*, is still an independent word and is often stressed. There are here two parts, one indicating the degree, the other the meaning. We are fond of using the analytic form since by means of it we can better shade our thought. We stress the adjective when we desire to emphasize the meaning, but stress the *more* or *most* when we desire to emphasize the idea of degree: "She is much more pléasant than her sister," but "She is indeed pléasant, but her sister is still móre pleasant."

b. Analytic Form to Express the Degrees of Inferiority. Here we put *less* before the positive to form the comparative and *least* to form the superlative: wise, less wise, least wise.

c. Two Qualities of One Person or Thing Compared. In comparing two qualities of one person or thing we usually employ *more:* She is *more proud* than *vain.* However, in the case of a few monosyllabics, *long, wide, thick, high,* we still regularly employ the old simple comparative, usually with full clause form in the subordinate clause: The wall was in some places *thicker* than it was high.

C. Different Form for Different Function. All degrees of the adjective usually have a different form in substantive (§ 103) function: "This is a much *more beautiful* day than yesterday," but "This is a beautiful day. A *more beautiful one* I have never seen." The *one* is not quite necessary in the comparative and the superlative since the comparative or the superlative sometimes of itself indicates a relation to a governing noun: John, *the older* of the two brothers; Mary, *the quietest* of the sisters.

The pure predicate adjective never takes a *one,* but there is often in the predicate a substantive form, so that the *one*-forms often occur in the predicate: "This line is *longer* (predicate) than that," but "This line is *the longer* (substantive form) of the two." "The lake is *deepest* (predicate) at this point," but "This lake is *the deepest,*" or "*the deepest one*" (substantive forms).

Instead of the simple predicate superlative the adverbial accusative (§ 68.B) of the noun (§ 108) made from the adjective superlative preceded by the definite article is sometimes used here: The rooks (Old World crows) settle where the trees are *the finest* (Lytton), instead of the usual *finest.* It was, perhaps, at this time that Mrs. Henry and I were *the móst uneasy* in mind (R. L. Stevenson), instead of the usual *móst uneasy.* As described in § 69.A.2, this form is sometimes used with verbs as the superlative of the adverb; hence it is also used here in the predicate, just as adverbs in general are often used in the predicate (§ 54.F). The preposition *at* is often placed before the adjective noun here: Things, however, were not yet *at the worst* (Macaulay). People are never *at their best* in a crowd (Sarah Grand).

D. ABSOLUTE SUPERLATIVE AND ABSOLUTE COMPARATIVE.

1. *Absolute Superlative.* This form expresses superiority in an absolute sense, indicating a very high degree in and of itself, not necessarily however the very highest. In lively style we here often place unstressed *most* before the stressed positive of the adjective or participle: "It is the *móst lovely* (relative superlative) of the flowers in the garden," but "He has *the most béautiful* (absolute superlative) of gardens." We shall soon see George and his *most béautiful* wife.

Instead of the absolute superlative with *most* we sometimes in the case of adjectives which admit of the terminational form employ the simple superlative, sometimes drawling it out and stressing it: Oh, he made the *rú-dest* remark. I am in the *best* of health. A stronger lens reveals to you certain *tiniest* hairlets. (G. Eliot). Our friendship ripened into *closest* intimacy. My *dearest* boy (address of a mother to her son in a letter).

The most common way to express the absolute superlative is to place *very, exceedingly, highly, absolutely*, etc. before the positive: very cold weather, an exceedingly intricate problem, a highly polished society. Compare § 69.B.*a*.

2. *Absolute Comparative.* The absolute comparative is not so common as the absolute superlative: the lower classes, the higher classes, higher education, the more complex problems of life. We usually employ an adverb here: a tolerably (or fairly or rather) long walk, somewhat talkative, etc.

E. COMPARISON OF COMPOUNDS. Here we compare the first element of the compound where this is possible, but if the first element is a word not capable of comparison we employ *more* or *most*: "the *biggest-chested* and *longest-armed* man I ever saw," but "This is the *most up-to-date* book I know." Even if the first element is capable of comparison, we employ *more* or *most* if the first element has fused with the other elements so closely that it is not felt as a separate element with a separate function: "*well*-known," "*better*-known," but "the *more* well-to-do tradesmen."

F. IRREGULAR COMPARISON.

Positive	Comparative	Superlative
bad } ill }	worse	worst
east, eastern	more eastern	easternmost
far	farther, further	farthest, furthest
fore	former	foremost, first
good } well }	better	best
hind	hinder	hindmost, hindermost
	inner	inmost, innermost
late	later, latter	latest, last
little	less, lesser	least
much, many	more	most
nigh	nigher	nighest, next
north		northmost
northern	more northern	northernmost
old	older, elder	oldest, eldest
	outer	outmost, outermost
south		southmost
southern	more southern	southernmost
top		topmost
	upper	uppermost, upmost
	utter	utmost, uttermost
west, western	more western	westernmost

In a few cases the variant forms indicate a differentiation of meaning or function. The usual comparative and superlative of *old* are *older, oldest,* always so in the predicate relation, but we may use *elder, eldest* in the attributive and the substantive (§ 103) relation and *elder* as a noun, especially of relationship and rank: the elder brother, the elder Pitt, I am the elder, He is my elder in service, the eldest brother, etc. He is an *elder* in the church.

We use *farther* and *further* with the same local and temporal meaning, but *further* has also the meanings, *additional, more extended, more:* The cabin stands on the *farther,* or *further,* side of the brook. I shall be back in three days at the *farthest*, or at the *furthest*. But: *further* details, without *further* litigation. After a *further* search I found her. Have you anything *further* (= *more*) to say? In adverbial use *farther* and *further* are used indiscriminately: You may go *farther*, or *further*, and fare worse.

Later and *latter* are now clearly differentiated in meaning.

The double comparative *lesser* replaces *less* in attributive and substantive function in certain expressions, especially with reference to concrete things: in *lesser* things, the *lesser* grammarians, the *lesser* of the two evils; but *less* with more abstract reference, as in "*less* degree," "at a *less* depth," also to express amount, quantity, and in adverbial use, as in "He works *less* than I."

The terminations in some of these forms, as in *innermost*, *outermost*, express the degree two or three times instead of once (G below).

G. PLEONASM AND EXCESS OF EXPRESSION IN COMPARISON. We have double comparison in *lesser*. Double comparison was not infrequent in older English: the *most boldest* and best hearts of Rome (Shakespeare, *Julius Caesar*, III, i, 120). This older usage survives in popular speech: *worser*, etc.

We no longer feel the double comparison in *near* (comparative of *nigh*, but now felt as a positive with regular comparison, *near*, *nearer*, *nearest*) and forms in -*most*, as in *foremost*, etc. This -*most*, now confounded with *most*, but in older English with the form -*mest*, consists of the two superlative suffixes -*m* and -*est*. In *hindermost*, *innermost*, *outermost* there is a comparative + the two superlative suffixes -*m* and -*est*.

While we today in general avoid pleonastic comparison, we do not feel such forms as *more perfect*, *most perfect*, *deader*, *deadest*, *more unique*, etc. as pleonastic, since we have in mind degrees of approach to something perfect, dead, or unique.

Somewhat similar to the pleonasm of older English was its excess of expression in using the superlative of two, which still survives in colloquial and popular speech, as in "the *smallest* of the two." We all say, "Put your *best* foot foremost."

105. Intensifying Adjectives. These limiting adjectives (§ 13.B), *myself*, *yourself*, *herself*, etc., never have a change of form. They serve as appositives to the noun or pronoun to which they refer: I *myself* think so, or I think so *myself*. We think we have hinted elsewhere that Mr. Benjamin Allen had a way of becoming sentimental after brandy. The case is not a peculiar one, as *we ourself* (= *I myself*) can testify (Dickens, *Pickwick Papers*). *We ourselves* think so. *Himself* an artist in rhetoric, he (Thoreau) confounds thought with style when he attempts to speak of the latter (J. R. Lowell).

As the intensifying adjective often emphasizes a personal pronoun or the indefinite pronoun *oneself* and is thus closely associated with it, it has gradually acquired the function of a pronoun in addition to its own, so that since the eleventh century the pronoun in certain categories drops out as useless and the intensifying adjective itself becomes a pronoun. It can perform this new function without endangering the thought since it can express person, number, and gender as accurately as the pronoun. It is most commonly thus used in the subject relation at the end of the sentence, introducing an abridged subordinate clause with the finite verb omitted: He saw that his antagonist was as strong as [he] *himself* [was]. Quite often also at the end of an independent proposition for emphasis: The poor boy of whom I have just related was [I] *myself*. It often serves as predicate: You are not [you] *yourself* today. One is not always [one] *oneself* (or *one's self*). We also say, "You can't do that *by yourself*." It occasionally occurs elsewhere: I am a stranger here *like yourself*.

This construction was once a favorite, but the simple personal pronoun now frequently seems more natural. The old heavy forms are entirely out of place where there is no emphasis whatever: There's only *myself* and Louisa here (H. Walpole), instead of "There are only Louisa and *I* here." Smith, Jones, and *myself* (instead of *I*) are the members of the committee.

a) The old simple form *self*, once in use where we now employ compounds, *myself*, etc., survives as a noun: love of *self*. I hope you are your old *self* again. He cares for nothing but his own precious *self*.

106. The Definite Article. The definite article is the weakened form of an old demonstrative adjective now represented by *that*.

A. Use. As a demonstrative it has a twofold function:

1. *Anaphoric* "*The*," pointing backward to a person or thing already mentioned: "There lived once in this old castle a powerful king. *The* king had a lovely daughter."

2. *Determinative* "*The*," pointing to a definite person or thing described usually by a following genitive, adverb, prepositional phrase, or relative clause: *The* hat of my brother, *the* tree yonder, *the* hat on the table, *the* hat which I hold in my hand. Determinative *the* has the following particular uses:

a. The modifier of the noun after *the* is often lacking because the person or thing in question is single in kind, hence needs no description: *the* King, *the* Queen, *the* Lord, *the* Savior, *the* Mayor, *the* schoolhouse (where there is only one in a town), *the* bridge (where there is only one), *the* Alps, *the* Hudson, etc. Outside of such cases of evident uniqueness we stress the *the* and put a short description after the noun: He is *thé* pianist of the day. That is *thé* hotel of the city.

b. The definite article often has generalizing force, i.e. the representative idea becomes more prominent than the conception of a sharp individualization, one individual representing the whole class: "*The* rat is larger than *the* mouse," or also "*A* rat is larger than *a* mouse." He is a lover of *the* beautiful. We sometimes still employ here the older style of individualization and generalization, i.e. the simple noun without an article: *Man* is mortal. *Woman* is frail.

The noun here often acquires abstract force, indicating the quality or trait that characterizes the class: He felt *the* patriot rise within his breast. *The* Englishman within him asserted itself. He acted *the* lord wherever he went.

c. *The* before a proper noun often gives it the force of a common noun: He is *the* Demosthenes (= finest orator) of our class. He is *the* Shakespeare of our time.

d. *The* has a different meaning according as it is repeated or dropped (§ 56.D).

e. *The* sometimes has adverbial force (§ 68.B).

227

B. OMISSION. A simple noun without the definite article has three quite different meanings:

1. The simple noun without the definite article is the old style of individualization, indicating something single in kind: *God, John, Mary, Milton, gold, silver, honesty, patience, gout, goodness, rheumatism, Shakespeare, London, New York, Mt. Everest, Lake Michigan,* etc.

As mentioned in A.2.b above, this form is also used for generalization: *Man* is mortal.

The old style of individualization still competes with the new style with the definite article described in A.2.a above so that usage is very uneven here: *God,* but *the Savior; Mars* (planet), but *the moon; Parliament, Congress* or *the Congress,* but *the House, the Senate; dropsy,* but *the measles* or simple *measles;* in formal style "the late Mr. Johnson," "the elder Pliny," but in familiar tone "poor Tom," "little Tom."

2. The absence of the definite article is often felt as a contrast to its presence and hence indicates an indefinite portion, amount, or extent: "*the* dust on the veranda," but in an indefinite sense "In these dry days we see *dust* everywhere."

3. A noun is often without the article when the noun does not denote a definite individual but something abstract, such as an estate, rank, relationship, calling, or capacity of any kind: He turned *traitor.* He fell *heir* to a large estate. Mr. Boyd is *Irishman* first, *critic* next. He is doing all that *mortal man* can do. Fully a century has passed since *mason's* hand has touched this building.

107. Form and Use of Indefinite Article. The indefinite article *a* or *an,* the reduced form of the numeral *one,* has preserved the *n* of the original word only before a vowel sound: *a* boat, *a* house, *a* union (yūnyŭn), not *a* one (wun); but *an* heir (with silent *h*), *an* apple, etc. There is a fluctuation of usage before a pronounced initial *h* wherever the syllable is unaccented. As the syllable is unstressed and the sound of the *h* not so distinct as in a stressed syllable, it is, often, especially in England proper, treated as a silent *h,* so that *an* is used before it: *an* historic character, *an* hotel, etc. In America, however, educated people pronounce the *h* also here distinctly and hence for the most part use *a* in accordance with the general rule, although some follow the English usage. As *h* was perhaps less strongly pronounced in older English than now, *an* was often used before *h* in accented syllables: *an* hundred crown (Shakespeare), *an* house (Matthew, V.14).

The indefinite article *a*, true to its origin, singles out one object, action, or quality from among a number. It designates an individual in different ways:

1) It points to an individual person or thing without fixing its identity: We met *an* old man on our way here. There is *a* book lying on the table.

2) In its more indefinite sense *a* is equal to *any*, designating no individual in particular: There isn't *a* man in our community in whom I have more confidence.

3) Like *the*, it often has generalizing force (§ 106.A.2.b).

4) It is often used as a determinative (§ 106.A.2) with the force of *such:* It was *a* sight that would make angels rejoice. He is *a* man that must be treated kindly.

5) Often with its original meaning: *a* (i.e. *one*) foot long.

6) It sometimes represents older *on*, hence is the reduced form of a preposition. This *a* occurs in adverbial expressions denoting repetition: He goes to the city several times *a* year.

7) It can stand before a proper name in only two cases: (1) to designate one member of a family: There isn't *a* single Jones in our village although it once seemed full of them; (2) to convert a proper noun into a common noun: He is *a* regular Hercules.

108. Descriptive Adjectives Used as Nouns. We must now say "the good *man*," "the good *woman*," "the good *thing*," "good *people*." Formerly it was possible to use the simple adjective here, since it had endings to express gender and number. There are still a large number of survivals of this older usage. The endings, of course, are gone, but the simple forms survive.

The situation alone now makes the meaning clear, so that they cannot be freely used. We now usually feel them as plurals but among them are a few singulars. Singulars: the deceased, the dear departed, the accused, the condemned, my intended, a lover clasping his *fairest*, my dearest (in direct address); especially neuters: the beautiful, the impossible, the genuinely (adverb) *lovable*. He is doing his *best*. Sometimes without a limiting adjective: There is *worse* ahead. Kindly *meant* is kindly taken. Especially in set expressions, with and without a limiting adjective: to go to *the bad*, to keep to *the right*, to go from *bad* to *worse*, etc.

Plurals: the rich, the poor, the really (adverb) poor; the seriously (adverb) wounded; a host of *workless* walking the streets; big and little, etc. These plurals usually have general or indefinite force and are differentiated in meaning from the new plurals: "the *poor* of our city," but "the two *poor men* entering the gate"; "the state of *the heathen* and their hope of salvation," but "Smith and Jones are regular *heathens*."

The terse simple forms have so appealed to English feeling that a large number of them have been retained and converted into regular nouns with regular inflection in singular and plural: a savage, *gen.* a savage's, *pl.* the savages. Similarly: *native, equal, superior, male, three-year-old, grown-up, Christian, German, Italian, American, daily* (paper), *weekly*, etc.

The old endingless plural, however, has become established in the case of foreign adjectives in *-ese* and the adjectives *Swiss* and *Iroquois: the Portuguese, Japanese, Chinese*, etc.; *the Swiss, the Iroquois*. We sometimes use the same form for the singular, just as we use "the deceased" for the singular, but we avoid these singulars since we feel these forms as plurals, and prefer to say "a Portuguese gentleman, lady," etc. In *Chinaman*, pl. *Chinamen* or *Chinese* we have, for singular and plural, forms that may become established. We also say *the English, the French*, or *Englishmen, Frenchmen*, but in the singular only *Englishman, Frenchman*.

Nouns made from adjectives may drop the article in a generalizing sense, just as nouns may drop it here, as in "*Man* is mortal": Sweet *seventeen* is given to day-dreams. Eleven years *old* does this sort of thing easily. *Slow and steady* wins the race.

SYNTAX OF VERBS

Voice

The voices — active and passive — have already been described in § 36 and in §§ 44–45. Here follows additional treatment.

109. Active Voice. A marked peculiarity of our language is the freedom with which a transitive (§ 15.A) verb is used without an object with reflexive (§ 15.A), intransitive (§ 15.B), or passive force: Mary *dresses* (with reflexive force) plainly. Her eyes *filled* (transitive used intransitively) with tears. The steam *is condensing* (active form with passive meaning = *is being condensed*).

In the case of many reflexive verbs where the subject plainly acts upon himself, the idea of a person acting on himself is often overshadowed by that of action pure and simple, so that we often drop the reflexive pronoun: "She *dressed herself* (or simply *dressed*) with care." Similarly, *behave*, *hide*, *wash*, *bathe*, etc. may be used reflexively or intransitively. Shakespeare said "He *basked him* in the sun," while we now say "He *basked* in the sun." Thus there has long been a trend from reflexive to intransitive form. In many cases we can now use only intransitive form, although the subject plainly acts upon himself: He *turned* around. He *pushed* forward.

The list of intransitives has increased from another source. Reflexive verbs were once common, and are sometimes still used, where the reference is to spontaneous action of any kind which seems to proceed of itself acting as it were on itself: The vine is *twining itself*, or simply *twining*, around the tree. A sweet smile *spread itself*, or more commonly *spread*, over his face. We now usually employ intransitive form here since the idea of action pure and simple is prominent in our mind: The door suddenly *opened*. Her eyes *filled* with tears. The wind *has turned*.

In this last group of intransitives there has in many cases a further development taken place. Since these intransitives represent something as naturally developing into a new state, or as entering a new state accidentally or as having the power or fitness to enter it, consequently as affected, or as capable of being affected, they acquire passive force, so that now passive force is often associated with intransitive form: Muscles, nerves, mind, reason, all *develop* (= *are developed*) under play. This cloth *feels* (= *is felt as being*) soft. The first consignment *sold out* (= *was sold out*) in a week. My hat *blew* (= *was blown*) into the river. Ripe oranges *peel* (= *can be peeled*) easily. These colors *do not wash* (= *cannot be washed*) well. This play *reads* better than it *acts* (= *should be read rather than acted*, or *is more adapted to reading than to acting*).

a) Causatives. From the above account it is evident that there is in English no sharp distinction in form between transitive and intransitive function. In older English, however, the two functions were often distinguished by their form. There are a few survivals of this old usage. There is in a few cases an intransitive verb alongside of a transitive with a little different form, a causative, i.e. a verb which indicates that somebody causes, brings about an action: "The tree *falls*" (intransitive), but "The woodman *fells* (causative) the tree," i.e. *makes* it *fall*. "John *is sitting* on the sofa," but "John *sets* his watch on the table." "The baby *is lying* on the bed," but "The mother *is laying* the baby on the bed." But we here as elsewhere usually employ the same form for both functions so far as a simple verb is used here: "The kite *flies*" and "The boy *flies* the kite." In most cases, however, the causative idea is now expressed by placing the auxiliary *make*, *have*, or *get* before the infinitive of the verb in question: I am trying to *make* both ends *meet*. Money *makes* the mare *go*. That hat *makes* you *look* miserable. I *made* him *take* it back. He will soon *have* his tailor *make* him a new suit, or He will soon *get* his tailor *to make* him a new suit. The passive form of the infinitive after *have* and *get* is always elliptical: He will *have* (or *get*) a new suit [to be] *made*. This peculiar construction after *have* and *get* is often used to express an entirely different idea — a suffering or experiencing something: I have often *had* gypsies *steal* my chickens. I *had* (or *got*) my right leg *hurt* in the accident.

In this construction a change of accent brings quite a difference of meaning: "They *háve* (or *gét*) their work *done*" (they employ other people to do their work), but "They have their work dóne" (their work is done) and "They get things dóne" (they accomplish a good deal).

110. Passive Voice. The forms of the passive and their use are presented in §§ 36.C.1, 2, 3 and 45.A,B.

The ways of changing a sentence from active to passive form are given in §§ 63.C; 67.A.1, B,C.1.a.i, b.i, D.1, E.1.

PROGRESSIVE PASSIVE. There are three progressive passive forms. They are described in §§ 36.C.4 and 45.B. Earlier in the present period the three progressive forms were: The house *is being built*, *is in building* (gerund), or *is building* (present participle). The second form, *is in building*, was gradually replaced by the third form, *is building*, surviving however in popular speech in contracted form, *is a-building*. The third form, *is building*, was the favorite until about 1825, when it began to gradually retire from the competition with *is being built*. The reason for this development is evident. The present active participle had been gradually acquiring the peculiar passive force described in §109, expressing the idea of spontaneous action, of a natural development, unfolding: Our plans *are working out* successfully. Dust *is blowing in* at the window. These books *are selling out* fast. The idea of spontaneity, so prominent here, made it unfit to express progressive action under resistance, so that in this meaning *is being built* gradually became the normal form of expression.

The form *is being built*, however, has become established only in the present and the past tense: The house *is being built*, *was being built*. In the compound tenses it would be too unwieldy, so that it has here never come into use. The form with the present active participle with passive force is the only form used here: The house *has been building*, *had been building*, *will be building*, *will have been building*.

Mood

The moods have been described in § 37. In the following articles the subjunctive and the imperative will be treated more fully.

111. Classes of the Subjunctive. The uses of the subjunctive naturally fall into two classes: (1) the *optative* subjunctive,
which represents the utterance as something desired or
planned; (2) the *potential* subjunctive, which represents the
statement, not as an actual fact, but only as a conception of the
mind.

These two subjunctives will be explained and illustrated
below.

112. Use of the Tenses in the Subjunctive. The tenses
of the subjunctive have a meaning quite different from those
of the indicative. The past subjunctive rarely points to the
past. It refers to the present or the future as regularly as does
the present tense. The present and the past here differ only
in the *manner* of the statement: "I am hoping that he *may come*
this evening," but "I think he *might* possibly *come* this evening,
but I am not expecting him." The past subjunctive suggests
doubt, uncertainty, while the present subjunctive implies more
hope.

By clothing our thoughts and wishes in the language of doubt
and uncertainty by the use of the past subjunctive, we frequently avoid a blunt expression of our opinions and wishes.
On this account the past subjunctive often loses in large measure the element of doubt and uncertainty and is used to state
an opinion or a wish modestly, politely, or cautiously: The
matter *might,* I should think, *be left* to his judgment. You *might
call* (polite command) at the baker's and get some bread.

This difference of meaning between a present and a past
subjunctive, however, is entirely lost after a past indicative,
for according to our English sequence (§ 118) a present tense
must here be changed to the past tense: "I *am hoping* that he *may*
come this evening," but "I *was hoping* that he *might* come that
evening." Here *might* does not have the usual force of a past
subjunctive, for it is a present subjunctive that has been attracted into the form of the past tense after a past tense.

The difference of meaning between the present and the past
subjunctive, as described above, holds also for any compound
form or any group of verbal forms that contains a present or a
past subjunctive: He *may* have come, He *might* have come. The

perfect infinitive *have come* here refers the time to the past. This idea does not lie in the subjunctive forms *may* and *might*, which merely indicate the *manner* of the statement, the present tense *may* expressing more probability than the past tense *might*.

113. Subjunctive Form. The simple subjunctive forms are presented in full in §§ 41.A,B; 42.A.1,B; 44; 45. For the most part, the simple subjunctive is in ordinary language not distinguished from the indicative by its form. It has, however, a few distinctive forms. In the present tense the absence of an ending in the third person singular marks the form as a subjunctive: he take*s* (indic.), he take (subjunc.). The present tense of *be* distinguishes subjunctive and indicative throughout. In the past tense only one verb distinguishes subjunctive and indicative: I *was* (indic.), I *were* (subjunc.). The time, however, always distinguishes here the two moods. The past indicative points to the past, the past subjunctive to the present or the future: "He came" (past indic. because it points to the past), but "If he *came*, it would be too late" (past subjunc. because it points to the future).

In general, the simple subjunctive is lacking not only in distinctive form but also in meaning. It is a bit of older English not suited to either our practical or our scientific needs. Even in its palmiest days in the Old English period it was a poor instrument of thought. It then had fuller forms, but it lacked expressive power and a movement away from it had already set in. The tendency to replace it by modal auxiliaries had begun. This development has culminated in the rich store of modal auxiliaries described in § 41.B.4. These modal auxiliaries in connection with an infinitive perform the same functions as the old simple subjunctive, only more effectively and with finer shades of meaning.

The old simple subjunctive would look shabby alongside of the modern subjunctive with a modal auxiliary if it were not surrounded by a halo of poetry. Its extensive use in poetry along with the other heirlooms of the past has given it a touch of elevation and a charm to which we are all susceptible. In this field we have a profound respect for it, but it should not be recommended for practical use outside of higher diction. It is, for accurate expression, far inferior to our modern subjunctive.

In the following articles the old simple subjunctive and the modern subjunctive with a modal auxiliary are given side by side. In general, however, the old form should be considered a little choicer English, a form especially adapted to poetic or solemn language, but here and there it is still a part of our everyday speech as a survival of older usage.

114. Optative Subjunctive. The optative (§ 111) subjunctive is used in the following expressions of will·

A. In Principal Propositions:

1. *Volitive Subjunctive.* This form is used in decided expressions of will. The old simple volitive is still used in a few expressions: *Suffice* it to say that, etc. Everybody *stand* up! The literary works that have fascinated mankind abound in strokes of invention: *witness* Homer, Shakespeare, etc. = *let* Homer, Shakespeare *bear witness*. The first person plural form survives only in poetry: *Part* we in friendship from your land (Scott, *Marmion*).

We now usually employ the modern subjunctive form with *let* and an infinitive: "There is some one at the door who wants to see you." — "*Let* him *come in!*" "*Let* us *hurry!*"

To convey still stronger force we employ auxiliaries that contain more imperative meaning: He *must* go! We *múst* go! We *must* gó! You *shall* do as I say!

On the other hand, we employ different auxiliaries to impart a mild force to our expressions of will: "*Will* you sit down?" or "*Won't* you sit down?" both with mild force, but in "*Will* you children *be* quiet?" the words and the tone have the force of a command, so that the form should be interpreted as the future indicative, often used in commands as described in § 116.D.1. In the first person plural, *will* is much used as a mild command, a little stronger however than *let us:* "We'*ll* carry these (i.e. the bookshelves) longwise," Sabre (name) directed when the first one was tackled (Hutchinson, *If Winter Comes*).

A mild form of expression of will is found in permissions:

236

"You *may* (or *can*) go into the garden," but "You *may not* (or here in negative form more commonly *cannot*) eat the fruit." If, however, the word *may* is used in a question, *may* is natural here in a negative answer: "*May* I go now?" — "No, you *may* not." In negative form *must* is used to indicate that permission is withheld because it is not advisable or proper to do the thing in question: You *must* not go out into this wind. You *must* not say such things. In questions we use *may* or *can: May* (or *can*) I go now? *May* and *can* are used in mild commands: Johnny, you *may* (or *can*) run along home now. At present there is in the literary language a distinct trend toward *may* as expressing the idea of permission more clearly, even in negative forms: Now the dilemma is acute and settlement *may not* be deferred (editorial in *Chicago Tribune*).

According to § 112, a past tense form is used as a modest or polite volitive: You *should* go at once! We *should* go at once! *Would* you tell me the time, please? You *might* call at the baker's and get some bread. The past tense, however, sometimes becomes sharp and emphatic: You *should* mind your own business! You *might* offer to help me!

2. *Subjunctive of Wish.* The present subjunctive, the sanguine subjunctive of wish, is often used to express a wish which in all probability may be realized: God *bless* you! The Lord *have* mercy on us! Heaven *forbid!* [God] *Hang* it! [God] *Confound* you!

In general, the new subjunctive with *may* is now more common: *May* you see many happy returns of this occasion! *May* I never see such a sight again!

A past tense, the unreal subjunctive of wish, conveys the idea of unreality, indicating that fulfilment is not expected: O *were* he only here! O *had* I wings!

Modal auxiliaries are more common here: *Could* we only look forward in life and see as clearly as we do looking backward! *Might* I see her just once more!

The past tense often expresses a modest wish: *Might* this little book contribute something toward arousing an interest in our language! I *had* (or *would;* see § 123.G.3.a.v) as soon walk as ride. I *had* (or *would*) rather stay than go. I *would* rather go now. "He *would* rather go now," but "I *should* like to go now." "He *would* like to go now." With the verbs *like, prefer,* which of themselves contain the idea of a wish, we avoid the use of the auxiliary *would* in the first person since it would express the idea of wish twice; hence we employ the auxiliary *should,* which expresses here merely the subjunctive force. In the third person we employ *would* here since we do not feel it as an optative but merely as a subjunctive, observing the distinction between the first person on the one hand and the second and the third on the other as in the future tense of the indicative.

For reference to past time we employ the past perfect subjunctive, or in the case of modal auxiliaries use the perfect infinitive instead of the present: O *had* he only *been* here! O *might* I *have known* it in time!

3. *Subjunctive of Logical Reasoning.* In logical reasoning in laying down one or more desired propositions from which conclusions are to be drawn, the present tense of the simple subjunctive is now entirely replaced by *let* with the infinitive: *Let* the figure "abc" *be* an isosceles triangle and "bd" a perpendicular line on the base, etc.

B. IN SUBORDINATE CLAUSES. Here the subjunctive represents the act *as conceded* or *as desired:*

1. *Action Conceded.* Here the subjunctive is a mild volitive (A.1 above). It is often used in propositions which in a mere formal sense are independent but logically are dependent: *Say* [he] what he will, or *let* him *say* what he will, he cannot make matters worse. A number of other examples are given in § 90.C.1.a. Often also in clauses formally dependent: Though he *make* (or more commonly *may make*) every effort, he cannot succeed. However hard it *may rain* (or *rains,* if we desire to indicate that we are reckoning with this factor), we shall have to go.

The past tense conveys the idea of unreality: Even though he *were* here, I would say the same thing. However hard it *might* rain, we should have to go. The past tense here usually points to the present or the future. But there is in this category a past subjunctive of entirely different character, a past subjunctive that refers to the past. If a sentence in which a *present* subjunctive is used for present or future time be referred to the past, after a past indicative, the past subjunctive must be used: (with reference to the present) "Stewart is, perhaps, the most beloved member of Trinity, whether he *be* feeding rugger blues on plovers' eggs or keeping an early chapel with the expression of an earth-born seraph," but with reference to the past: "Stewart was, perhaps, the most beloved member of Trinity, whether he *were* feeding rugger blues on plovers' eggs or keeping an early chapel with the expression of an earth-born seraph" (Compton Mackenzie, *Sinister Street*, Ch.V). We more commonly employ the past indicative here since we feel that we are dealing with facts.

2. *Action Desired*. This is a large category with many subdivisions:

a. Substantive Clauses. In these clauses, which have the force of a noun clause in the object or subject relation, or in the attributive relation of an appositive, a prepositional phrase, or a genitive, the subjunctive expresses various shades of the volitive and the sanguine subjunctive described in A.1–2 above, with the same use of the tenses: She desires that he *do* (or *may do*) it, or with milder force, She begs that he *will* (consent to) do it, that I *will* do it. See to it that my boots *be* (or *shall be*) blacked, but more commonly *are blacked*, to indicate that we are counting on it. It is my ardent wish that he *come* (*may come*, or *shall come*) at once. The auxiliary *shall* here has stronger imperative force than the others: The committee presents the recommendation that each of these students *shall* report each week to the Dean.

A past tense, here as elsewhere, often conveys the idea of unreality: I wish I *were* dead! It often also is a modest expression of desire: I wish you *would* stay a little longer! Which would you rather *took* you over the crossing? I or Papa?

After a past indicative the distinction of meaning between the present and the past tense forms usually, according to § 112, disappears entirely: She desired that he *might* come at once. She demanded that action *should* be postponed, that they *should* take no action at present. There is, however, a strong and just tendency here at present to break through our rigid sequence

(§ 118) and employ the simple present subjunctive even after a past tense, since the simple present subjunctive with its implication of early or immediate execution has become associated with the expression of will in general without reference to the tense of the principal verb: I *desire, demand, suggest,* or *I desired, demanded, suggested,* that action *be* postponed, that they *take* no action at present.

b. Relative Clauses: Its interest to be paid to her if she's a spinster at thirty — which Heaven *forbid!* (Barker, *The Madras House*). Often in relative clauses of purpose: I desire only such books as *shall* instruct the children. Envoys were sent who *should* sue for peace. I am hunting a man who *may* take my place for a week. I desire something that *may* relieve my pain.

c. Adverbial Clauses. It is especially common in clauses of purpose: I'll go early that I *may* get a good seat. I went early that I *might* get a good seat. There is a tendency here to disregard the old sequence (§ 118) where the idea of present or future time is prominent: And lest she *disobey* (or *should disobey*), he left her (Amy Lowell, *Men, Women, and Ghosts,* p. 111). Compare § 91.A.

Clause of result: He is so badly hurt that he *shall* (or more modestly *should*) be taken to the hospital.

In temporal clauses after *until, till, when, whenever, before, against* (= *before*), *ere,* we employ in choice English the modern subjunctive with *shall,* in older English and in poetry also the simple subjunctive, to represent a future act, not as a fact, but only as the outcome of circumstances, the result of a development, or as planned, desired:

Is she going to keep a lonely vigil till that time *shall* come?

Your father is going to wait till your uncle *shall* come.

The most forward bud
Is eaten by the canker ere it *blow.*

— Shakespeare.

We more commonly employ the indicative here: When he *comes,* bring him into the room. I'll wait until he *comes.*

The subjunctive of wish is used in conditions and concessive clauses. For example see §§ 89.C.3: 90.C.1.c.

115. Potential Subjunctive. The potential (§ 111) subjunctive represents something as not actually belonging to the domain of fact or reality, but as merely existent in the mind as a conception, thought, in the present tense associated more or less with the idea of probability, in the past tense associated with the idea of possibility, bare possibility, unreality, disagreement with the facts, or, on the other hand, much used to state facts modestly or cautiously.

This subjunctive is widely used in both principal propositions and subordinate clauses.

A. In Principal Propositions. Here only the modern form with an auxiliary is now used: It *may* rain. We *may* (or with stronger force *can*) expect opposition. It *cannot* (or with much weaker force *may not*) be true.

Shall is sometimes used in rhetorical questions (§ 9.F), indicating doubt in the mind of the speaker as to the outcome or the solution of the matter in question: When doctors disagree, who *shall* decide? What *sháll* I do?

The past subjunctive is widely used here. Possibility that lies in the ability of a person or in circumstances: He *could* easily do it. It *couldn't* possibly be done. It *might* possibly be true. Doubt or uncertainty: *Could* he mean it? Why *should* he stay so long?

The polite subjunctive of modest or cautious statement: It *were* wise to be silent. I *had* (§ 123.G.3.a.v) better do it. I *should* hope so. This *would* seem to confirm his statement. A man's first care *should* (or *ought to*) be to avoid the reproaches of his own heart. Under these circumstances you *must* (old past subjunct.; see § 41.B.4), or *ought* (§ 41.B.4) *to*, or *should* act at once. The tone of modest assurance in the past subjunctive is sometimes intensified to that of positive affirmation: "Is anybody deceived by such words?" "I *should* say not." He *must* be a fool to even think of such a thing. For the use of *must* for reference to the past see B.1.*b* below.

For reference to the past the perfect infinitive is usually employed instead of the present: He *could* easily *have done* it. He *must have come* by this time. He *ought to have known* better than to speak.

a) In popular speech *ought* is much used here as a full verb, an infinitive dependent upon subjunctive auxiliaries which express the potential idea: A woman *should ought* (= *ought*) to be modest. You *should ought* (= *ought*) to have seen it. He *had ought* (= *ought*) to know better.

B. In Subordinate Clauses. The potential subjunctive is widely used here. Attention is directed here to the principal categories.

1. *Potential Subjunctive in Substantive Clauses.* Here, i.e. in clauses used as a subject, object, or attributive noun, the subjunctive represents the thought which is busying the mind as a mere conception: It seems quite probable that it *may* (or with different meaning *will*) rain. Whoever *shall* (a future contingency) violate the law shall (optative) pay the penalty. It is possible that it *might* (possibility) rain. It is easily conceivable that he *might* (modest statement) outstrip them all. We doubt whether it *be* (in plain prose *is*) possible to mention a state which on the whole has been a gainer by a breach of faith (Macaulay). "I fear that he *may* not recover," but we say "I fear he *will* not recover" when we desire to indicate that the statement is felt not as a mere conception but as a reality, a sure result. I see that that *might* (possibility) have proved disastrous. I don't know what I *should* (doubt) do. I think that that *might* (or *should*) please anybody (modest statement). It is high time that he *go*, or more modestly *went*, or *were going*, or *should go* (attributive substantive clause).

After a past tense form, however, the distinctions of meaning between present and past tense forms are usually lost, since the present tense subjunctives are all attracted into a past tense in accordance with the law of sequence (§ 118): He decided that he would go and see whether Rachel *were* (or in plain prose *was*) in. There is a modern tendency after *lest* to disregard the old sequence where the idea of present or future time is prominent: Each was playing a part and dreading lest the other *suspect* it (G. Atherton, *Sleeping Fires*, Ch. XX), or *should suspect* it.

a. Indirect Discourse after Verbs of Saying, Reporting, Etc. In reporting indirectly the words of another we employ the indicative or subjunctive as in the original utterance, only changing the persons to suit the circumstances:

Direct

I come as often as *I can.*
I will do it *for you.*
I would come if *you should* ask *me.*
It *may* rain.

Indirect

He says *he comes* as often as *he can.*
He says *he will* do it *for me.*
He says *he would* come if I *should* ask *him.*
He thinks it *may* rain.

There is no difficulty here except in the case of the pure future, which has different forms for the different persons. In the indirect statement we here usually, without regard to the auxiliary used in the direct statement, employ *shall* in the first person and *will* in the second and the third in accordance with the usual way of using these forms in the future tense:

Direct

You *will* surely fail.
I *shall* return tomorrow.

Indirect

He says I *shall* surely fail.
He says he *will* return tomorrow.

There is, however, a tendency here, especially in the third person of the indirect statement, to retain the auxiliary used in the direct, just as elsewhere in indirect discourse:

Direct

I *shall* come to stay at Diplow.

Indirect

Sir Hugo says he *shall* (usually *will*) come to
stay at Diplow. — G. Eliot.

Of course, after a past indicative, according to our sequence (§ 118) every present tense becomes a past: He said he *came* as often as *he could*. He said I *should* surely fail. He said he *would* return tomorrow.

If the past subjunctive is used in the direct discourse, it, of course, undergoes no change in the indirect: He said he *would* come if I *should* ask him (indirect) and I *would* come if you *should* ask me (direct). *Must* and *ought* do not change their form after a past tense since, according to § 41.B.4, they are in fact past subjunctives: I thought it *must* kill him (Meredith). I thought he *ought* to do it and told him so.

b. Independent Form of Indirect Discourse. In a lively style the author often strips off all signs of subordination, i.e. drops the principal verb *says*, *reports*, etc., along with the entire principal proposition and relates the thoughts, musings, reveries of another, employing past tense forms as in narrative in general: "James looked at his daughter-in-law. That unseen glance of his was cold and dubious. Appeal and fear were in it. Why *should he* (direct *should I*, with reference to the moment described by the writer) be worried like this? It *was* (direct *is*) very likely all nonsense; women *were* (direct *are*) funny things! They *exaggerated* (direct *exaggerate*) so, you *didn't* (direct *don't*) know what to believe" (Galsworthy, *The Man of Property*).

According to § 112 the past subjunctive regularly refers to present or future time. It can refer to the past only in a subordinate clause after a past indicative, where the idea of past time is suggested by the past indicative, as in the last two sentences in a above. As there is in the independent form of indirect discourse no principal proposition with a past indicative, the idea of past time is indicated by the situation, by the preceding description, which usually contains a past indicative: "John fell to thinking. If he *should* let another opportunity go by unused, his father *would* never forgive him." Similarly, in regular narrative the past subjunctive *must* (see A above) sometimes stands in the principal proposition seemingly pointing to the past, but this idea really comes from the situation, from some past indicative in the sentence which indicates past time: A commander like Mansfield, who could (past indic.) not pay his soldiers, *must*, of necessity, plunder wherever he was. As soon as his men had eaten up one part of the country, they *must* go to another, if they were not to die of starvation (Gardiner, *Thirty Years' War*).

2. *Potential Subjunctive in Attributive Relative Clauses:* It is a book that *may* (or the indic. *will*, to indicate that the speaker is counting on a favorable result) help many a poor struggling fellow. Here is a book that *may*, or more modestly *might*, interest you. I offer a reward to anyone who *shall* (future contingency) give me the desired address.

In a relative clause introduced by a *why* that stands in a question, we often use *should* to give expression to the doubt in our mind as to the proper explanation of a contemplated act, or often also the doubt as to the proper explanation of an actual fact: Can you give me one good reason why you *should* do this? (contemplated act). Can you give me one good reason why you *should* always answer so peevishly? (actual fact). We often use the declarative form of this type of sentence to state an opinion modestly: There is no good reason why you *should* do that = You surely should not do that.

3. *Subjunctive and Indicative in Conditional Sentences.*

a. Practical Condition.

(i) Future Time. When the action or state expressed in the condition seems of practical importance to us, something which in the near or remote future will concern us, hence something well within the domain of reality, we usually employ the present indicative, which here, as so often elsewhere, has future force; in the conclusion we use *will* to express intention and the future indicative to indicate a future result: If it *rains*, or *is stormy*, I'*ll* not go. If I *can't* pray, I'*ll* not make believe (Longfellow). If it *rains*, or *is stormy*, we *shall* all *be* very much discouraged.

In older English, the present tense of the potential subjunctive was common here in the condition instead of the present indicative, with virtually the same force, only presented from a little different point of view. The indicative recognizes as a practical working basis the reality of state or act, but does not commit us to this view; the subjunctive represents state or act as a mere conception, but at the same time recognizes the reality of state or action as a practical working basis. The older use of the subjunctive survives in rather choice language: Let him go, so (= provided) only he *come* (or more commonly *comes*) home with glory won (G. M. Lane, *A Latin Grammar*, p. 338).

Instead of the simple present potential subjunctive the newer form with *shall* was much used in older English and in choice language is still employed:

If annihilation *shall end* (or *end* or *ends*) all our joys, it will also end our griefs.

If you *shall fail* to understand what England is . . .
On you will come the curse of all the land.
— Tennyson.

(ii) Present and Past Time. Often also a present or a past state or act is of practical importance to us. Here we often employ in both condition and conclusion a present, past, or present perfect indicative, thus for the time being recognizing as a practical working basis the reality of state or act, but not finally committing ourselves to this view: If he *is doing* this, he *is* in the right. If this *is* true, that *is* false. If he *did* this, he *did* wrong. If it *has thundered*, it *has lightened*. Condition and conclusion are often in different times: If he *did* this, he *is* in the right.

Alongside of the present, past, and present perfect indicative in the condition here, we sometimes in rather choice English, as a survival of a once common usage, still employ the present, past, and present perfect subjunctive, with virtually the same force, only presented from a little different point of view, the subjunctive representing act or state as only conceived, but at the same time recognizing the reality of act or state as a practical working basis: If God so *clothe* the grass . . . how much more will he clothe you? (Luke, XII.28). "My friend should have taken you along with him. But the slight, if there *be* one, was unintentional" (Stevenson, *Treasure Island*). If ever poet *were* a master of phrasing, he (Tennyson) was so (A. C. Bradley, *Commentary on Tennyson's In Memoriam*, Ch. VI). It ought to weigh heavily on a man's conscience, if he *have been* the cause of another's deviating from sincerity (W. J. Fox, *Works*, III, 283).

b. Theoretical Condition. The time is always future. The
action or state seems less near to us, seems to us of only theoretical nature with no prospect of our having to deal with it prac-
tically, hence we employ here a past tense form of the subjunctive, namely, *should* to indicate that the situation is only conceived, and in the conclusion we use the past subjunctive *would*
to express intention and *should* in the first person and *would* in
the second and the third person to indicate a future result: If it
should rain tomorrow, I *wouldn't* go. "If he *should* go away without speaking to me, I *should* be grieved"; but "If I *should* go
away without speaking to him, he *would* be grieved."

In the subordinate clause of all these conditional sentences
we normally use *should*, but instead of *should* we may employ
the simple past subjunctive or *were to*, usually however with the
differentiation that the simple past subjunctive, *should*, and
were to indicate decreasing grades of probability: If we *missed*,
should miss, or *were to miss*, the train, we should have to wait an
hour at the station.

The past subjunctive *could* and *might* are often used to express
the idea of possibility, the former the possibility that lies in the
ability of a person, the latter the possibility that lies in circumstances: He *could* do it if he tried. We *might* miss the train if we
walked more slowly.

c. Condition Contrary to Fact. In conditions contrary to
fact, or unreal conditions, as they are often called, we employ
the simple past subjunctive in the condition and in the conclusion use *would*, *should*, *could*, *might*, as described in b above:
If he *were* here, I *would* speak to him. If father *were* here and
saw this, we *should* have to suffer for it. If father *were* here and
saw this, he *would* punish us.

In poetry and rather choice prose we sometimes still use the
old simple past subjunctive *were* in the conclusion instead of the
newer, now more common *should be*, *would be:* It *were* (= *would
be*) different if I had some independence, however small, to
count on.

When the reference is to past time, we usually employ in the
condition the past perfect subjunctive and in the conclusion
the same auxiliary used for present time, *should*, *would*, *might*,

247

but put the dependent infinitive into the perfect tense instead of the present: If it *had rained*, I *would* not *have gone*. If he *had gone* away without speaking to me, I *should have been grieved*. We *might have missed* the train if we *had walked* more slowly. The past perfect subjunctive in the condition is a poor form because it is not different in form from the indicative and hence does not give formal expression to the idea of unreality. This defect of the literary language often leads many in informal language to insert a *have* (often contracted to *of* or *a*) after *had*, just as *have* so often stands after *would*, *should*, or *might* in the conclusion: He would have gone if he had *have* had a chance. The literary language demands the form without *have* in the condition, although it is inferior in expressive power to the popular and colloquial form.

In older English, the past perfect subjunctive was used in both propositions: If thou *hadst been* here, my brother *had* not died (John, XI.21). This older usage lingers on in poetry and choice prose: It *had been* no surprise to him if she *had fallen* dead at his feet (Max Pemberton).

(i) Optative in Conditions. In unreal conditions the past tense forms are often optative instead of potential: *Were* he here, I would give all that I have.

d. Elliptical Conditional Sentence. A sentence that is seemingly independent is often in fact the conclusion of a conditional sentence with the condition suppressed: He could easily do it [if he tried]. I should say [if I were asked] that it were better to say nothing about it. In this sentence *that it were better* serves as an object clause, but *it were better* is also the conclusion to the condition *to say nothing about it* = *if one said nothing about it*. He was not the kind of man whom a servant would ever have dared to express any sympathy with [if he had felt inclined to do so]. Here the conclusion serves also as a relative clause.

4. *Potential Subjunctive in Clauses of Result*. For examples see § 87.B.

5. *Potential Subjunctive in Clauses of Cause*. Let us act and not shrink for fear (or lest) our motives *be* misunderstood. I trem-

bled lest you *should* be seen. Sometimes after a past tense there is a tendency to disregard the old sequence (§ 118) where the idea of present or future time is prominent: She was afraid to breathe lest she *break* (or *should break*) the wonderful spell of the magic (Ellen Glasgow, *Life and Gabriella*, Ch. V).

116. Forms of the Imperative. The simple imperative, as in *see*, *give*, antedates inflection. It is an old uninflected form which along with interjections, like *O! Ouch!*, belongs to the oldest forms of spoken speech. Though the oldest imperative form, it is still widely used, but now it is only one of many forms, for today the expression of one's will is no longer a simple matter as in the earliest period when men were less differentiated and less sensitive.

The following categories indicate the means we now employ to express our will:

A. OLD SIMPLE IMPERATIVE. In direct address we usually employ in commands, admonitions, requests, supplications the simple stem of the verb without a subject, since the direct address of itself suggests the subject: *Hurry! Shut* the door! *Study* your failures and *be instructed* by them! *Give* us this day our daily bread (prayer).

The subject is often expressed:

1. *In Older English: Enter ye* in at the strait gate (Matthew, VII.13). There are survivals of this older usage: *Mind you*, he hasn't paid the money as yet. The subject here follows the imperative.

2. *In Present-Day English* to indicate a contrast, usually with the subject before the imperative: "*I* don't know what to say. Norah, *yóu go!*"

3. *In Lively Language* to indicate that the person addressed should take an interest in something, or that it is intended especially for his good or for his discomfiture, or that it should concern or not concern him especially: "Yóu márk my words. It's a certainty." "It'll never work." — "Just yóu wáit and sée!" "Yóu léave that alone!"

B. Modern *Do*-Form.

1. *Negative Commands* are expressed by the form with un-stressed *do:* Don't tálk so lóud!

In older English the simple imperative is employed here. This older usage survives in connection with the adverb *never* and sometimes elsewhere in solemn language and in poetry: Never *mention* it again!

Tell me *not* in mournful numbers...

2. The form with *do* is also employed in entreaties and as an *emphatic prohibition* or *negative command*, here usually with stressed *do:* Dó go, please! When the tone becomes that of an emphatic prohibition or negative command, the subject according to A.3 is often expressed: Dón't yóu do that! Dón't yóu forget!, or, to call attention to the verbal activity, Don't forgét!

For an explanation of the stress or stresslessness of *do* see § 53.A.3.a–b.

C. Subjunctive Forms in Commands. The old imperative has forms only for the second person. When we have to give commands, admonitions, etc. in the first and the third person, we employ the volitive (§ 114.A.1) subjunctive: *Let us part* (or in older English *part we*) in kindness! Please *forgive* me every-body! We use the volitive subjunctive not only in the first and the third person, but also in the second, for the employ-ment of various auxiliaries in the modern subjunctive makes it capable of shading our thought and feeling more accurately than the old imperative. For these subjunctive forms see § 114.A.1. As described in § 90.C.1.a, the simple subjunctive imperative forms are much used in concessive clauses in the first and third persons.

D. Future Indicative with Imperative Force. We em-ploy the future indicative when we desire to speak courteously and at the same time indicate that we are confidently expect-ing that our wish will be fulfilled: Heads of departments *will submit* their estimates before January first. When spoken in earnest tone the future indicative becomes almost a command: She (grandmother to grandchild) said, "You *will do* nothing of the kind!" (Galsworthy). On the other hand, since we feel here a certain bluntness, we often soften the force of the expression by the use of *please*, *kindly*, *perhaps*, etc.: As you are going to the post office, you *will perhaps* (or *I know*) mail these letters for me.

E. PROGRESSIVE FORM AS IMPERATIVE. As described in § 120 the progressive form often has modal force, hence its imperative is often charged with feeling: Up, *be doing* everywhere, the hour of crisis has verily come (Carlyle).

As the present indicative of the progressive form often indicates a prospective action which is to take place in the immediate or near future, it is often used in expression of will to indicate that the command is to be carried out at once or soon and is usually charged with feeling: John, you'*re going* to bed early tonight!

F. PREDICATE INFINITIVE AS IMPERATIVE. The predicate infinitive in connection with the present indicative of the copula is much used to convey the will of someone other than the subject, representing the order as something that has already been determined upon and here is merely transmitted: You are *to be up* at six! You are always *to shut* the door when you enter this room! "You are *to come down!* Mama wants you."

G. IMPERATIVE IN ELLIPTICAL CONSTRUCTION. In lively language, expression is often elliptical since the situation makes the thought clear: [sit] Down in front! [take your] Hats off! All [come] aboard! A noun or a noun and an adjective often serve as a warning: Danger! Fresh paint!

The gerund preceded by *no* has the force of a negative command: No parking here = Do not park here.

117. Tenses of the Imperative. The present tense is the only form of the old imperative that is much used. We sometimes employ the present perfect tense to represent the action as already performed: Have done! In the tone of entreaty, the imperative of *do* is used here in connection with the perfect infinitive: Do have done with this nonsense!

Tense

118. Sequence of Tenses. In English there is a general rule of sequence when a past indicative precedes. When the principal proposition has a past indicative, a past tense form must usually follow: "He *wants* to do it before his father *comes*," but "He *wanted* to do it before his father *came*." "He *says* he *will* do it sometime," but "He *said* he *would* do it sometime." This usage, though very old, is still for the most part firm.

The old sequence, however, is not observed if it is desired to represent something as habitual, customary, characteristic, or as universally true: He *asked* the guard what time the train usually *starts*. He *did*n't seem to know that nettles *sting*. Columbus *proved* that the world *is* round.

The old sequence is not infrequently disregarded to emphasize the relation of the act or state in question to the present or the future. The present perfect is used after a past indicative to represent the statement as something general which holds for the past as well as the present, or holds for the past life of the person in question up to the time of speaking: He brought vividly to their minds that honesty *has* always *been* the best policy. The old conductor told me that he *has* not *missed* a single trip since he entered the service of the road. The present perfect is often used to emphasize the close relation of the act or state in question to the present: I learned this morning that they *have begun* work on the bridge.

The present tense is often used after a past indicative to represent a state or activity as still continuing: He told me this morning that the men *are* still at work on the bridge.

The present or future is often used after a past indicative when the reference is to a point of time still vividly felt as future at the time of speaking: He told me this morning that he *is going*, or *will go*, with us tomorrow.

There is a tendency to disregard the old sequence in certain subjunctive categories where the idea of present or future time is prominent: She lowered her voice lest the children *hear* (Rupert Hughes, *Clipped Wings*, Ch.1), or *should hear*. For other examples of this tendency see § 114.B.2.a (3rd par.), § 115.B.1 (2nd par.).

119. Tenses of the Indicative.

A. PRESENT TENSE.

1. *It Refers to Present Time:* He *is writing.*

2. *It Expresses a General Truth:* Twice two *are* four.

3. *Historical Present.* In narrative, especially in a lively style, the historical present is much used to make past events more vivid and bring them nearer the hearer: Soon there *is* a crowd around the prostrate form, the latest victim of reckless speeding. A strong man *holds* the little fellow in his arms. The crowd *makes* room for a slender woman who *cries* out. "Give me my boy."

The preceding example is narrative, but also elsewhere we often bring something from the near or remote past up to the present moment by the use of the present tense: "Mr. Smith, we *read* in the newspapers that you are going to Europe soon." Similarly we quote an old author when we feel that his words have weight in the questions of the hour: Homer *says* that, etc.

4. *Use of the Present Tense for the Present Perfect.* The present is sometimes used instead of the present perfect to express that an action or state that was begun in the past is still continuing at the present time, usually accompanied by some adverbial element, such as *these many years, these forty years, long since, long ago*: Nicholas Vedder! Why, he *is* dead and gone these eighteen years (Washington Irving).

5. *Use of the Present Tense for the Future.* As in oldest English, when there was no distinct form for a future tense, the present is still often used for the future, especially when some adverb of time, or conjunction of time or condition, or the situation makes clear the thought: He *is coming* soon. The ship *sails* tomorrow. We are waiting until he *comes.* If you *move, I shoot.*

The present tense form *am (is) going* in connection with a dependent infinitive often has the force of a pure future auxiliary: I *am going to call* on him soon = I *shall call* on him soon. This auxiliary, however, has also other meanings (§ 121.A.3. and B.3).

6. *Use of the Present Tense for the Future Perfect*. The present tense form is often used in adverbial clauses instead of the future perfect: Telegraph me as soon as he *arrives*.

B. PAST TENSE. This form refers to time wholly past at the present moment, be it a remote time or the second just past: Columbus *discovered* America. I *lost* my pencil a second ago and can't find it. This is the common tense of narrative.

C. PRESENT PERFECT TENSE. This form refers to time now past but in some way connected with the present. In the afternoon we can say "I *have bought* a new hat this afternoon" provided the afternoon is not yet wholly past, but if we report this same purchase in the evening, we say "I *bought* a new hat this afternoon." We say "England *has had* many able rulers," since England is still in existence, but we say "Assyria *had* many able rulers," since it is no longer in existence as an independent country.

The present perfect is much used of past time provided the time is indefinite and general, but cannot be used at all if a definite date is mentioned which is now wholly past. The indefinite statement may be something which holds for the past life of the speaker up to the moment in which he speaks: I *have* never *met* a man more just. "I *have seen* England three times," but "I *saw* England when I was a boy, but *have* not *seen* it since." It is much used in general statements where the reference is to timeless events, i.e. events that occur in all ages, the past as well as the present: It was one of those epidemic frenzies which *have fallen* upon great cities in former ages of the world (Hall Caine).

The present perfect is often used to indicate that an action or a state that has begun in past time is still continuing: He *has been working* hard all day. He *has been* sick all week.

The close relation of the present perfect tense to present time is explained by its origin. It was once a present tense: I *have* the letter *written*, lit. I *have* the letter *in a written state*. The participle *written* was originally an objective predicate (§ 67.C.1.a) and is still, as in this example, so used, but by a slight change of the word-order this expression became the present perfect tense: I *have written* the letter. Similarly, out of the past tense

"I *had* the letter *written*" developed the past perfect tense "**I** *had written* the letter."

Intransitive verbs did not participate at once in this new development, but long remained present and past tenses: The tree *is fallen* (= *in a fallen state*), The tree *was fallen*. The perfect participle is here merely a predicate adjective. Shakespeare still used this old form of the present perfect tense for intransitives: The King himself *is rode* to view their battle (*Henry the Fifth*, IV, iii, 2). It is even still occasionally used, but now only when the participle is felt more as an adjective than as a verb: My money *is* all *gone*. Our friend *is*, or *has, departed* (i.e. is dead). We *are*, or *have, assembled* to discuss a difficult problem. This morning the police found the nest of the thieves, but the birds *were*, or *had, flown*. Gradually, as the perfect participle was felt more as a verb than as a predicate adjective, the auxiliaries *is* and *was* were replaced by *has* and *had*, since intransitives naturally followed the example of transitives, which had developed a real present perfect and a real past perfect tense: The tree *has fallen, had fallen*. The King *has ridden*, etc.

With one verb, namely *get*, the present perfect form is often still a present tense, as originally with all verbs: I *have got* (= *have*) a cold, a new car, etc. I *have got* (= *have*) to do it. *Have got*, however, is not an exact equivalent of *have;* it has more grip in it, emphasizing the idea of the possession or necessity as the result of recent circumstances: "He *has* a blind eye," but "Look at John; he *has got* a black eye."

D. PAST PERFECT TENSE. This form represents a past action or state as completed at or before a certain past time: After he *had finished* the book, he returned it. In colloquial speech, the past tense is still often used for the past perfect, as in the early period before the creation of a past perfect: After he *finished* the book, he returned it. For the origin and earlier form of the past perfect tense see C above (4th par.).

E. FUTURE TENSE. Future time was originally expressed by the present tense, and this older usage is still common where the context makes the thought clear, as described in A.5 above. The need of more accurate expression here has called forth an especial form — the future tense. There are three uses of this form:

1. *As a Pure Future.* The two auxiliaries employed here are *shall* and *will*, the latter of which is often contracted to *'ll.* Both *shall* and *will* were originally modal auxiliaries and are still often used as such, so that there are peculiar difficulties connected with the use of these words as pure future forms. The rules given below for their use have gradually become established in the literary language since the seventeenth century. They were, however, not widely observed before the nineteenth century, so that they do not apply to our older literature.

The pure future form for the first person is *shall*, for the second and third persons *will:* I *shall* die, We *shall* die, You *will* die, He *will* die, They *will* die. *Will* is only used in the first person as a pure future when in a compound subject *I* or *we* is preceded by a pronoun in the second person or by a noun or pronoun in the third person: You and I *will* get on excellently well (Dickens). Eddie and I *will* be delighted to come on Monday (Archibald Marshall).

If *will* is used in the first person, it must be a modal auxiliary, not a pure future, while, on the other hand, a *shall* in the second or the third person must be a modal auxiliary, not a pure future. *Will* is used in the first person to express an intention, desire, threat, resolution: I'*ll* send it to you next week (promise). "I'*ll* do it for you," but "I *shall* be glad to do it for you," for we do not desire to say that we are willing to be glad, but that we shall be glad, employing a pure future to express confidently a future result. I *will* punish you if you do that again (threat). I'*ll* never give my consent to that! (resolution). Resolutions in the first person expressed by *will* are usually such as are formed under the impressions of the moment. We employ modal *shall* for resolutions that are the result of deliberation or deeply rooted feeling: I *shall* not give up the Lord even for you (Eggleston, *Circuit Rider*, Ch. XIX).

In the second and the third person, *shall* as a modal auxiliary, indicates the will of someone other than its subject, representing its subject as standing under the will of another who commands him, promises or assures him something, wishes something to be arranged to suit him, threatens him, or it represents the speaker as determined to bring something about or prevent it: Thou *shalt* not kill (commandment). "I won't do it" — "You *shall* [do it]." You *shall* pay me at your convenience, i.e. you *are to* pay me, it is my desire that you pay me at your convenience. You *shall* have some cake (promise). If you pursue this course, you *shall* be pleased with the results (a promise as it were, a strong assurance that the result in question will follow, a once common usage, now usually replaced by *will*, the future tense auxiliary). You *shall* pay for that (threat). She *shall* not regret her kindness (resolution). I mean it; nothing *shall* stop me. The constraint is often that of authority: Immigrants *shall* be treated with kindness and civility by everyone (notice posted at different points on Ellis Island). The constraint of circumstances: I'll sell my new red cloak rather than you *shall* go unpaid. Constraint of destiny, with the same force as *is to:* The time *shall* (= *is to*) come when Egypt *shall* (= *is to*) be avenged (Lytton, *Last Days of Pompeii*, II, Ch. VIII). Often in rhetorical questions (§ 9.F): When doctors disagree who *shall* (= *is to*) decide?

In older English, *shall* was used as a future in all three persons, but the idea of compulsion, constraint, so intimately associated with it in the second and the third person, as in all the examples just given, aroused the feeling that it was here not a suitable form to express the pure future, so that it was here gradually replaced by the more polite *will*. The new usage of employing *shall* in the first person and *will* in the second and the third has by reason of its expressiveness become more or less established in the literary language, but as it is a natural expression only to the people of England proper, who have developed it, deviations from the rule are not infrequent. Outside of England proper there has come into wide use in colloquial speech a simpler pure future, formed by employing *will* in all three persons. As this is a natural American expression we have considerable difficulty in learning the literary future.

In independent questions, the literary pure future form for the first person is *shall* and for the third person *will*, just as in the declarative form; but in the second person that auxiliary is used which is expected in the answer, so that also in questions we must carefully distinguish between tense and modal auxiliaries: *Shall* (tense aux.) we have the pleasure of seeing you tomorrow? *Will* (tense aux.) he come tomorrow? *Shall* (tense aux.) you come tomorrow? i.e. Are you to come tomorrow?, corresponding to the expected answer: "I *shall* come tomorrow"; but "*Will* (modal aux.) you do this for me?" corresponding to the expected answer: "I *will* do it for you." In asking after the will or desire of another we employ *shall*, not *will*, as so often heard in the language of Irishmen and Scotchmen: What *shall* I do next? = What do you want me to do next?

After a past indicative, of course, in accordance with the usual sequence (§ 118) *shall* becomes *should* and *will* becomes *would*: "He says I *shall* fail," but "He said I *should* fail." "He says he *will* return tomorrow," but "He said he *would* return tomorrow." For a fuller description of the form that the pure future assumes in indirect discourse see § 115.B.1.a.

a. Modal "Will." Stressed *will* expresses determination in all three persons: I *will* go, no matter what you say. You *will* (or he *will*) act foolishly, in spite of my advice. Unstressed *will* is often used in one of its old meanings, *inclined to* when we desire to represent an action as customary: Courage *will* come and go. A strong stress indicates a strong inclination: Accidents *will* happen.

2. *As an Imperative.* The future tense is often used as an imperative (§ 116.D).

3. *To Indicate Present Probability.* The future tense sometimes indicates a present probability, the future form implying that upon investigation the truth of the statement will become apparent: "This *will be* your luggage, I suppose," said the man rather abruptly when he saw me, pointing to the trunk in the passage.

F. FUTURE PERFECT TENSE. This form represents that an action or state will be completed at or before a certain time yet future. The rules for the use of *shall* and *will* here are the same as those for the future tense (E above): I *shall* have completed my task by evening. He *will* have completed the task by evening.

In principal propositions, the future perfect is used in choice accurate language, but in colloquial speech it is avoided as too formal. This form is a late and learned development which has not yet become established in simple expression. It is not found in the language of Shakespeare. In informal speech we employ here the future in connection with a perfective adverb or a perfect participle: I *shall have finished* the work before you return, or in colloquial speech "I *shall be through* with the work, or I *shall have* the work *finished*, before you return."

In the subordinate clause, the future perfect is usually replaced by the present, future, or present perfect: He is standing there reasoning out the steps to be taken when the fog *lifts*, *will lift*, or *has lifted*.

Aspect

120. Terminate and Progressive Aspects. These are the forms which the verb assumes to represent the act as a finished whole, as an actual fact, or as going on. They are the two main aspects; they are modern but now widely used. The terminate form, the common form of the English verb (I *walk*, *work*, etc.), represents the act as a finished whole, an actual fact, hence called terminate, i.e. finished: "Last Saturday I *worked* (terminate, a fact) in the garden," but: "Last Saturday I *was working* (progressive) in the garden when he went by." The progressive form represents the act as going on.

In Old English "He *works*" meant either "He *works*" or "He *is working*." The form *is working* was in those days little used. It was a foreign construction that came into English from the Vulgate. In the early history of this foreign form in England it did not become differentiated from the common form of the verb. The later slow development of progressive force in it brought new things into our language — terminate and progressive aspect. The progressive form has at last taken deep root. It is now often impossible to avoid it where we use a finite verb, but still as in older English we often cannot use it at all with verbs of infinite predication (§§ 122–125): "In *correcting* (progressive = when I *was correcting*) his exercise I

259

found many mistakes." "After *correcting* (terminate = after I *corrected*) the exercises I went to bed." "I met him *driving* (progressive = as he *was driving*) his cattle to pasture." "I am proud of him *acting* (terminate = as he *acted*) so unselfishly." The infinitive is the only verb of infinite predication that has developed progressive form: We were wearily trudging along the hot dusty highway, but we all expected *to be resting* in cool clean beds before midnight.

The common form of the verb, as a terminate form to express fact, now freed from the function of expressing progressive action, has become one of the most distinctive features of our language, which very few languages possess. The progressive form is now well established as a progressive, but it was originally not always progressive. It had both terminate and progressive force just as the common form of the verb had both terminate and progressive force. The old terminate force of the progressive form still lingers on and is even common in animated language, as we shall see below.

The common form of the verb is used also to represent the act as habitual, customary, characteristic, as a general truth, always with terminate force, for the common form is now always terminate: I *get* up early. Dogs *bark*. Water *runs* down hill. In animated language also the progressive form is used here with terminate force, as explained below.

As the present participle in the progressive form has not only verbal force, but is also a predicate adjective, it often like an adjective has descriptive force: "There he *comes*" (a fact), but "He *is coming* down the road" (descriptive). We *are tramping* over the hills and *reading* and *writing* and *having* a restful time. The simple present tense here would be only an objective statement of fact. Both the simple and the progressive form represent the acts as habitual, but the latter has warmth of feeling in it.

The warmth of feeling associated with the progressive form, as in the last example, often becomes so marked that we now often feel it as a modal form expressing joy, sorrow, pleasure, displeasure, praise, censure, also emphasis, implying that the person in question is convinced of the truth or importance of the statement: "John bothers me a good deal" (fact), but "John *is bothering* me a good deal of late and *keeping* me from work" (spoken in a complaining tone). "John *is* now *doing* fine work at school" (spoken in a tone of praise). You are helping me, darling. You *are being* an angel (Noel Coward). "When Elizabeth put Ballard and Babington to death, she *was* not *persecuting*" (Macaulay), spoken in a tone of conviction.

"Twice two are four" (general truth), but it is also common to employ the progressive form here in lively style when we feel the truths as living forces always at work: True taste *is* for ever *growing, learning, reading, worshiping, laying* its hand upon its mouth because it is astonished (Ruskin).

Past habit: "Even when a little girl she *ran, used to run*, or *would run*, after the boys," but in a tone of censure "Even when a little girl she *was* always *running* after the boys."

Somewhat similar to the progressive form is modal *will* (§ 119.E.1.a), much used in lively expression to represent an act as customary, oft occurring, since the subject is inclined to this activity, but it is not associated with praise or censure, for the form is not progressive but terminate and hence has factual force: John *will* sit on the veranda alone for hours. They *were wont*, or *used*, to discuss politics together by the hour, and often they *would* become quite excited. As in this example terminate *were wont* and *used* can also be employed here, but *used* is now found here only in the past tense.

Often to emphasize the idea of duration as a fact we add *on* or *on and on* to a terminate form. The prayers and talks (in the prayer-meeting) *went on and on* (W. S. Cather).

When we desire to report simply as a fact without descriptive force, but yet in lively tone, that an activity is proceeding, we place a terminate form of *continue, keep*, or *keep on* before a predicate appositive present participle with progressive force, or an objective predicate present participle with progressive force: They *continued fighting*. The fire *kept burning*. He *kept whistling* to cheer himself up. He didn't mind the rain; he *kept on working*. He *keeps* things *moving*. These sentences show clearly that in one and the same statement English can by the use of a terminate and a progressive form represent in lively tone a continuing activity as a fact. Usually the progressive form imparts descriptive force to the whole statement.

261

But when we desire to state as a fact, but in calm objective language, that an activity is proceeding, we employ two terminate forms, *continue* + infinitive: During the whole day the army *continued to advance*.

We may see from the foregoing description of terminate and progressive aspects that (1) we can represent the act as a whole, as a fact, either objectively or in warm tones of praise, censure, or of deep conviction, or (2) we can represent the activity as going on, with descriptive force, or (3) we can report simply as a fact, but in lively tone, that an activity is proceeding, or (4) we can report simply as a fact, but in calm objective language, that the activity is proceeding.

121. Point-Action Aspect. The two point-action classes described in § 39.C are here treated a little more fully.

A. INGRESSIVE ASPECT. The ingressive (§ 39.C.1) aspect is expressed in various ways:

1. The beginning of an activity is indicated by a number of ingressive auxiliaries with different shades of meaning, *begin*, *commence*, *start in*, *start out*, *set about*, *set in*, etc., in connection with an infinitive, gerund, or participle: When we scold her, she *begins to cry*. It *is beginning*, *starting to rain*. As soon as the flood was over they *set about repairing* (or *to repair*) the damage. It *set in to rain* (or *raining*).

2. The present tense of *to be about* in connection with a *to*-infinitive and the present tense of *to be on the point* (or *verge*) *of* in connection with the gerund indicate an action that will take place in the immediate future in accordance with some plan, or as the result of circumstances or a natural development: I *am about to leave* for Europe. He *is about to break down*. It *is about to rain*. She *is on the point* (or *verge*) *of breaking down*.

3. The *to*-infinitive dependent upon *am* (*is*, etc.) *going* was originally an abridged clause of purpose, but *am going* has lost its original concrete force and has become a mere auxiliary, often an ingressive auxiliary indicating that the subject is getting ready to act, sometimes still with the original idea of purpose strongly pronounced: Look out! I *am going to shoot*.

It *is going to rain.* I *am going to put* my foot down on that! On the other hand, *am going* is often used as a pure future auxiliary (§ 119.A.5) and as an effective auxiliary (B.3 below).

4. The ingressive idea is often expressed by *be* (see next par.), *get, grow, fall, turn, wax, become, go, come, set, start, take* (of habitual actions) in connection with an adjective, participle, noun, or a prepositional phrase: She *turned* (*became, got, grew*) *pale.* He *fell asleep* (from older *on sleep*). He *took to drinking.*

Be, now usually terminate (§ 120), had originally point-action force, ingressive or effective, and sometimes still has this older force: Up, *be doing* everywhere, the hour of crisis has verily come (Carlyle). We must *be going.* We usually employ ingressive *get* here: I had better *get going.* Get going!

Verbs made from adjectives have a similar force: They went out the moment it *cleared.* The milk *soured.*

5. We often use *catch* here in connection with an object: I *caught sight* of him. I *caught a cold.* The rug before the hearth *caught fire* from a spark.

6. Ingressive force often lies in the adverbs *up, down, off,* etc., in the prefix *a-,* and the suffix *-en:* The children hurried *up,* quieted *down.* At first he was very mad, but after a little he calmed *down,* or cooled *off.* Then a heated discussion *arose.* He quick*en*ed his pace. Foreign verbs often have ingressive force by virtue of their prefixes: *ap*pear, *intro*duce, etc.

B. EFFECTIVE ASPECT. The effective (§ 39.C.2) aspect is expressed in various ways.

1. We often call attention to the final point of an activity by the use of the verbs *cease, stop, leave off, finish, quit, do* with an infinitive or gerund as object, or by the use of the predicate adverb *through* followed by a predicate appositive present participle: She *ceased to cry* (or *ceased,* or *stopped, crying*). I *have left off sleeping* with the windows shut. I *have* just *finished reading* the book. I *have quit smoking.* I *have done packing* (or often in American English *am done packing,* where *done* is a predicate adjective participle followed by a predicate appositive present participle). I *am through trying* to please her.

2. By means of adverbs and prefixes we often call attention to the final point of the activity, thus indicating the result or the attainment of the end in view: We have burned our coal all *up*. The problem was difficult, but I kept at it until I worked it *out*. He put the rebellion *down*. Many borrowed verbs with prefixes are used here: *ef*fect, *ob*tain, *ac*quire, *per*fect, *ar*rive, etc.

The same form is often used for both point-action aspects. The context alone can then indicate whether the expression is ingressive or effective: "The children *quieted down*" (ingressive), came into a quiet state, but "He *put* the rebellion *down*" (effective), the final result of the action.

The English adverbs used here have in general strong concrete force, but they are acquiring abstract ingressive or effective force, as can be clearly seen in *up*. We say "I ate the apple *up*," although we know very well that the apple went *down* and not *up*. This shows that *up* has lost here its old concrete force and has become a point-action particle, in this example an effective particle.

3. After point-action verbs like *to be* (A.4, 2nd par.), *become*, *get*, *turn*, etc. we use a noun or an adjective to indicate the final goal or state: He wants *to be* (effective = *become*) *a lawyer*. He *became a lawyer*. He *got to be rich*. He *turned out to be a great rascal*. He *turned traitor*.

The infinitive is much used after *to get, grow, come, is going* to indicate the actual result, outcome of some action, influence, development, or state of things: I *got to talk* with him. I *got him to do* it. I *got* the machine *to run*. I *am growing to believe*, or *am coming to believe*, that my sacrifice has been in vain. He *is going to be rich* some day.

The infinitive here is regularly replaced by the gerund or the present participle when the force becomes descriptive, i.e. when it is desired to represent the resultant activity as proceeding steadily rather than to state a bare result as a fact: I got the machine *to running* (or simply *running*) smoothly.

4. The final result, goal is often indicated by an object, or an object in connection with an objective predicate (§ 67. C.1.a): He has won *great fame*. He has made *himself skilful* in this kind of work.

The Infinite Forms of the Verb

The infinite (p. 52) forms of the verb — the participle, the infinitive, and the gerund — are forms which partake of the nature of verbs and have in addition the function of adjectives or nouns.

122. The Participle. The participle, true to its name, participates in the nature of an adjective and a verb.

A. As an Adjective. It is still often used as an adjective with more or less verbal force.

1. *Attributively:* with active meaning and descriptive stress (§ 56.B): a *gràsping* náture, a *càptivating* mánner, the *rìsen* sún; with passive meaning and descriptive stress: a *bròken* cháir, a *wèll-dressed* little gírl (i.e. a little girl who *has been* well *dressed*, while in a "*wèll-dressed* mán" the participle has active meaning); with classifying stress and active meaning: *círculating* líbrary; with classifying stress and passive meaning: *wáshing* tíes (ties that can be washed), *cóoking* àpples (apples that can be cooked), *róast* (§ 42.A.2) bèef.

2. *Predicatively:* He is always *reserved*. It is *interesting*. As objective (§ 67.C.1) predicate: I consider the matter *settled*. I found him *reading* a book. As predicate appositive (§ 53.C): He awoke next morning *trembling* all over, or *rested* and *refreshed*.

3. *As a Noun.* As an adjective the participle can be used as a noun: the *wounded* and the *dying* (§ 108).

4. *As an Adverb.* The participle is also used as an adverb: *boiling* hot, *piercing* cold.

a) Participle and Gerund. The identity of form in the present participle and the gerund makes it often difficult to distinguish them: the form -*ing* a gerund in din*ing*-car (i.e. a car for dining), iron*ing*-board (i.e. board for ironing), but a present participle with passive force in *cooking* apple (i.e. an apple that can be cooked), breech-*loading* gun (i.e. a gun that is loaded at the breech).

In a number of cases the adjective nature of the participle has entirely overshadowed the verbal nature, so that the words are now felt as adjectives pure and simple and, in the case of the perfect participle, have become differentiated in form from the participle by the retention of the older participial form in *-en*, while the participle with verbal force has developed a new form, if it is preserved: a *cloven* hoof, *sunken* eyes, a *graven* image, a *drunken* man, a clean-*shaven*, or clean-*shaved* face, etc. Sometimes the present participle is a pure adjective in force: She is very *loving* (= *affectionate*).

B. With More Verbal Force. On the other hand, the participle now for the most part has more verbal force than formerly. The present participle in connection with a copula (§ 53.B) is much used in the progressive form of verbs: He *is writing*. As described in § 110, this form often has passive force: These books *are selling out* fast.

Also the perfect participle is much used in verbal forms as a predicate adjective, namely in the passive: The house is *painted*.

The use of the participle as a predicate appositive is illustrated in A.2 above. In these examples the original adjective nature is still prominent. In this function the participle in older English gradually assumed more and more the character of verbs, so that it now has tenses and voices like verbs. Hampered by their original adjective nature and form, they have not yet developed forms for mood and have not as many tenses as verbs have, but on the other hand they are terser forms of expression and are often much more convenient. They are adjectives and hence without the formality of framing a full clause with a nominative subject and a finite verb as predicate they as adjectives in the relation of a predicate appositive need merely to be placed alongside of their governing noun to explain it and at the same time as predicate appositive to serve as an adverb indicating some adverbial relation, such as time, cause, manner, condition, concession, etc.: *Going down town*, I met a friend = *While I was going down town*, I met a friend. *Having finished my task*, I went to bed = *After I had finished my task*, I went to bed. *Being sick*, I stayed at home = *As I was sick*, I stayed at home. *Born in better times*, he would have done credit to the profession of letters = *If he had been born*, etc. Compare § 45.A.*a*.

The present participle, widely used here, has quite commonly progressive force, but it is not infrequently also terminate (§ 120): You ought to be ashamed *stealing* (referring to a single act as a whole) from a poor widow. Compare § 120.

For the time relations of these participles see §§ 41.A.4, 45.A.*a*.

The idea of time, cause, manner, condition, etc. in such clauses is suggested only by the situation. In the full clause there is a conjunction, *when, while, as, because, if,* etc., which indicates the adverbial circumstance of time, cause, condition, etc. Since the sixteenth century it has become common to introduce this feature of the full clause into the participial clause to give more precision to the statement: Experience, *when* dearly bought, is not thrown away. He will do it, *if properly* approached. The new form is more accurate in expression, but the simple participle is still a favorite in lively style since it is more concrete and impressive: *Passing* through crises, *struggling* and *suffering*, we get large views of life. Compare § 76.A (7th par.).

C. OUTLINE OF THE FUNCTIONS OF THE PARTICIPLE. The different functions of the participle are treated in: §§ 53.C; 54.B, D.3; 56.B; 67.C.1.a; 73.A, B; 74; 76.A.; 80.G; 81.A; 84.B; 85.B; 86.A.1, E.2.a; 87.A.1.c.i; 88.C; 89.B; 90.B; 91.B.

123. The Infinitive.

A. *Origin.* The infinitive originally was a noun and had the inflection of a noun. The infinitive without *to* is the nominative or the accusative of this old noun. The old simple nominative is sometimes still used, although we do not now feel the original force: [it is] Better *ask* than *go* astray = It is better *to ask* than *to go* astray = *To ask* is better than *to go* astray [is]. Simple *ask* and *go* here are the subjects of the two propositions, but we now feel them as imperatives.

The old accusative is still common after modal auxiliaries, but we do not now feel it as an object, as it originally was: I will *play*, (i.e. I wish *to play*, or I desire *a playing*).

The infinitive with *to* was originally the object of the preposition *to*, and we can sometimes still feel the original force: Some-

thing impelled me *to do it* = *toward the doing of it*. We do not
now usually feel the *to* before the infinitive as a preposition, but
construe it as the sign of the infinitive, so that we now employ
the infinitive with *to* as the subject or the object of the verb, as
once the old simple infinitive was used, as illustrated above.
The *to*-infinitive has in large measure supplanted the old simple
infinitive since it is a more distinctive form.

An outline of the present functions of the infinitive is given
in § 123.G.

B. INFINITIVE CLAUSE AND ITS SUBJECT. By reason of the
great simplicity of its form the *to*-infinitive has had a wonderful
development. Instead of forming a full clause with a nominative subject and a finite verb as predicate, we now need only
lay the infinitive clause alongside of the principal proposition:
He wrote me *that I should come at once*, or *to come at once*. The
infinitive has here no subject expressed. Originally, it was always implied in some word in the principal proposition, just
as in this example it is implied in *me*.

The compact convenient form of the infinitive construction
won it favor in older English, so that in the fourteenth century
there arose a desire to extend its boundaries, i.e. to use it with
a subject of its own if there was no word in the principal proposition that could serve as its subject. When the infinitive
has a subject of its own, the subject is usually introduced by
for: He was eager *for me* to come at once. The *for* + noun or
pronoun here developed out of a sentence dative, the dative
of reference described in § 64.C.2. The construction originated
in such sentences as "It is difficult *for me* to pronounce the
word" = The pronunciation is difficult *for me*. Compare
§ 76.A. For exceptions to the rule that the expressed subject
of the infinitive is introduced by *for* see § 82.B.

Besides the *for — to* described above there is another
for to with an entirely different force. In older English *for*
was placed before the *to* of the infinitive in clauses of purpose to emphasize the idea of purpose: Are ye come out as
against a thief with swords and staves *for to* (now simple
to or *in order to*) *take* me? (Matthew, XXVI.55). This *for to*
early lost its original force and was frequently used as a mere

variant form of *to* and could stand wherever simple *to* could stand. This older usage has passed entirely away in the literary language, but survives in popular speech: It's not manners *for t'help* (instead of *to help*) oursel's (Mrs. Gaskell, *Sylvia's Lovers*, Ch. XXVII).

C. SPLIT INFINITIVE. The *to* before the infinitive was originally a preposition, as described in § 123.A, but we now feel it as the introduction to the infinitive clause, just as we feel *that*, *if*, etc. as introductions to the full clause with a finite verb. Hence there is a strong tendency today to put the sentence adverb (§ 70), not before *to*, i.e. outside of the clause, but within the clause immediately before the infinitive, just as we put it in the full clause immediately before the verb containing the verbal meaning: I wish the reader *to clearly understand this* (Ruskin), just as we say "I wish that the reader *may clearly understand this*." It would have overburdened the text *to there incorporate many details* (G. Hempl, *Modern Language Notes*, XIII, 456) just as we say "It would have overburdened the text *if I had there incorporated many details*." Other examples: without permitting himself *to actually mention* the name (Matthew Arnold), of a kind *to directly stimulate* curiosity (Walter Pater), *to bravely disbelieve* (Robert Browning, *The Ring and the Book*, Cambridge ed., p. 570), things which few except parents can be expected *to really understand* (Oliver W. Holmes, *Elsie Venner*, Ch. XIX). An infinitive separated from *to* by an adverb, as in these examples, is called a split infinitive. Compare § 70.B.

Older usage with the adverb before *to* is often ambiguous: He failed *entirely to comprehend it*. This sentence is ambiguous since we do not know whether *entirely* modifies *failed* or *comprehend*. If it belongs to *comprehend*, many split the infinitive, i.e. put the adverb between *to* and the infinitive: He failed *to completely comprehend* it. Thus the much censured split infinitive is an improvement of English expression. It first appeared in the fourteenth century and has since been gradually gaining favor as it has become better understood. At present it is widely used by our best writers, who feel its advantages. It is avoided by many, especially our minor writers, who here follow the instructions of their school-teachers.

D. TENSES OF THE INFINITIVE. Although the infinitive was originally a noun, it has in the course of time acquired the properties of tense, voice, and aspect. It has two tenses, the present and the perfect. The use of these tenses depends upon whether the governing verb is a full verb or an auxiliary.

1. *Governing Verb a Full Verb*. Here the present tense indicates time contemporaneous or future with reference to that of the principal verb: I wish *to go* at once. I intend *to write* a line or two to her soon. Yesterday I intended *to write* a line to her, but forgot it.

The perfect tense indicates time prior to that of the principal verb: I am proud *to have been* able to help. I met two students whom I did not remember *to have met* before. He disclaimed authorship of the poem, but at the same time declared that he would have been proud *to have written* it.

Where, however, the situation clearly shows that the reference is to the future, the perfect infinitive expresses completed action: He expects *to have written* the last chapter by tomorrow evening.

Where it is desired to indicate that a past intention has not been realized, we employ the past perfect subjunctive of the principal verb in connection with the present infinitive: I *had meant, thought, intended, wanted, wished* to write a line to you. With verbs of wishing we may use instead of the past perfect subjunctive the past subjunctive *should* in the first person and the past subjunctive *would* in the second and the third person in connection with a dependent perfect infinitive: "Yesterday I was under the constraint of circumstances. I *should have wished* (or *preferred*) *to act* otherwise." He *would have wished to act* otherwise.

Instead of a past perfect subjunctive here in connection with a present infinitive, many incorrectly employ a past subjunctive in connection with a perfect infinitive: I *intended to have written* a line to you. This form would be correct if *intended* were a modal auxiliary. The only way to express an unrealized past intention with a modal auxiliary is to put the infinitive into the perfect tense, for these auxiliaries cannot of themselves indicate past time: I *ought to have written* a line to you. But *intend, think*, etc. are not modal auxiliaries, hence they should not be used with this construction.

The incorrect past subjunctives *intended, thought*, etc. are now felt as past indicatives, as we can see when we use *was to* with the same construction: She *was to have dined* with us here the day after her father's death (Gissing, *A Life's Morning*, Ch. XIV). This expression, though incorrectly formed, has become established in the language. We have to resort to an incorrect form here because the correct past perfect subjunctive is impossible. The infinitive here, standing after a form of *be*, has modal force and an infinitive with modal force cannot stand after a compound tense form. Compare § 54.D.2.

In another respect this construction is sometimes improperly influenced by that found after modal auxiliaries. After modal auxiliaries the perfect infinitive is necessary to convey the idea of past time. After the past perfect subjunctive of *intend, mean, think, hope, want, desire, wish, like, long for*, or after the longer subjunctive form with *should* or *would* with the perfect infinitive, we sometimes, after the analogy of usage with modal auxiliaries, find the perfect infinitive instead of the present, which here is sufficient and the proper form, since the preceding subjunctive clearly indicates past time:

> I had thought, sir, *to have held* (instead of the correct *to hold*)
>> my peace until
> You had drawn oaths from him not to stay.
>> — Shakespeare, *The Winter's Tale*, I, ii, 28.

He would have liked *to have hugged* (instead of the correct *to hug*) his father.
>> — Hughes, *Tom Brown*, I, Ch. IV.

Of course, the perfect infinitive is in order when it is desired to indicate that the intention at the time was that a contemplated act should take place prior to another act that is mentioned in connection with it: I had meant *to have visited* Paris and *to have returned* to London before my father arrived from America.

2. *Use of Perfect Infinitive with Auxiliaries.* As the modal auxiliaries express only the manner of the action without distinctions of time, reference to the past can only be secured here

by using a perfect infinitive: He *may have come.* He *might have come.*

With auxiliaries that point to the future the perfect infinitive indicates completed action: I *shall have completed* it before you return.

E. REPETITION OF "TO" WITH THE INFINITIVE. When there are several infinitives with the same or similar construction, it is common usage to employ *to* with the first infinitive and understand it with the next one or the following ones: I wished to finish my business and [to] get away.

But wherever the second or later infinitive becomes important by reason of a contrast or a wish to emphasize it in any way, it becomes at once more natural to repeat the *to:* It is better to laugh than to cry. To be or not to be, that is the question. In involved constructions it is always desirable to repeat *to* to make the grammatical relations and the thought clear.

F. "TO" EMPLOYED TO REPEAT A THOUGHT. In colloquial speech, when we desire to repeat briefly something that has already been said, we employ the convenient infinitive construction, suppressing all the words in it except its distinctive sign *to*, which of itself suggests the thought: I shall go to the celebration tomorrow, or at least I am planning *to* [*go to it*].

In older English, it was more common here to place *to* before the neuter pronoun *it*, which pointed back to the thought previously expressed: But shall we dance, if they desire us *to* '*t*? (Shakespeare, *Love's Labour's Lost*, V, ii, 145).

Besides the common *to*-form described above there is now another less common elliptical construction, which has no distinctive mark and consists simply in suppressing the infinitive clause entirely and leaving us to gather the thought from the context: "Do you write to him!" — "I will since you wish me" (Marryat, *The Settlers in Canada*).

G. FUNCTIONS OF THE INFINITIVE. The infinitive is now used:

1. *As Subject: To err* is human. It is better *for you to go.* Now rarely with its simple form: [it is] Better *bend* than *break*. Compare §§ 123.A and 77.B.

2. *As Predicate*, always with *to:*

a. Normal Form:

(i). After linking verbs: To do good is *to be* happy. Compare § 54.D.1.a.

(ii) After passive verbs: He was made *to shut* the door. Compare § 54.D.1.b.

b. Modal Form:

(i) After linking verbs with the modal force described in § 54.D.2: This story is not *to be repeated*. He is soon *to be married*. Compare § 54.D.2.

(ii) As objective predicate: I have much *to do*. Compare § 54.D.2.

c. After linking verbs to express purpose: I have been down town *to buy* me a new hat. The infinitive here sometimes has the force of the predicative present participle in the progressive form: The baby started *to cry*, or *crying*. Compare §§ 54.D.3 and § 121.A.1.

d. In the nominative absolute construction (73.B).

3. *As Object:*

a. With its simple form:

(i) After the auxiliary *do:* I do not *know*.

(ii) After the modal auxiliaries, *will, would, shall, should, may,* etc.: I *will* do it, i.e. I desire the doing of it. Also after *shall* and *will* when used to form the future tense: I shall *go*, He will *go*.

(iii) After *dare*, which not only is treated as a full verb with the *to*-infinitive after it, but often also, when not standing in the form of a present participle or in a compound tense, is used as a modal auxiliary with the simple infinitive after it, especially in the negative and interrogative forms of statement and in the now rare old past tense form *durst* and the new past subjunctive form *dare*, which is now often employed where the context

273

makes the thought clear: He lay flat on his face not daring *to look* (not *look*) up. He has never dared *to say* (not *say*) it. Who *dare set* (or *dares to set*) a limit to woman's tenderness? Didn't he *dare do it?* or Didn't he *dare to do* it? He *dare not* (or *does not dare to*) tell the truth. If I *durst* (usually *dared to* or *dared*) *speak*, I should have something interesting to say. He felt that he *didn't dare venture* (or *didn't dare to venture*), or *dared not venture*, or *dare* (past subjunctive) *not venture*, upon the subject.

The past subjunctive *dare* has arisen under the influence of the past subjunctive *must* (§§ 41.B.4; 115.A).

(iv) After *need*, which frequently still as in older English is treated as a full verb with a *to*-infinitive after it, indeed regularly so in positive indicative form, usually also in negative statements and questions in its newer periphrastic form with *do;* or on the other hand, when not standing in the form of the present participle, or in a compound tense, or in the form with *do*, it may be used as a modal auxiliary with a simple infinitive after it when negatived, qualified, used in a question, and when it has the new past subjunctive form *need*, which is now often employed where the context makes the thought clear: Not needing *to hurry* (not *hurry*), I walked along leisurely. He has never needed *to hurry* (not *hurry*) more than now. "He needs *to hurry*," but "He *need* not *hurry*," or "He *doesn't need to hurry*." "*Need* he *hurry?*" or "*Does he need to hurry?*" He only *need* (or *needs to*) inquire of the porter. Had he done his duty in that respect, Lydia *need* (past subjunctive) not have been indebted to her uncle. The waiter was told that he *need* (past subjunctive) *not stay* (or *did not need to stay*).

The past subjunctive *need* has arisen under the influence of the past subjunctive *must* (§§ 41.B.4; 115.A).

(v) After the subjunctive (§§ 114.A.2; 115.A) groups *had* (or *would*) *rather* (or *sooner*), *had* (or *would*) *as soon*, *had as lief* (not now so common as formerly); *had better* (or *best*), *had as good:* I had (or would) rather *wait* a day. I had (or would) rather *die* than do it. I had (or would) as soon (or lief) *go* as *stay*. "He had (or would or might) better *go*"; but we cannot use *would* here in the first person, where *had* or *might* must be used: I had (or might) better *go*. A man had as good *go* to court without a cravat as appear in print without a preface.

(vi) After the verbs in § 67.C.1.b, but only as objective predicate: I heard him *say* it.

(vii) After the one preposition *to:* Anger impelled him to *do* it. Compare § 123.A.

b. With the *to*-form.

(i) After verbs other than those mentioned above: I wish *to go*. Often in connection with an objective predicate (§ 67.C. 1.a): "I find *it* difficult *to do* that, i.e. I find the doing of that difficult. Here anticipatory *it* points to the following infinitive.
The infinitive as object has a wide field of usefulness in abridged clauses: He begged *to go*, begged me (acc.) *to go*. I told him (dat.) *to go*. I planned *for him to go*. For the form of the subject of the infinitive here see §§ 76.A; 123.B; 82.B.

(ii) After adjectives: He is eager *to go*, eager *for you to go*. The question is difficult *to answer*. He is hard *to approach, to understand, to cook for, to get along with*.

4. *As an Adjective Element Modifying a Noun* (§§ 60, 80.G; 79.A.1, B.1, C.1; 124.C.4.a).

5. *In Elliptical Constructions:* I [should] *ask* his pardon? In older English the *to*-infinitive was used in such exclamations, but this construction is not elliptical. This older usage still lingers: I *to marry* before my brother, and *leave* him with none to take care of him! (Blackmore, *Lorna Doone*). This is an old loose type of expression once common.
The infinitive is much used in another elliptical exclamatory construction, an abridged conditional clause (§ 89.B) with the conclusion suppressed: *Oh to be in England* (= *if I were only in England*) now that April's there! (Browning).
Especially common are elliptical constructions after the conjunctions *but* (= *except*), *save, than:* She does nothing *but* [that she does] *laugh*. I'll do anything to show my gratitude *except* [that I do] *marry* the daughter. You can't do better than [that you do] *do* that.

6. *As an Adverbial Element.* This is one of the most common uses of the infinitive. It is described in §§ 85.B: 86.E.1.a, 2.a; 87.A.1.a, 2.a, B.a; 88.C; 89.B; 90.B; 91.B.

124. The Gerund. The gerund was originally a verbal noun in -*ing*, thus differing from the participle in -*ing*, which was originally an adjective. The gerund is still often a simple noun without any of the characteristics of a verb except its verbal meaning. The noun gerund usually preserves its original active form even where it has strong passive force and is usually formally distinguished by a preceding adjective, descriptive or limiting, and often also by a following genitive object: He has not committed any act worthy of *hanging* (active form with passive force). His forearms and clean-shaven face were brown from *prolonged tanning* (passive force) by the sun. The *shooting of birds* (gen. object) is forbidden.

A verbal gerund, aside from possessive adjectives, never has an adjective before it and may take after it an accusative, dative, or prepositional object and adverbial elements of all kinds: *Shooting birds* (acc. object) is forbidden. *Lending him* (dat. object) *money* (acc. object) is useless. It is fun *shooting at a mark* (prepositional object). It is dangerous *playing recklessly with fire* (two adverbial modifiers). The gerund of a copula takes after it a predicate, which in the case of a noun or pronoun is in the nominative: I never dreamed of *its being he*. I never dreamed of *his being sick* (predicate adjective). Compare § 54.A.1.a.

A. TENSE AND VOICE. As the gerund in the sixteenth century was felt as having strong verbal force, it began to appear with forms for tense and voice, which have become established.

The active forms now usually indicate tense although the older use of the present tense for past time occasionally occurs: I have heard of his *doing*, or *having done*, it before.

Passive force today usually requires passive form and an appropriate tense, although in older English we find active form, and we may still use a present tense for past time, as originally: Shall we send that foolish carrion, Mistress Quickly, to him and excuse his *throwing* (now *being thrown*, or *have been thrown*) into the water? (Shakespeare, *The Merry Wives of Windsor*, III, iii, 205).

B. Subject of the Gerund. As the gerund was originally a noun, its subject was a genitive, the subjective genitive (§ 57.C.3). As in older English we still use only the simple form of the genitive here, never the prepositional form. The loss of many distinctive genitive endings in the Middle English period has often made it impossible to comply with the old rule that the subject of the gerund must be put into the genitive. The old rule is now best observed with the possessive adjectives, which were originally the genitives of the personal pronouns. They have kept their old distinctive form, which always makes the grammatical relations clear, so that they are still widely used as the subject of the gerund: I don't like to think of *his*, or *her*, or *their*, doing that. Also proper names always have a clear genitive and hence are still often used as the subject of the gerund: I don't like to think of *John's* doing that. In case of common nouns, however, the genitive subject is usually ambiguous in the spoken language, since to the ear the singular and the plural are alike: I don't like to think of *my boy's doing that* and *my boys' doing that*, where in print there is a distinction, but in the spoken language no difference at all.

Where the genitive is impossible on account of the lack of a genitive ending, it is replaced by the accusative: He awoke to examine the first principles of world politics with some sense that the safety of his home would depend on *these* being rightly understood and treated.

The subject of the gerund, when modified by another noun, be it a genitive or an appositive, is invariably in the accusative: There is danger of a woman's *head* being turned (Meredith, *Diana of the Crossways*, Ch. VI). Did you ever hear of a *man* of good sense refusing such an offer? I am counting on *him* as a man of honor doing the right thing.

We always use the accusative — never the genitive — when the subject follows the gerund: He would always ignore the fact of there being a *backdoor* to any house (Mrs. Gaskell, *Cranford*, Ch. VIII).

Our best writers feeling that the genitive subject of the gerund is a poor means of expression avoid it, often even when the genitive would be a clear form, as in the case of proper names: At *Elizabeth Jane* mentioning how greatly Lucetta had been

277

jeopardized, he exhibited an agitation different in kind no less than in intensity from any she had ever seen in him before (Hardy, *The Mayor of Casterbridge*, Ch. XXIX). The evident trend of the present is toward the accusative subject, not only in colloquial speech but also in choice English.

C. FUNCTIONS OF THE GERUND. The gerund is used:

1. *As Subject: Seeing* is believing. *Having done one's duty*, or *to have done one's duty*, is a great consolation in misfortune. It is no use, or of no use, or useless, or there's no use, *to say anything*, or *for me to say anything*, or *for you to say anything*, or *for Father to say anything*, or *saying anything*, or *my, your, father's, saying anything*.

2. *As Predicate:* Seeing is *believing*, or To see is *to believe*.

3. *As Object:*

a. Accusative object: I like *getting up* early, or I like *to get up* early. Compare § 82.B.

b. Dative object: He came near *being killed*. Next *to being married* a girl likes to be crossed in love a little now and then (Jane Austen). I don't feel like *laughing* over it.

c. Prepositional object: He spoke about *my*, or *John's*, or John's *brother* (accusative subject; see § 124.B), returning so late.

In the predicate relation after an ingressive (§ 121.A.1) or an effective (§ 121.B.3) verb, such as *get, fall, burst out, set*, the gerund is used after the preposition *to* or *on* with the same force as the predicate present participle, namely to indicate *entrance* into a state of activity: The machine got *running* (participle), or *to running* (gerund). He fell again *speculating* (part.), or *to speculating* (gerund). Similarly in the objective predicate relation, i.e. when the activity is predicated of an object: I got the machine *running* (part.), or *to running* (gerund). That set me *thinking* (part.), or *to thinking* (gerund). The present participle and gerund here have descriptive force, representing the resultant activity as proceeding steadily. When it is desired to state a bare result, the infinitive is used here: I got the machine *to run*. I got *to talk* with him.

In the same way participle and gerund were once used in the predicate to represent the activity as *continuing:* He is *writing* (participle) *a letter*, or *in* (or *on*) *writing* (gerund) *of a letter.* The gerundial construction is no longer used here in the literary language but survives in popular speech: He is *a-writing* (from older *in*, or *on*, *writing*) *of a letter.* Though the preposition *in* or *on* of the gerundial construction has been retained in the contracted form of *a* in popular speech, it has entirely disappeared in the literary language. Through the suppression of the presposition here the old gerundial construction has merged into the participial. That the preposition has been suppressed here can be seen in older English by the objective genitive which often followed the form in *-ing*, thus clearly indicating that the preceding form in *-ing* was a gerund, not a present participle: as she was [*in*] *writing of it* (Shakespeare, *As You Like It*, IV, iii, 10), now *writing it*, the *of* having dropped out under the influence of the participial construction *was writing it.* Similarly, when the activity is predicated of an object: I found her [*in*] *writing of it*, now *writing it.* Thus in the predicate relation to indicate a continuing activity the participle has entirely replaced the gerund in the literary language, although the gerund survives in popular speech.

Similarly in the passive: of the two older constructions "The house *is building* (participle) or *in building*" (gerund) only the participle survives as a living construction. Still more common, however, is "The house is *being built.*" Compare § 110.

The parallel use of the present participle and the gerund, as seen above, is also found where the participle is a predicate and the gerund an accusative object: She began *crying* (a predicate part. or an acc. gerund). Older "He went *on hunting*" (gerund) has been replaced by "He went *hunting*" (pres. part.; see § 91.B, last par.).

4. *As an Attributive Element:*

a. As an attributive genitive: the love *of indulging self*, the fear *of losing his friendship.*

Though the attributive genitive gerund is very common, it cannot be used at all when the idea of desire, wish, demand, intention, or modality is present, in which cases the prepositional infinitive is usually employed: There is a strong public demand *for him to take the place*, not *of his taking the place*. She has a strict charge *to avoid the subject*. It is not his intention *to injure you*. He is the man *to do it* = *who should do it*.

b. As an appositive, agreeing with its governing noun in case: I now have very pleasant work, *preparing* boys for college. This construction is often replaced by the appositive genitive: I now have the very pleasant work *of preparing* boys for college.

c. As an attributive prepositional phrase: his joy on account of *my* — or *John's*, or John's *brother* (acc. subject; see § 124.B) — coming.

5. *In Abridged Adverbial Clauses*. This common construction is described in §§ 85.B; 86.C.1; 87.A.1.a.i; 88.C; 89.B; 90.B; 91.B.

125. Infinite Predication. For five centuries infinite predication, i.e. predication by means of the participle, infinitive, and gerund instead of the finite verb, has been coming into wider use and has been improving its means of expression to meet the growing demand for a simpler English. To bring about simpler expression it seemed at the start necessary to employ adjectives and nouns that had some verbal force. Adjectives and nouns were felt as appropriate since they had lost almost all their distinctive endings and were now ready to assume the new function of predicating like finite verbs. This was possible because they originally had some verbal force. The rapid spread and wide use of the new constructions are explained by the great simplicity of their forms. In simplicity also lies vigor. Simplicity and vigor are qualities that appeal to the English people. In §§ 122–124 we see the old and the new functions of these forms lying side by side and we can see there also the means by which the English people gradually converted these forms into terser expressions than their old finite verbs. It is interesting to see how we are still working on these problems — for example, the case of the subject of a gerund (§ 124.B). The English language is not a fixed thing. It is always developing and changing to make the thought clear or more simple. Some grammarians usually feel that a change is something bad, but the tremendous development of infinite predication in recent times shows clearly that the English people believe that change is good. In spite of the wide employment of infinite predication in modern English there is one limitation to its use. It can be used only in the subordinate clause. In the clause with a finite verb there is usually some conjunction to indicate the nature of the clause, but in infinite predication the nature of the clause is inferred from the context: "*When* I was correcting his exercise I found many mistakes," but in infinite form: "In correcting his exercise I found many mistakes." Often, as here, the subject of the clause is not expressed but only inferred. Terseness is the soul of infinite predication.

A glance at the infinitive clauses shows that they are more accurate than the finite clause. The power of the English sequence is broken in the infinitive clause while it holds tenaciously in the finite clause. The English sequence — a past must follow a past — is the stupidest thing in English expression: "It was reported to us here in the office a moment ago *that he was* sick in bed," but in infinite predication: "A moment ago he was reported *to be* (present with reference to the principal verb) sick in bed." The powerful sequence of tenses is powerless in infinite predication. In older English, however, there are indications that attempts have been made to introduce the old sequence into it (§ 123.D.1). But these attempts have not proved successful, although in colloquial speech the old sequence still lingers here.

Notice that mood is wholly disregarded in infinite predication: "I think that he *should go*" (subjunctive), but "I want him to go."

Infinite predication is often very simple. It is forceful and accurate in spite of its great simplicity, but it can never be polite. Now this should not suggest anything disrespectful: it simply means that infinite predication is the language of the English people in its working hours. It is the very embodiment of English business spirit. It cannot express some of our milder, gentler feeling that comes to us in our hours of leisure. But although it is plain and simple, it is always quite accurate, for it fits into the situation closely and derives from that what it lacks in its own form: We shall arrive too late to catch the train *leaving* (*which will leave*) at eight. I want you *to go* to the store. He is very fond *of skating*.

SYNTAX OF PREPOSITIONS

126. Nature and Functions. Very closely allied in nature to adverbs are prepositions, which, like adverbs, limit the force of the verb as to some circumstance of place, time, manner, degree, cause or reason, purpose, result, means — in short the same circumstances as are expressed by the adverb. Thus a preposition in connection with its dependent substantive is exactly equal in force to an adverb, but a preposition and an adverb differ in this, that the latter limits the force of the verb in and of itself, while the former requires the assistance of a dependent noun or some other word: "Mary is *in*" (adverb), but "Mary is *in* (preposition) *the house*."

Similarly, as the adverb is not limited to expressing adverbial relations, so is the prepositional phrase widely used in expressing other than adverbial relations, as described in § 19.

127. List of Prepositions.

The most common prepositions are:

abaft	aside from
aboard	aslant
about	astern of
above	as to
according to	at
across	athwart
after	barring
against	bating
along	because of
alongside of (or alongside)	before
along with	behind
amid or amidst	below
among or amongst	beneath
apart from	beside
around	besides
as against	between
as between	betwixt
as compared with	beyond
as for	by

by dint of

by means of

by reason of

by virtue of

by way of

concerning

considering

despite

down

during

ere

excepting (or except)

exclusive of

for

for the sake of

from above

from among

from behind

from beneath

from between

from over

from under

in

in accordance with

in addition to

in behalf of

in case of (= in the event of)

in the case of (= as regards)

including

inclusive of

in comparison to

in comparison with

in compliance with

in consequence of

in consideration of

in default of

independently of

in front of

in lieu of

in opposition to

in place of

in preference to

in regard to

inside of (or inside)

in spite of

instead of

into

like (§ 86.B)

notwithstanding

of

off

on

on account of

on behalf of

onto (or on to)

opposite to (or opposite)

out of

outside of (or outside)

over

owing to

past

pending

regarding

regardless of

relating to

relative to

respecting

round

round about

saving

short of

since

through

throughout

to

touching

toward (or towards)

under

underneath

until (or till)

unto

up

upon

via

with	with (or in) regard to
within	without regard to
without	with a view to
with the intention of	with the view of
with reference (or respect) to	in view of

128. Omission of Prepositions. In colloquial speech, prepositions are often omitted in set expressions since they are lightly stressed and are of little importance to the thought: He must never treat you [*in*] *that way* again. In such expressions the element as a whole is felt as an adverb, like the adverbial accusatives *the following day, little, more,* etc. described in § 68.B, so that the preposition really has no function any more and drops out. In the same way, *of* often drops out of many prepositions, as in *inside* instead of *inside of*. The moment that such a group of words is as a whole felt as a preposition, *of* ceases to have a function and naturally drops out as superfluous.

On the other hand, when we say *Sunday* instead of *on Sunday*, we do not drop *on* but employ another construction, the adverbial accusative described in § 68.B.

129. Contraction of "On" to "A." The preposition *on* is often contracted to *a: asleep, afire, aflame,* etc. Aside from such established set expressions, this usage is characteristic of popular speech (§ 124.C.3.c).

130. "Onto," "Into." The preposition *onto* or *on to* corresponds closely to *into*. As it indicates motion to the upper surface of something, it differs distinctly from *on* or *upon:* The boys jumped *onto* the ice and played *on it* until sundown. The use of *onto* or *on to* ought not to be discouraged, as is done by some grammarians, but strongly encouraged, for it enables us to express ourselves more accurately. Even with friendly encouragement improvements of speech often spread slowly. No one discourages any longer the use of *into* as a form now differentiated in form and meaning from the older form *in*. But in spite of the general recognition of *into* as an independent preposition we still often employ the older form *in* with the meaning of *into:* I put it *in* (instead of the better *into*) my pocket.

131. Preposition at End of Clause or Sentence. The preposition usually stands immediately before its object; but, as explained in § 80.A.1–2, it is often at the end of a relative clause: This is the pen I write *with*, originally This is *the* pen I write with |it]. The position of the preposition at the end of the clause is explained by the omission of the personal pronoun, the object of the preposition. The clause is closely related to the antecedent, so that the situation makes the thought clear without the expression of the personal pronoun. Compare § 132.

The suppression of the pronoun is not confined to relative clauses, but occurs also in adverbial clauses: The case is as sad as I have ever heard *of*. He writes with a worse pen than I write *with*.

As we no longer feel the force of the original construction in such sentences, we now interpret the position of the preposition at the end of the clause as a device to make the important first place available for an emphatic word or group of words. Hence, we now often put emphatic words at the beginning of the sentence and the unimportant preposition at the end, even where originally this construction was impossible: Which pen do you write *with?* Where did he come *from?* We even put the dative sign *to* at the end in order that the emphatic dative may have the first place: These reports he does not seem to have paid much attention *to*.

132. Prepositional Adverbs. Similar to the prepositions that stand at the end of a proposition, as described in the first two paragraphs of § 131, are the prepositional adverbs that often stand at the end of a proposition because of the suppression of the governing noun or pronoun, which is omitted since it is suggested by a preceding noun or by the situation: I threw the ball at the wall, but I threw too high and it went *óver*. We soon reached the park and strolled *through*. These adverbial prepositions differ from the prepositions that stand at the end only in having a heavier stress: This is the park we strólled through (preposition). The strong stress on the adverbial preposition shows that it stands in a closer relation to the verb than does the ordinary preposition.

The adverbial preposition once had in a number of cases a little different form from the ordinary preposition and in several cases still has: "This is the house I saw him gó *into*" (preposition), but "Come *in*" (spoken by some one from the window of a house to someone passing by). "This is the house he cáme *out of*" (preposition), but "I saw him go into the house, but he will soon come *óut* again." "This is the car he júmped *onto* (prep.), but "Just as the car started, he jumped *ón*."

If, in older English, there was no antecedent, the adverbial preposition followed its object. This older usage survives in poetry: Soft went the music the soft air *along* (Keats). Sometimes also in plain prose: I have read the letter *throúgh*. I want to think the matter *óver*. Let us pass the matter *by*. As the prepositional force has for the most part overshadowed the adverbial, we now usually put the adverbial preposition before its object, like a preposition proper, but we stress it heavily to distinguish it from a preposition proper: He stood bravely *bỳ* my brother. It becomes necessary to look *ínto* this matter. As in these two examples, the prepositional adverb is so closely related to the verb that it often forms a compound with it with a somewhat altered, figurative meaning of the components. Even where the meaning is concrete, a strong stress upon the preposition indicates a close relation to the verb, hence adverbial force: I haven't gone *óutside of* the house today. He went *dówn* the hill.

INDEX

References are to section unless page is specified

Attributive relative clause, 80; 115.B.2

Attributive substantive clause, 79

Aught, indef. pron., 9.E

Auxiliary verb, *do* as, 44.C; 53. A.3; 116.B; modal, 41.B.4.*a*; 113; in passive voice, 36.C.1–2; in tense formation, 43.A–D

Awake, prin. pts., 42.B.2

Axis, plur. of, 24.B.4

Bacillus, plur. of, 24.B.2

Bacterium, plur. of, 24.B.3

Bad, comparison of, 104.F

Badly, comparison of, 69.A.1

Be, as passive auxiliary, 36.C.1,4; 44.B; 45.B; as terminate and point-action auxiliary, 121.A.4. B.3; as copula, 15.C; 53.B; inflection of, 41.B.1; 42.B.*a;* 44.B; as linking verb, 54.A.1.a,A.4; principal parts of, 42.B.2

Be-, prefix, 16.A

Bear, prin. pts., 42.B.2

Beat, prin. pts., 42.B.2

Beau, plur. of, 24.B.9

Become, as passive auxiliary, 36.C.3; point-action auxiliary, 121.A.4, B.3; predicate complement with, 54.A.4; principal parts of, *see Come*, 42.B.2

Before, conjunc., 85.A; 114.B.2.c; prep., 59.A; 80.B; 127

Beget, prin. pts., 42.B.2

Begin, as ingressive auxiliary, 121.A.1; principal parts of, 42.B.2

Behold, prin. pts. 42.B.2

Bend, prin. pts., 42.A.2

Bereave, prin. pts., 42.A.2

Beseech, prin. pts., 42.A.2

Besides, coördinating conjunc., 75.A.1

Bespeak, prin. pts., 42.B.2

Bet, prin. pts., 42.A.2

Bid, prin. pts., 42.A.2; 42.B.2

Bind, prin. pts., 42.B.2

Bite, prin. pts., 42.B.2

Bleed, prin. pts., 42.A.2

Blend, prin. pts., 42.A.2

Blending, of clause, 76.A; 89.A; of direct and indirect discourse,

82.A; of partitive genitive, **57.** C.8.b

Bless, prin. pts., 42.A.2

Blow, prin. pts., 42.B.2

Both, demon. adj., 13.C; pron., 9.G.2

Both — and, 75.A.1

Both of, 53.C.6

Break, prin. pts., 42.B.2

Breed, prin. pts., 42.A.2

Bring, prin. pts., 42.A.2

Broadcast, prin. pts., 42.A.2 (p. 65)

Broke, colloquial for *out of money*, 42.B.2

Brother, plur. of, 24.A.2,C

Build, prin. pts., 42.A.2

Building, after the copula a progressive passive, 110

Burn, prin. pts., 42.A.2

Burst, prin. pts., 42.A.2

But, for *but because*, 88.A; as coördinating conjunction, 75.A,A.3; nominative case after, 76.A.1; 89.A (p. 190); number of verb after, 55.A.1.b; as relative pronoun, 80.B; as subordinating conjunction, 77.A; 82.A; 86.C, E.2; 87.B; 89.A; 123.G.5

But that, rel. pron. and sub. conjunc., *see* entries under *But*

But then, 75.A.3

But what, rel. pron. and sub. conjunc., *see* entries under *But*

Buy, prin. pts., 42.A.2

Calyx, plur. of, 24.B.4

Can, inflection of, 41.B.4; and *may*, 114.A.1

Candelabrum, plur. of, 24.B.3

Canoe, pres. participle of, 41.A.2

Cardinal numeral, adj., 13.D.1; indef. pron., 9.G.3

Case, 25; agreement of complement and subject in, 54.A.1.a; 55.D; agreement of relative pronoun and antecedent in, 80.E; errors in, 89.A (p. 190); of noun, 25; of pronoun, 27–34 *passim;* 80.E. *See also* Accusative, Dative, Genitive, Nominative

Cast, prin. pts., 42.A.2

97; omission of, 109; for reciprocal pronoun, 98

Reflexive use of transitive verb, 15.A; 109

Relative adjective, 13.E

Relative adverb, indefinite, 18.A.3; 77.A

Relative clause, 80; abridgment, of, 80.G; attributive, 80; 115.B.2; descriptive, 80.C; restrictive, 80.C; subjunctive in, 114.B.2.b; 115.B.2

Relative comparison, of adjectives, 104.B; of adverbs, 69.A

Relative pronoun, 9.D; 77; 78; 79; 80.B; 82; 83; 99; agreement of, with antecedent, 80.E; case of, 80.E; false attraction of, 80.F.3; inflection of, 31; omission of, 80.A.1; personality and form in, 80.D; position of, 31; 80.F; repetition of, 80.F

Rend, prin. pts., 42.A.2

Repeated subject, 77.A.*b*

Repetition, of limiting adjective, 56.D; of relative pronoun, 80.F

Restriction, clause of, 87.A.1.c.i

Restrictive relative clause, 80.C

Result, adverb of, 18.B.6; degree clause of modal, 87.B; manner clause of, 86.E

Retained accusative object, 67.A.1, C.1.a.i

Retained phrase, 67.C.1.a.i

Rhetorical question, 9.F; *shall* in, 115.A; 119.E.1 (4th par.)

Riches, sing. and plur., 55.A.2.c

Rid, prin. pts., 42.A.2

Ride, prin. pts., 42.B.2

Ring, prin. pts., 42.B.2

Rise, prin. pts., 42.B.2

Rive, prin. pts., 42.A.2

Roast, prin. pts., 42.A.2; adj., 42.A.2

Run, prin. pts., 42.B.2

S-genitive, 57.A.1

Same, demon. adj., 13.C

Same, same one(*s*), pron., 9.G.2; 34.B

Save, saving, saving that, sub. conjunc., 89.A

Saw prin. pts., 42.A.2

Say, prin. pts., 42.A.2

See, past tense of, 42.B; principal parts of, 42.B.2; syntax of, 67.C.1.b

Seeing that, sub. conjunc., 88.A

Seek, prin. pts., 42.A.2

Seethe, prin. pts., 42.A.2

Self, noun, 105.*a;* for reflexive pronoun, 97

Sell, prin. pts., 42.A.2

Send, prin. pts., 42.A.2

Sentence, p. 97; as adjective, 56.C; appositive to, 58.A.3; classes of, 75–92; complex, 76–92; compound, 75; declarative, 48.B; definition of, p. 97; essential elements of, 49–55; exclamatory, 48.A; independent elements of, 71–74; interrogative, 48.C; kinds of, 48; predicate of, 49, 53–55; subject of, 49–52; 55; subordinate elements of, p. 120; 56–70; syntax of, 48–92

Sentence adverb, 18.A.2; 70; position of, 70.B, stress of, 70.B

Sentence modifier, adverb as, 18.A.2; 70; *as*-phrase with force of, 53.C.4

Separable compound verb, 16.B

Sequence of tenses, 118; and infinite predication, 125 (2nd par.)

Seraph, plur. of, 24.B.10,C

Series, plur. of, 24.B.7

Set, causative, 109.*a;* principal parts of, 42.A.2

Set in, 121.A.1

Several, indef. adj., 13.F; indef. pron., 9.G.3; 34.C

Sew, prin. pts., 42.A.2

Shake, prin. pts., 42.B.2

Shall, 41.B.4; in commands, 119.E.1; as future auxiliary, 119.E.1; as future perfect auxiliary, 119.F; in indirect discourse, 115.B.1.a; as modal auxiliary, 114.A.1; 119.E.1; in rhetorical questions, 115.A; 119.E.1 in subjunctive, 112–115; and *will*, 115.B.1.a; 119.E.1

Shape, prin. pts., 42.A.2

Shave, prin. pts., 42.A.2

303